T0306036

How to Create a
Sustainable Food Industry

This book presents a practical guide to help businesses navigate the complex topics of sustainability in the food industry.

The book takes you on a journey along the food value chain, from farm to fork, exploring key opportunities to increase positive impacts and circularity at each step of the journey. Written by a team of authors with decades of experience in the food industry and academia, it provides guidance on how to analyse sustainability across the value chain and life cycle of a food product and how to design, implement and communicate strategies to customers. Furthermore, the book shows that there are not always straightforward solutions, but rather choices and trade-offs that require an understanding of what is best suited to the product, customers and business in question. It demystifies a variety of topics, such as local sourcing, regenerative agriculture, plant-based protein and the environmental impact of meat production, and draws on a wide range of case studies from across the globe, to provide concrete, real-world examples. While a perfect food system may not exist, informed decisions can go a long way to reshape and transform the food industry as we know it.

This book will be of great interest to professionals working in the food and agriculture industries, as well as students and scholars of sustainable food systems and sustainable business.

Melissa Barrett is Global Managing Director, Practices and Impact at dss⁺. She has twenty years of experience in consulting on food system and value chain sustainability, and as a board advisor to a number of startups. She holds a PhD in Environmental Sciences from the University of Adelaide, Australia, and has worked and taught in a number of research institutions including at the University of Cambridge, UK, the British Antarctic Survey and the South Australian Research and Development Institute.

Massimo Marino is an environmental engineer, specialist in Life Cycle Assessments (PhD) and Principal at dss⁺. He is the author and co-author of many publications, including the *Life Cycle Analysis Manual* (2008).

Francesca Brkic is a Manager at the sustainability consultancy dss⁺ and the Founder of an early stage start-up in the circular economy of infant food, Little Origins. She has an MSt in Sustainability Leadership from the University of Cambridge, UK, where she focused on frontier approaches to sustainability, such as circular economy and regenerative agriculture, and a BSc in Economics and Politics from the University of Bath, UK.

Carlo Alberto Pratesi is a Professor of Economics and Business Administration at the University of Roma Tre, Italy, where he leads courses on Marketing, Innovation and Sustainability. On the same topics, he consults for businesses, with a particular focus on the food and agriculture industry. He is the Founder and President of EIIS – the European Institute of Innovation for Sustainability.

Routledge Studies in Food, Society and the Environment

For more information about this series, please visit: www.routledge.com/
Routledge-Studies-in-Food-Society-and-the-Environment/book-series/
RSFSE

How to Create a Sustainable Food Industry
A Practical Guide to Perfect Food

Melissa Barrett, Massimo Marino, Francesca Brkic and Carlo Alberto Pratesi

Routledge
Taylor & Francis Group
LONDON AND NEW YORK

earthscan
from Routledge

dss⁺

Designed cover image: © Yü Lan/stock.adobe.com

First published in English 2024
by Routledge
4 Park Square, Milton Park, Abingdon, Oxon OX14 4RN

and by Routledge
605 Third Avenue, New York, NY 10158

Routledge is an imprint of the Taylor & Francis Group, an informa business

© 2024 DSS Sustainable Solutions Italy S.R.L. and Carlo Alberto Pratesi

Published in Italian as *Il Cibo Perfetto: Aziende, consumatori e impatto ambientale del cibo* by Edizioni Ambiente 2022

British Library Cataloguing-in-Publication Data
A catalogue record for this book is available from the British Library

ISBN: 978-1-032-58359-4 (hbk)
ISBN: 978-1-032-51688-2 (pbk)
ISBN: 978-1-003-44974-4 (ebk)

DOI: 10.4324/9781003449744

Typeset in Times New Roman
by codeMantra

Contents

Foreword

How do we transform our global food systems at the pace needed to nourish humanity today before the Earth gives up on us tomorrow?

FAO's vision for sustainable agriculture and food is one in which food is nutritious and accessible for everyone, and where natural resources are managed in a way that maintains ecosystem functions to support current, as well as future human needs.

Our global food system is currently designed to produce huge amounts of food, using a limited variety of commodities, at the lowest possible economic cost. We need to be honest. We are collectively overusing finite resources in an inefficient, detrimental manner without fully considering the food system externalities, i.e. the total social and environmental costs to people, society and the planet.

Food prices have been skyrocketing this year. Inflation is at a 40-year high with everything from cereals to sugar, oils and eggs impacted. Coupled with shortages in supply, these high prices are having devastating consequences on communities in our poorest countries, those that are already food insecure. Hundreds of millions of families who were just about keeping their head above water are now severely under-nourished.

Recently, the secretary general of the UN FAO has been engaging with multiple stakeholders, including governments and senior executives in the private sector, warning of a growing food crisis, with increasing food inflation and supply shortages which started during the pandemic and are now being exacerbated by the war in Ukraine.

And the overwhelming scientific evidence is that the industry is also not yet innovating at the pace needed to address both the global food crisis AND the food system sustainability.

So how do we design a food system that is able to feed 10 billion people with tasty and healthy nutritious food choices every day, that is culturally acceptable and fair to people, that is not contributing to non-communicable diseases for billions of people, that is not wasting 30% of the food produced, that is not depleting 70% of the water available and that is able to regenerate soils and bio-diversity while limiting global warming to below 1.5°?

Recent events have highlighted the fragility of our industry, but it has also provided confidence and optimism that under pressure we can deliver solutions to immense problems in record speed. This however begs the question – are we future focused enough to take the courageous steps to deliver transformational change? Diverting the best of human ingenuity to transform the food systems and coupling this expertise with leaders who will make the right decisions is a winning combination.

As leaders we have the influence and platform to cultivate a culture change within our businesses, to create the excitement and urgency to solve this crisis. We have a responsibility to do this as individuals in our businesses, and collectively as an industry. We have a duty to be role models of moral courage, and audacious in our approach. I challenge you to consider what decisions you will take within your business to positively impact our planet.

After reading this book, I am more optimistic. The authors are very successful in educating us on the challenges and opportunities, and in highlighting a possible path for the agri-food industry to address and answer this fundamental question for future generations. They have my most sincere admiration for their undertaking, and I am honoured and humbled to have had the opportunity to write this brief foreword.

All life is precious; now is the time to seize this moment, to transform by using our collective power to contribute to a better world, to invent the Perfect Food.

Yours Sincerely,
Juan Aguiriano, Group Head of Sustainability, Kerry Group

Preface

The concept of 'Perfect Food' intrigued me from the outset. The very idea of 'Perfect Food' – coming from the cleverly positioned title of the previous Italian edition 'Il Cibo Perfetto' (written by Massimo Marino and Carlo Alberto Pratesi) – is more than a discussion starter and comes across as a challenge, or question, to the food industry. Does perfect food exist, can it even be attainable? I believe the concept is helpful for us all to consider as we find ways to advance towards an improved global food system and make better choices as citizens, consumers and businesses.

Perfect Food is nonsensical; it does not exist. One person's perfect will be different from another's. We also know there are both positive and negative impacts, as well as trade-offs throughout the food-value chain, with challenging decisions to be made at every stage. Whether it is a question of how to eat better for ourselves and the planet, choosing one ingredient over another or balancing taste with carbon emissions or circularity – even with innovation in food science and technologies – the decision is never simple.

This book brings together a depth of experience, data and tools to help uncover the facts, simplify decision-making and guide actions that support the sustainable transformation of food systems. There may be no one recipe, and there is no *perfect* recipe, but developing an understanding of 'who' or 'what' we are making choices for, and having a clear view across the whole product, can reveal answers. Consumers are citizens with both nutritional and ethical desires. The decisions of food sector professionals must balance quality, traceability, footprint and end of life of products. There is a sweet spot that is found between food science, environmental science and behavioural science that can inform action and review who and how we need to engage.

The book is written for those wishing to understand sustainability holistically and apply it within the context of their business, be it agriculture, food or beverage. It is designed as a guidebook to support the non-sustainability expert who is approaching the topic in depth for the first time: useful to those whose company is yet to embark on a comprehensive sustainability transformation, or those who are part of a company with significant sustainability ambitions but have not yet, due to their profession, been fully immersed in the subject matter.

As a food system sustainability consultant, I support farmers, processors, R&D teams and marketeers who bring sustainability to their day-to-day decision-making.

The concept of Perfect Food, and the topics discussed in this book have prompted me to think differently. From regenerative agriculture, low-carbon farming and local sourcing through to packaging, circularity and consumer engagement, there is an immense need and opportunity to simplify the food system challenge.

When we welcomed the Perfect Food consulting team to dss+ last year, I was excited to connect with their deep expertise in food and agronomy and the practical guidance in support of the food system transformation. There is a simplicity here that can support industry professionals to build the capabilities and the culture for the change the industry needs.

Successfully building sustainability impact and business value through a single product is one thing, creating a sustainable business or portfolio takes much deeper thought and effort. In the fast-moving food products industry, decisions must be made quickly. An executive team must determine strategy and launch new business models, while ensuring everyone is engaged from finance, brand and marketing to sourcing leads, deciding on ingredient credentials and R&D teams creating the next meal. This means a whole organisation approach is needed, building on core values, levers for change and rules for success. Developing a 'perfect portfolio' of products is also about creating an enabling environment for change.

When reading this guide, be specific about the product or context you are interested in. What does 'perfect' mean for you? For this product, this ingredient, this consumer, this farmer? Even for this meal? Everything lies in the goals that we set ourselves as consumers and producers.

This book is perfectly positioned to build awareness and to dip in and out of to support our decisions as we work together to drive transformational change through our ingredient, product, producer and citizen choices.

Dr Melissa Barrett

1 Introduction – towards perfect food

With some 5 billion metric tonnes produced every year, food is at the centre of global production systems. As population growth and consumption patterns increase demand, the search is on for sustainable food. But there are complexities specific to food that can make it more challenging to find solutions than in other sectors.

Food is a basic human need and essential to people's health and well-being. Unlike other sectors – like energy or transport – we cannot dramatically reduce the consumption of food. It is also not only its availability and accessibility that impact sustainability; aspects such as quality, safety, human rights, nutritional value, diets and consumption habits are all part of the overall sustainability of the food system.

In many cases, food production involves animals. Regardless of whether we are consuming animal products or managing animal waste, animal welfare must also be evaluated. To further complicate matters, while technical elements can be quite easily quantifiable (the health of an animal can be measured, for example), ethical considerations (is it right to eat animals?) depend on subjective and individual values. Then there are interconnected factors – deforestation, biodiversity, water quality and availability, soil health and emissions – all of which depend on, and are impacted by, agri-food production.

Today's industrial food system is a major driver of environmental issues, but it doesn't have to be this way. Food comes from nature and the food system has the potential to provide powerful nature-based solutions.[1] Methods used to objectively evaluate the impact of a food product or system are often based on life cycle thinking. This approach analyses the steps 'from field to table' to provide a holistic view of impact across the life of a product.

Calculations must consider two very different types of production. The agricultural part of the value chain is made up of an infinite number of small companies and smallholder farmers: this doesn't allow for the precise collection of data, nor is this data easily verifiable. In contrast, the industrial processing stage is carried out in a few complex plants and involves tightly controlled industrial processes. This duality presents challenges for achieving traceability and transparency, given the number of value chain players, for delivering large-scale, complex projects, such as rolling out decarbonisation technologies, and for protecting the socio-economic

DOI: 10.4324/9781003449744-1

well-being of farmers and their communities. Anyone interested in sustainability in the world of food must be aware of these complexities when reflecting on and delivering actions to support the transformation to a sustainable food and agriculture industry:

1   There is no simple recipe for reconciling environmental, social and economic needs in food production, distribution, consumption and post-consumer end of life. Payoffs exist at every stage and solutions may solve one problem whilst unintentionally creating another. For example, if actions to protect animal welfare and cut emissions were to drastically reduce meat consumption, coupled with a reduction in food waste, there could be a reduction in the availability of fertiliser needed to grow organic food.

2   When it comes to impact, the sum makes up the total. We must consider the entire supply chain and set objective indicators that consider each step, from field to table and beyond. A full-system view at the product level is a precondition for responsible consumption. Agri-food chains are closely interconnected, and it is almost impossible to think of transforming one without impacting others.

3   It is necessary to choose values on which to base choices. This may seem simple, but we often find ourselves facing dilemmas whereby a choice may be advantageous in one aspect, but not another. Producing eggs from caged hens reduces CO_2 emissions but raises concerns over animal welfare. Conventional palm oil production is a driver of deforestation but can be better than other vegetable oils in terms of its environmental impact if grown sustainably. Choosing Ecuadorian oranges may support the fair-trade market but may generate higher emissions due to transport miles. Plastic packaging protects food and reduces food waste, but plastic pollution is a serious concern. These are just a few of the many dilemmas we can face.

To reach the best decision we must identify our priorities and carefully consider different impacts and aspects of sustainability. Companies and their customers – both business clients and consumers – should begin this journey by defining their objectives. This means asking what is truly sustainable for you and your stakeholders. You may need to accept the fact that, in many cases, your decision will be questioned by others.

In this book, we try to relate the technical aspects of sustainability, particularly environmental aspects, with the market and consumer behaviour. Consumers are one of the food sector's most influential stakeholders – their decisions guide markets in directions which may, or may not, be logical or sustainable.

In order for a transition to a sustainable food industry to take place, it needs to be tackled by changing the demand (what products are eaten) as well as the supply (how these are produced). We begin this exploration in Chapter 2, looking at the scale of challenge the food industry has in feeding a growing population and what are the social and environmental variables within that, from food quantity, to quality and health. Within this chapter we briefly focus on the demand side – what a sustainable and healthy diet is and how companies can influence what is being eaten in the first place. The rest of the book is dedicated to the supply side, focusing on what companies can influence the most – how food is produced.

Chapter 3 introduces sustainability as a business concept, exploring the evolution of sustainability as a concept and how it has been integrated in the economy over time. This chapter sets the scene for how sustainability is valuable and commercially necessary. This chapter highlights key steps one can go through to build a robust strategic approach to transitioning towards a sustainable food system: each of the key questions raised is answered in the following chapters.

Chapter 4 defines what and where your social and environmental impact is, exploring with a technical eye what analysis methodologies and impact indicators are available – the language and tools of sustainability. In Chapter 5 we hone in on challenges specific to each situation along the value chain: analysing different aspects, from field to table, to show how when we use technical rigour (such as a life cycle assessment approach) to understanding sustainability, it can lead to dilemmas, requiring decision-making that is not always simple or unambiguous.

Chapter 6 is fully dedicated to stakeholder engagement and communication. These are important first and foremost to understand who is guiding decision-making and how to make product and business decisions that resonate within your company. This chapter also analyses strategic communication tools, important for establishing a favourable brand position in the market.

In the final two chapters, we shift our attention from analysis to solutions. After decades of discussion, it is time to act decisively to secure the sustainability of food-production systems. In Chapter 7 we explore how food production can go from being a problem to being part of the solution through approaches such as

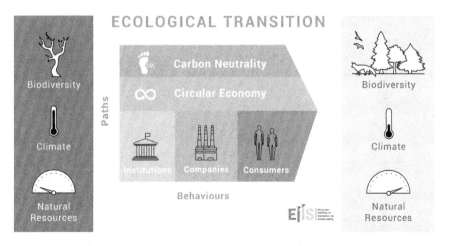

Figure 1.1　The path for the ecological transition. Authors' elaboration. Originally published in the first edition of this book, *Il Cibo Perfetto*, published in Italian in 2022.

regenerative agriculture, the circular economy and decarbonisation (Figure 1.1). Chapter 8 then explores how to design and set in motion a sustainability transformation, leveraging unique capabilities unique to your organisation.

Note

1 *Three Things to Know about Nature-Based Solutions for Agriculture*, The Nature Conservancy, February 2021, https://www.nature.org/en-us/what-we-do/our-insights/perspectives/three-things-nature-based-solutions-agriculture/.

2   The challenge of feeding the world

While the challenge of transitioning to a sustainable economy is universal, the food and agriculture industry finds itself in a unique position. On the one hand, it must reduce its negative impacts. The industry accounts for 31% of greenhouse gas (GHG) emissions,[1] 70% of global freshwater use,[2] 38% of land use,[3] 80% of biodiversity loss[4] and 78% of eutrophication of waterways[5] due to excessive mineral fertiliser application and mismanagement. On the other hand, it must deliver an essential good that we all need: nutrition. Demand for nutritious food is growing with the global population set to reach 9.1 billion by 2050 and the rise in living standards driving up demand for resource-intensive foods, such as animal products. It is predicted that we will need a 70% increase in food production by 2050[6] to satisfy demand.

This poses a unique challenge for the food and agriculture industry; it must radically transform to meet higher-production demand and steward a significant proportion of the world's natural resources. Food and agriculture are also inextricably linked to other industries, from textiles and leather production to furniture, paper and biofuel. For these industries to be commercially viable, they must secure a sustainable supply of resources and raw materials alongside developing innovative business models that promote environmental health.

Achieving this requires a systemic rethink of the entire food industry – one that spans agriculture and manufacturing all the way through to consumer choice and diets. The relationship between diet and environmental sustainability is an increasingly salient topic in scientific and media arenas, motivating food innovations and dietary shifts – of which plant-based protein has been a central focus.

This chapter focuses on the demand side of food: understanding the challenges facing the food industry which must feed a global population and influence what consumers eat to support sustainable and nutritious diets. We summarise various positions on this issue and aim to provide an overview from a global perspective.

DOI: 10.4324/9781003449744-2

Box 2.1   How many mouths do we need to feed?

Reflections on the sustainability of food (and beyond) must take into account an undisputable fact: the number of people on the planet is growing exponentially, rapidly increasing the demand for food.

Currently, there are approximately 8 billion people on Earth. This is projected to rise to 9.1 billion by 2050. In addition to the total population, it is important to consider the rate of growth at which it was reached: effectively, it all happened in the past 300 years, causing a sudden strain on the environment and its ability to produce natural resources and maintain the integrity of ecosystems (Figure 2.1).

The most noteworthy phenomenon, however, is the rate of growth – reaching exponential levels since the industrial revolution.

We must also consider that the world's population is not evenly distributed, creating challenges for food distribution networks in both highly populated metropolitan areas and remote areas with a small number of inhabitants. Over 50% of the world's population lives in North America, Europe, China and India, yet these regions represent just 30% of the Earth's land area.

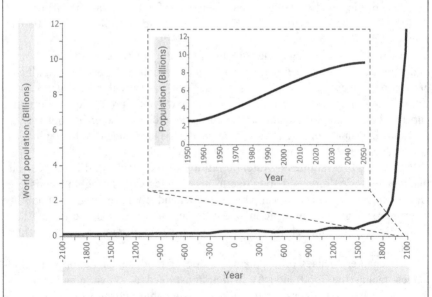

Figure 2.1 World population growth. Authors' elaboration. Data processed from M. Roser, H. Ritchie, E. Ortiz-Ospina, L. Rodés-Guirao, *World Population Growth*, Our World in Data, 2013, https://ourworldindata.org/world-population-growth. Originally published in the first edition of this book, *Il Cibo Perfetto*, published in Italian in 2022.

2.1 A perfect balance: food availability and quality

In November 2022, the global population reached 8 billion[7] and it is expected to peak at 10.4 billion during the 2080s.[8] In 2021, 29% of the global population faced food insecurity while 10% went hungry.[9] The Covid-19 pandemic exacerbated the situation for those already facing serious hardship, impacting employment, disrupting food supply chains and driving up food prices due to rising fertiliser and fuel costs.[10]

But feeding the global population is not only a question of food quantity, it also hinges on nutritional quality, access and distribution. While more than enough food is produced to feed everyone, it is ensuring that there is enough nutritious food available for everyone, at the right place and at the right time; that is the problem (Figure 2.2).

This isn't helped by the fact that around 30% of all food produced goes wasted. Preventing food loss and redistributing food waste to those who need it most could significantly address the current food gap. Food waste occurs in the supply chain due to weather-related losses, processing inefficiencies, damage during transit and poor inventory planning at the retail level due to excess supply and at the consumer level by going uneaten.

There have been significant positive developments over the last century, with a significant drop in the number of people living in extreme poverty,[11] increased economic welfare and better health, resulting in longer lifespans.

The food industry has also become incredibly efficient as the Green Revolution of the 1960s brought about new irrigation systems, large-scale mechanisation and use of fertilisers and other agrochemicals. These developments led to massively increased yields; from 1961 to 2014, global cereal production increased by 280%.[12] Increased

Term	Definition
Hunger	Hunger is an uncomfortable or painful physical sensation caused by insufficient consumption of dietary energy. In this report, the term hunger is synonymous with chronic undernourishment and is measured by the Prevalence of Undernourishment, i.e., an estimate of the proportion of the population that lacks enough dietary energy for a healthy, active life. Hunger is synonymous with chronic undernourishment.
Malnutrition	An abnormal physiological condition caused by inadequate, unbalanced or excessive intake of macronutrients and/or micronutrients. Malnutrition includes undernutrition (child stunting and wasting, and vitamin and mineral deficiencies) as well as overweight and obesity.
Food Security	A situation that exists when all people, at all times, have physical, social and economic access to sufficient, safe and nutritious food that meets their dietary needs and food preferences for an active and healthy life. Based on this definition, four food security dimensions can be identified: food availability, economic and physical access to food, food utilisation and stability over time.

Figure 2.2 Food and nutrition glossary. FAO, IFAD, UNICEF, WFP, WHO, *The State of Food Security and Nutrition in the World 2022. Repurposing Food and Agricultural Policies to Make Healthy Diets More Affordable*, Rome, 2022, https://www.fao.org/3/cc0639en/online/cc0639en.html.

food volumes became available for distribution to global regions via long supply chains, enabled by technological advancements such as refrigeration and cooling technologies. As the food supply chain became highly globalised, supermarkets were able to stock fresh fruits and vegetables from far-away regions, every month of the year, regardless of the local season. However, these positive developments had unforeseen impacts that the food industry must now grapple with.

First, as people become richer, diets tend to diversify. Combined with population growth, this has led to increased demand for animal products. Global meat consumption is now five times higher than it was in 1961,[13] largely driven by rising incomes in developing countries.[14] As demand for animal products increases, so does the need for land to produce animal feed and graze livestock. This now accounts for 77% of all agricultural land globally.[15] These trends raise important questions. How can we significantly increase production of some of the most resource-intensive food products to meet rising demand? And is it feasible to do so within current environmental constraints? The market has responded in multiple ways to manage demand for animal products, from intensifying and industrialising feed and livestock production to innovating lab-raised alternatives and diversifying into alternative proteins such as tofu, mycoproteins (e.g. Quorn), seitan, tempeh and other soy- and legume-based products.

Second, despite the rise in global wealth, significant inequality affects access to food and education. A staggering 3.1 billion people could not afford a healthy diet in 2020[16] while adult obesity nearly doubled in absolute value in the last two decades, estimated at 13% of the global adult population in 2016.[17] Non-communicable diseases such as heart disease, cancer, chronic respiratory diseases and diabetes have become the world's single largest killer, estimated to be responsible for 71% of deaths globally. A huge proportion of these have diet-related causes.

One of the factors contributing to malnutrition is the decline in the nutritional content of certain foods. This is driven by several factors such as the development of high-yield crop varieties and high-volume food products that provide mass, but relatively low nutrition. A 2004 US study found that across 43 vegetables analysed, important nutrients were up to 38% lower than mid-20th-century levels, including a 16% decline in calcium and a 15% decline in iron content.[18] The body of scientific evidence linking soil health and human health is also growing, with studies pointing to industrial agriculture's negative impact on soil fertility and a subsequent decline in the nutritional quality of food.[19] Hyper-processed and fast foods are also often designed to maximise flavour and volume, leading to calorie-rich but nutrient-poor food products.

2.1.1   *The crucial role of business*

These scientific developments apply a new lens through which to look at food production and its associated impact – optimising not for volume but for nutritional value. Food security, health and well-being are being addressed through the concerted effort of governments, international institutions and food providers. Business arguably has the most important role to play with its deep understanding of food science, technological innovation and influence over customers. Today's food industry is largely made up of crafters who are able to design taste, texture and nutritional profiles of food products from scratch. Given this, food businesses have the capability and resources to be able to create products and supply chains that promote access to safe, healthy and sustainable food at affordable prices, while influencing people's dietary choices.

Food businesses are in a unique position to be able to provide affordable nutritious food by formulating products that promote good health and positively influence consumer dietary choices. The World Health Organisation (WHO) has put together a list of guidance of what companies and policymakers can endeavour to do to alter the nutritional composition of food products to reduce non-communicable disease[20]:

- reduce the level of salt/sodium added to food (prepared or processed)
- increase availability, affordability and consumption of fruits and vegetables
- reduce saturated fatty acids in food and replace them with unsaturated fatty acids
- replace trans-fats with unsaturated fats
- reduce the content of free and added sugars in food and non-alcoholic beverages
- limit excess calorie intake, reduce portion size and energy density of foods

2.2   What is a sustainable and healthy diet?

In the early 1980s, researchers began studying the relationship between food and the environment. This was the beginning of a long journey, with a hallmark publication in 2010 that saw the Food and Agriculture Organization (FAO) define the concept of sustainable diets for the first time:

> Sustainable Diets are those diets with low environmental impacts which contribute to food and nutrition security and to healthy life for present and future generations. Sustainable diets are protective and respectful of biodiversity and ecosystems, culturally acceptable, accessible, economically fair and affordable; nutritionally adequate, safe and healthy, while optimising natural and human resources.[21]

The health aims of sustainable diets are to achieve optimal growth and development of all individuals of all ages, for present and future generations. They should promote good health and work to prevent all forms of malnutrition as well as reduce the risk of diet-related diseases. These nutritional requirements need to be provided in a way that supports the preservation of biodiversity and planetary health well into the future.

Since the 1980s, the international community has officially recognised the need to identify a set of guiding principles for sustainable healthy diets. Such guidelines would aim to solve the problems of access to food and nutrition and environmental sustainability at each stage of the food value chain. Fortunately for humans and the planet, research shows that a sustainable diet is also largely a healthy one, capable of meeting nutritional needs through foods that support planetary health.

Box 2.2   Diet or nutrition?

Before diving into sustainable healthy diets, it is helpful to summarise the functional properties of food for the human body. It is worth remembering that there is a difference in meaning between the terms 'diet' and 'nutrition', which are too often used synonymously. Diet can be understood as the simple act of providing food to the body which, through metabolism, extracts energy and other substances it needs to regenerate and stay healthy. Meanwhile, nutrition is the science that studies the correct intake of nutrients through food and diet, such as the intake of macronutrients (carbohydrates, fats, proteins) and micronutrients (vitamins and minerals). Each contributes in different ways to keeping the body healthy, but while our diet simply looks at what food we ingest, nutrition ensures our diet meets our body's true nutritional needs.

2.2.1   *The FAO sustainable healthy diet*

In 2019, the FAO and WHO partnered on a report that defined sustainable healthy diets. The report was specifically requested by countries that acknowledged the existence of diverging views on nutrition and sustainability at a time when debates were high on the agenda of civil society, governments, international institutions and academia (Figures 2.3).

Figure 2.3 Nutritional models from all over the world. The shape might change but the substance remains the same. Various graphics based on typical local foodstuffs and diets always recommend eating a lot of fruit, vegetables and cereals. *Food-Based Dietary Guidelines*, FAO, https://www.fao.org/nutrition/education/food-dietary-guidelines/regions/en/. Originally published in the first edition of this book, *Il Cibo Perfetto*, published in Italian in 2022.

Two series of international expert consultations led to the development of the *Sustainable Healthy Diets Guiding Principles* (Figure 2.4). Interestingly, the two UN agencies do not prescribe a recommended set of food products or types, such as the often famous 'plates' represented in national dietary guidelines (Figure 2.5). Rather, they focus on guiding principles that can be applied in the context of local food cultures.

According to these principles, a sustainable healthy diet is one primarily made up of fresh, unprocessed foods such as fruits, vegetables, legumes and wholegrains. Poultry, fish, eggs and dairy can be included in moderation alongside small amounts of red meat.

2.2.2   National dietary guidelines

National dietary guidelines are documents issued by each country to advise its population on what to consume, and in what quantities, to ensure adequate and sufficient nutrition. These documents are issued alongside policy documents and government consultation. Sustainability is not always directly addressed, sometimes as a result of the political process. An example is the political decision to exclude sustainability considerations from the US 2015 National Dietary Guideline against advice provided during the expert consultation process.

The guidelines of different countries are generally very similar and resemble the well-known food pyramid, first used in the early 1990s by the US government to launch a nutritional education programme for its citizens. In 2014, the Barilla Centre for Food & Nutrition published the Double Food Pyramid. This tool ranks foods based on their relative health and environmental impact, with the lowest impact at the bottom and the highest impact at the top of the scale. Environmental impacts, measured per kilogram of food, are assessed in terms of their carbon footprint (GHG emissions). The diagram shows that the food types recommended to be consumed in the largest quantity are also those with the lowest environmental impact. This demonstrated how a healthy diet can be synonymous with a sustainable one (Figure 2.5).

The original Double Food Pyramid was adapted to be culturally relevant for the local populations of different geographic regions: Nordic countries and Canada; US; South Asia; East Asia; Africa; Latin America and Mediterranean countries. The Barilla Center for Food and Nutrition's (BCFN's) work also led to the development of a large database that includes over 1,000 sources of impact data for foods included in the food pyramid. The database was assembled using data available internationally from public databases and scientific articles concerning the environmental impacts of food, calculated according to the life cycle assessment (LCA) method.

It is likely that the importance placed on food sustainability by national dietary guidelines will increase in the coming decades. At the time of writing, Brazil, Canada, Germany, Norway, Sweden, Switzerland and Qatar have initiated work to address key areas such as fish traceability and certification, household food waste and red meat consumption. In 2021, China – which consumes 28% of the world's meat and 50% of the world's pork[22] – set a national target to cut meat consumption

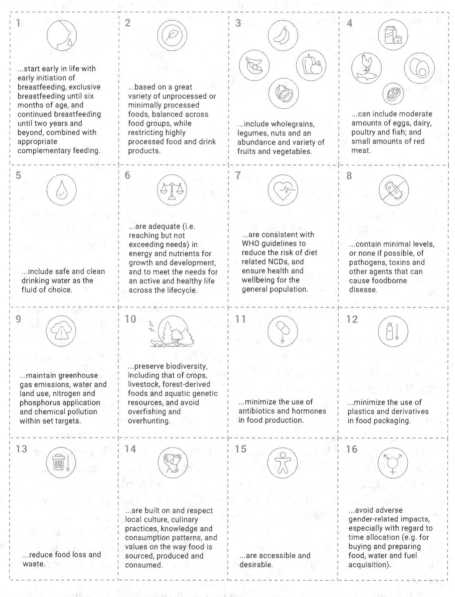

Figure 2.4 Summary of the FAO-WHO guiding principles of a sustainable healthy diet (2019). *Sustainable Healthy Diets*, WHO, FAO, 2019, https://www.who.int/publications/i/item/9789241516648.

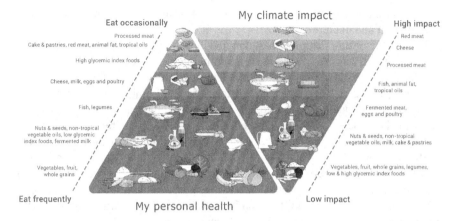

Figure 2.5 The food and environmental double pyramid. Published by the Barilla Center for Food and Nutrition (BCFN) in 2010 and reviewed in the following years. BCFN Foundation, 2014, https://www.fondazionebarilla.com/doppia-piramide/. Originally published in the first edition of this book, *Il Cibo Perfetto*, published in Italian in 2022.

by half by 2030[23] and amended its national dietary guidelines to recommend a reduced meat intake from 75 g to 40 g of meat per person each day.[24]

2.2.3   *Plant-based diets*

The rise of plant-based meat substitutes – a market valued at $910 million in 2018 and projected to grow 20% to 25% annually[25] – is a trend that could accelerate the meat reduction target by providing appealing meat alternatives. Interest in plant-based diets has grown significantly in recent years with the growth in popularity of vegan, vegetarian and flexitarian diets. Plant-based foods are estimated to make up to 7.7% of the world's protein market by 2030 – growing from a valuation of $29.4 billion in 2020 to $162 billion in just a decade.[26]

The move towards more plant-based diets has been influenced by health, animal welfare and environmental concerns. Limiting consumption of conventionally produced meat and dairy can significantly reduce GHG emissions and land, water and fertiliser use. However, the entire population moving to plant-based diets is not a panacea, due to the health and environmental benefits livestock provide when reared regeneratively. From a health perspective, animal products also provide essential nutrients such as vitamin B12, DHA and biotin in high density. This makes small quantities of meat, fish, eggs and dairy beneficial for health.[27]

There is growing evidence from the field of regenerative agriculture of the importance of integrating livestock in the farming system. They provide a natural source of fertiliser and improve soil health, structure and fertility. Good soil health is essential for maximising soil's ability to draw carbon dioxide from the atmosphere (through plants' photosynthesis) and lock it in the soil. Livestock can also valorise food waste streams – such as crop residues and by-products of food manufacturing – helping to recycle nutrients back into the system through their consumption and manure.

It is vital to ensure that plant-based ingredients themselves have been produced in a sustainable way. Soy is the most used alternative-protein ingredient. It has a long history of sustainability challenges, ranging from intensive farming to deforestation. Quinoa, at first sight a promising sustainable ingredient, has also had unintended consequences. Traditionally grown in Bolivia and Peru, quinoa is a staple food for local populations in the Andes that has seen a dramatic increase in global demand due to its health benefits, with production growing by more than 400% since the 1970s.[28] This boom in demand boosted the price of quinoa, positively impacting the welfare of many farming communities but making the crop unaffordable to many indigenous communities who relied on it as a staple crop.[29] When assessing the sustainability of an ingredient, it is fundamental to look at both the environmental and the social impact to ensure that it is produced and managed in a sustainable way.

As companies research the environmental impact of food crops, it is helpful to focus on the environmental footprint per unit of nutrient. This ensures that nutritional quality if considered when categorising one ingredient as more 'environmentally friendly' than the next. For example, eggs and dairy provide disproportionately high nutrition compared to their environmental impact, especially when produced organically or regeneratively, when compared with other alternatives.

Plant-based foods are an important piece of the sustainable food solution which must be viewed as a whole. We explore additional angles in the following chapters.

Chapter 2 Summary

Key takeaways

- The food industry is one of the most resource-intensive industries in the world, with a significant footprint, responsible for 31%[30] of GHG emissions, 70%[31] of global freshwater use, 38% of land use,[32] 80% of biodiversity loss[33] and 78% of eutrophication.[34]
- The food industry is tasked with the challenge of feeding a growing population. This involves not only producing more and sufficient food, but simultaneously tackling issues of quality and distribution to ensure that people are food secure, have a varied diet and that operational issues such as food waste are minimised.
- A transformation towards a sustainable food industry requires a dual approach: shifting towards sustainable and less wasteful production methods on farm and throughout the value chain (supply side), whilst also shifting the design of recipes and influencing eating habits to ensure we are eating more sustainable crops (demand side).

- Businesses play a fundamental role in ensuring that people eat sustainable and healthy diets, by being able to influence recipe design, the nutrient profile of food, taste and desirability through positive marketing, and in particular, by reducing sugar, salt and saturated fat content.
- Sustainable diets are healthy diets and vice versa, as they are focused on primarily fresh produce, plant-based and wholegrain-rich diets. The environmental impact of different food groups, from meat to fresh plants, is inversely proportional to the recommended quantity to consume.
- The general guidelines for a Sustainable & Healthy Diet have been defined by the FAO & the WHO, allowing for enough flexibility for these to be personalised to local and cultural eating habits.

Key questions for reflection

- Have you factored in your organisation's role in shaping sustainable production as well as influencing sustainable consumption within the food industry?
- What topics within health and nutrition are applicable and material to your business and brand vision?
- If you are a consumer-facing business, how can the FAO-WHO Sustainable Diet Guidelines be reflected in your business model?

Notes

1 *New FAO Analysis Reveals Carbon Footprint of Agri-Food Supply Chain*, United Nations News, November 2021, https://news.un.org/en/story/2021/11/1105172.
2 *Water for Sustainable Food and Agriculture. A Report Produced for the G20 Presidency of Germany*, 2017, Food and Agriculture Organization of the United Nations, https://www.fao.org/3/i7959e/i7959e.pdf.
3 *Land Use in Agriculture by the Numbers*, Food and Agriculture Organization of the United Nations, May 2020, https://www.fao.org/sustainability/news/detail/en/c/1274219/.
4 *Secretary-General's Chair Summary and Statement of Action on the UN Food Systems Summit*, United Nations, Food System Summit 2021, September 2021, https://www.un.org/en/food-systems-summit/news/making-food-systems-work-people-planet-and-prosperity.
5 J. Poore, T. Nemecek, Reducing Food's Environmental Impacts Through Producers and Consumers, in *Science*, Vol 360, Issue 6392, pp. 987–992, June 2018.
6 *Global Agriculture Towards 2050*, High Level Expert Forum – How to Feed the World in 2050, 2009, https://www.fao.org/fileadmin/templates/wsfs/docs/Issues_papers/HLEF2050_Global_Agriculture.pdf.
7 *Population, United Nations, Peace, Dignity and Equality on a Healthy Planet*, https://www.un.org/en/global-issues/population#:~:text=Our%20growing%20population,and%202%20billion%20since%201998.
8 *Ten Key Message, World Population Prospects 2022: Summary of Results*, 2022, United Nations, Department of Economic and Social Affairs, https://www.un.org/development/desa/pd/sites/www.un.org.development.desa.pd/files/undesa_pd_2022_wpp_key-messages.pdf.

9 FAO, IFAD, UNICEF, WFP, WHO, *The State of Food Security and Nutrition in the World 2022. Repurposing Food and Agricultural Policies to Make Healthy Diets More Affordable*, Rome, 2022, chrome-extension://efaidnbmnnnibpcajpcglclefindmkaj/ https://www.fao.org/3/cc0639en/cc0639en.pdf.

10 B. Farmer, Soaring Fertiliser Prices Causing More Global Hunger Than Russia's Grain Blockade, *The Telegraph*, January 2023, https://www.telegraph.co.uk/global-health/climate-and-people/soaring-fertiliser-prices-causing-global-hunger-russias-grain/#:~:text=Researchers%20modelled%20the%20combined%20effects,to%20 2021%20levels%2C%20they%20found.

11 Z. Christensen, *Economic Poverty Trends: Global, Regional and National*, Development Initiatives, February 2023, https://devinit.org/resources/poverty-trends-global-regional-and-national/#:~:text=In%202021%20an%20estimated%20698,live%20 below%20%245.50%20a%20day.

12 H. Ritchie, *Yields vs. Land Use: How the Green Revolution Enabled Us to Feed a Growing Population*, Our World in Data, August 2022, https://ourworldindata. org/yields-vs-land-use-how-has-the-world-produced-enough-food-for-a-growing-population.

13 H. Ritchie, Which Countries Eat the Most Meat? *BBC*, February 2019, https://www.bbc. co.uk/news/health-47057341.

14 A.M. Komarek, S. Dunston, D. Enahoro, H.C.J. Godfray, M. Herrero, D. Mason-D'Croz, K.M. Rich, P. Scarborough, M. Springmann, T.B. Sulser, K. Wiebe, D. Willenbockel, Income, Consumer Preferences, and the Future of Livestock-Derived Food Demand, in *ScienceDirect*, Vol 70, p. 102343, September 2021, https://www.sciencedirect.com/ science/article/pii/S0959378021001229.

15 H. Ritchie, *How Much of the World's Land Would We Need in Order to Feed the Global Population with the Average Diet of a Given Country?*, Our World in Data, October 2017, https://ourworldindata.org/agricultural-land-by-global-diets.

16 FAO, IFAD, UNICEF, WFP, WHO, *The State of Food Security and Nutrition in the World 2022. Repurposing Food and Agricultural Policies to Make Healthy Diets More Affordable*, Rome, 2022, chrome-extension://efaidnbmnnnibpcajpcglclefindmkaj/https:// www.fao.org/3/cc0639en/cc0639en.pdf.

17 *Obesity and Overweight*, WHO, June 2021, https://www.who.int/news-room/fact-sheets/ detail/obesity-and-overweight.

18 R. Lovell, How Modern Food Can Regain Its Nutrients, *BBC*, https://www.bbc.com/ future/bespoke/follow-the-food/why-modern-food-lost-its-nutrients/.

19 D.R. Montgomery, A. Biklé, Soil Health and Nutrient Density: Beyond Organic vs. Conventional Farming, in *Frontiers in Sustainable Food Systems*, Vol 5, November 2021, https://www.frontiersin.org/articles/10.3389/fsufs.2021.699147/full.

20 *Global Action Plan for the Prevention and Control of Noncommunicable Disease 2013–2020*, WHO, 2013, https://www.who.int/publications/i/item/9789241506236.

21 *Sustainable Diets and Biodiversity – Directions and Solutions for Policy, Research and Action*, FAO, Roma, 2012, https://bit.ly/3qlV3oQ.

22 C. Campbell, How China Could Change the World by Taking Meat Off the Menu, *Time*, January 2022, https://time.com/5930095/china-plant-based-meat/.

23 Ibid.

24 *Food-Based Dietary Guidelines*, FAO, https://www.fao.org/nutrition/education/food-dietary-guidelines/regions/en/.

25 C. Campbell, How China Could Change the World by Taking Meat Off the Menu, *Time*, January 2022, https://time.com/5930095/china-plant-based-meat/.

26 *Plant-Based Foods Market to Hit $162 Billion in Next Decade, Projects Bloomberg Intelligence, Bloomberg*, August 2021, https://www.bloomberg.com/company/press/ plant-based-foods-market-to-hit-162-billion-in-next-decade-projects-bloomberg-intelligence/.

27 R. Obeid, S.G. Heil, M.M.A. Verhoeven, E.G.H.M. van der Heuvel, L.C.P.G.M de Groot, S.J.P.M Eussen, Vitamin B12 Intake From Animal Foods, Biomarkers, and Health Aspects, in *Frontiers in Nutrition*, Vol 6, Issue 93, June 2019.

28 *Quinoa 2013 International Year*, https://www.fao.org/quinoa-2013/faqs/en/.

29 L. Fotso, The Sustainability of Superfoods: The Case of Quinoa, *Environbuzz Mag*, June 2022, https://environbuzz.com/the-sustainability-of-superfoods-the-case-of-quinoa/.

30 New FAO Analysis Reveals Carbon Footprint of Agri-Food Supply Chain, *United Nations News*, November 2021, https://news.un.org/en/story/2021/11/1105172.

31 *Water for Sustainable Food and Agriculture. A Report Produced for the G20 Presidency of Germany*, Food and Agriculture Organization of the United Nations, 2017, https://www.fao.org/3/i7959e/i7959e.pdf.

32 *Land Use in Agriculture by the Numbers*, Food and Agriculture Organization of the United Nations, May 2020, https://www.fao.org/sustainability/news/detail/en/c/1274219/.

33 *Secretary-General's Chair Summary and Statement of Action on the UN Food Systems Summit*, United Nations, Food System Summit 2021, September 2021, https://www.un.org/en/food-systems-summit/news/making-food-systems-work-people-planet-and-prosperity.

34 J. Poore, T. Nemecek, Reducing Food's Environmental Impacts Through Producers and Consumers, in *Science*, Vol 360, Issue 6392, pp. 987–992, June 2018.

3   The pathway to a sustainable transition

The need to meet the nutritional needs of a growing global population is clear – but how can this be achieved and who is responsible? Rising economic inequality, climate disruption, pandemics, international migration, war, extreme weather events and scarce and polluted resources have led to growing questions over current models of economic development.

For too long, we have been under the illusion that achieving well-being makes it necessary – and sufficient – to pursue economic growth at all costs by maximising production and incentivising consumption without considering the environmental and social impacts.

It is clear this model is no longer sustainable; exponential growth does not guarantee an increase in human well-being. Instead, we need a model of sustainable development that allows people's well-being and economic welfare to thrive within the boundaries of the planet, which are essential to life on Earth.

When it comes to food and agriculture, this means driving a holistic transformation that reconciles business interests, consumer needs and planetary boundaries. This transition will take time and must be supported by strategic processes at the company level to develop sustainable products and supply chains, and to engage stakeholders – including consumers – to build a sustainable food industry.

3.1   The evolution of 'sustainability'

To develop a model of economic development that is sustainable through time, the first step is to understand the social and environmental boundaries within which economic activity can take place. For centuries, companies have focused on a narrow definition of economic value – increasing profits through the sale of products that satisfy consumers. Now, many realise that failure to account for social and environmental impact is one of the most serious risks facing their business.

Taking care of these impacts is no longer seen as an ethical or moral imperative, but as a business issue. Environmental and social risks can threaten the long-term viability of a company. For example, if a production process consumes too much water for its operations in an area affected by drought, its commercial viability may be threatened by water scarcity and increased cost. And, if a company does not value its employees, it can fail to attract talent and reduce its brand equity and

DOI: 10.4324/9781003449744-3

outlook in financial markets. Finally, if biodiversity is not safeguarded, there is a risk that disease will threaten the annual harvest and overall crop viability, with significant economic consequences.[1]

When a company takes responsibility for its impacts across the value chain, these risks become core strategic, operational and marketing considerations. The commercial viability of a business requires a constant focus on environmental and social issues, but what is the relationship between economic, social and environmental priorities? How do you make decisions when a trade-off must be made between social welfare and the competitiveness of the business, or when an environmental safeguard puts people's jobs at risk?

The image historically used to illustrate the concept of sustainability displays three circles of equal size. This is the concept of the *Triple Bottom Line*, coined by John Elkington in 1994.[2] The well-known and widely shared diagram suggests that sustainability is the small area where the three circles intersect. This implies that the goal is to find solutions and actions that respect all three domains, that no one sphere is more important than the other and that there are no interdependencies between them (Figure 3.1). As sustainability discourse has evolved, this interpretation is clearly misleading. It assumes that an economy can be predominantly independent from society, and that society can prosper regardless of the environment.

One of the best alternative models to be proposed to date is that put forth by Kate Raworth[3] in *Doughnut Economics*, in which the three circles are concentric. The largest represents the environment, the smallest represents society, and the economy is the 'doughnut' that is contained within the environmental boundaries and the minimum social requirements it must provide for. In this model, an economy cannot be sustainable over time unless it provides social well-being and does not overstep planetary boundaries.

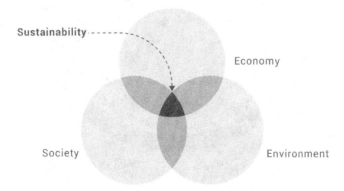

Figure 3.1 The most commonly used diagram to illustrate the concept of sustainability, which suggests that anything that simultaneously meets environmental, social and economic requirements is sustainable. Widespread representation. Originally published in the first edition of this book, *Il Cibo Perfetto*, published in Italian in 2022.

Until now, many assumed that economic activity existed alongside, or irrespective of the environment, rather than considering that there are essential ecosystem services that are fundamental to sustain economic activity and life on Earth. Extreme weather events, droughts and wildfires remind us that society, and the economy, can go haywire because of small environmental changes. We can only imagine what would happen to the economy and society if natural resources – such as freshwater or lithium, to cite just a couple – ran out or became prohibitively costly to extract. The long-term effects that could emerge from the unstoppable flow of microplastic pollution impacting the health of marine fauna and humans are similarly concerning (Figure 3.2).

More recent concepts that have entered the sustainability discourse are revolutionary in nature, including that of regenerative business and a circular economy. These recognise that 'sustainable' is no longer enough, as it limits our ambition by enabling business to continue as usual.

Recognising that there are significant issues that must be addressed, companies have taken the lead by aiming to become regenerative. By regenerating

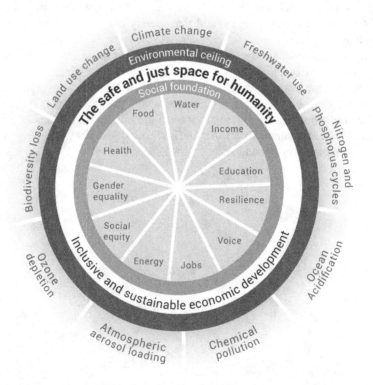

Figure 3.2 Doughnut economics: a sustainable economy between social and environmental boundaries. K. Raworth, *Doughnut Economics: Seven Ways to Think Like a 21st Century Economist*, Random House Business Books, London, 2018. Originally published in the first edition of this book, *Il Cibo Perfetto*, published in Italian in 2022.

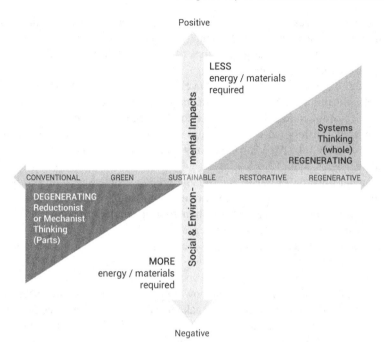

Figure 3.3 Comparison of sustainability concepts and their impact. Authors' adaptation from J. Fullerton, *Regenerative Capitalism*, Capital Institute, Greenwich (CT, USA), 2015.

environments and communities, business activities have a net positive impact. Similarly, a circular economy aims to create an economy that functions like nature – using resources and repurposing them continuously for new uses and in new forms, so that waste is avoided in the first place (Figure 3.3). We explore these approaches in significant depth in Chapter 7.

When a company sets out its strategy, it must understand the environmental and social contexts in which it operates – not necessarily because environmental or social issues are the most critical business challenges in the short term, but because their medium- to long-term management is a prerequisite for societal well-being and the survival of the economy and business.

While we recognise the breadth and complexity of sustainability issues, the focus of this book is primarily the environmental and social issues that affect the agriculture and food industries, and how companies can evolve so that these no longer form risks but are used to drive innovation and growth that is fit for the future.

3.2   Business as a driver of change

Throughout the 20th century, companies viewed the environmental impacts of their activities as marginal, mostly in response to legal requirements. If a company voluntarily went beyond this, it did so to capture a relatively small market segment, such as idealists willing to spend more for product features that benefit the environment or community. Sustainability was a niche proposition that was often weakened by consumer perceptions of 'eco' or 'fair trade' options being of inferior quality and performance.

Attitudes began to change around 20 years ago within the context of Corporate Social Responsibility (CSR). Environmental impact started to be seen as a reputational indicator for companies who understood that ignoring it could be detrimental to business. Publishing an environmental or social report became a prerequisite for any company interested in proactively managing its stakeholders, brand and reputation.

Consumer appetite for green and organic products increased, with eco product lines appearing on the shelves of major retailers and in the names of major brands. Sustainability evolved beyond being a branding or reputational issue to be a lens through which to re-evaluate products, ensure security of supply of the raw materials and create products that did not cause excessive waste or harm during or at the end of their life.

Some of the world's largest global corporations began announcing comprehensive sustainability strategies, covering how they sourced and communicated about ingredients along with the design and makeup of products. Examples include the renowned cases of Unilever, under Paul Pollman's leadership, and Danone.

In 2015, the UN launched the 17 Sustainable Development Goals (SDGs), outlining areas we must all focus on to achieve economic prosperity and well-being for society that is 'sustainable' through time. Many businesses have since launched sustainability strategies that directly align with the SDGs, in particular those signatories to the UN Global Compact whose mission is to galvanise business action towards achievement of the goals.

Since then is no longer seen as a choice or point of differentiation, but as a prerequisite for staying competitive and resilient to market disruptions and external trends. The EU and many national governments have made reporting on social and environmental issues compulsory, whether through integrated reporting or formal disclosure to investors, such as the EU's Sustainable Finance Disclosure Regulation (SFDR).[4]

There is still a long way to go before we have an accurate and comprehensive understanding of the environmental and social performance of companies across the entire value chain. However, the direction of travel is set. Industries are no longer talking about 'if' sustainability should be done, but 'how'. This is especially true for the agri-food sector, where a shift in public opinion can accelerate quickly through media channels and social networks to trigger boycotts, accusations of greenwashing and demand for change – touching on issues ranging from palm oil to pesticides and plastics.

For change to happen, sustainability must be a viable, marketing proposition that makes good business sense. Transitioning to sustainable business takes time and begins with identifying priorities and determining the most impactful changes to make. It can require significant innovation and investment to develop and implement new ways of working, processes and technologies. It also calls for the careful orchestration of employees and other stakeholders to implement change across the value chain.

We have reached a tipping point and doing nothing is no longer an option. There are many examples of companies receiving clear signals from the market that business as usual is no longer valued due to sustainability concerns. The incredibly low market valuation of coal-sector businesses is one example[5] and shifts in consumer demand towards sustainability products, incentives to de-risk supply chains in response to environmental volatility, the rising costs of natural resources and ongoing policy developments are spurring significant change to business models and products worldwide.

3.2.1   *Value drivers of sustainability*

Having understood the need for transformation, businesses must approach it from the perspective of what matters most to them and their stakeholders. The Sustainability Business Value Drivers framework (Figure 3.4) summarises the different types of value which sustainability may provide to a business. Historically, sustainability was seen to predominantly affect the bottom line as a way to reduce costs through material and energy-efficiency improvements. It was also relevant to mitigate risk, such as consumer boycotts or supply chain risks. Some more innovative companies recognised that sustainability builds customer trust and brand equity with investors, leading to financial facilitation in the market and increased revenue (Figure 3.5).

Sustainability is a key driver for innovation and market competitiveness, even if a product is not overtly marketed as sustainable. A famous example is Airbnb, which revolutionised the hospitality sector by making use of idle resources (a form of waste) by renting out spare rooms and homes. Circular economy approaches, explored further in Chapter 7, also show how new products and services can be borne out of innovation when we attempt to eliminate all waste from a business model, ensuring that the life of products and materials is extended for as long as possible.

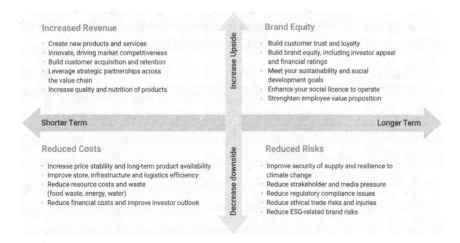

Figure 3.4 The value drivers of sustainability for businesses. Authors' elaboration.

Figure 3.5 The SDGs. The SDGs comprise 17 targets, set by the UN in 2015 (to be achieved by 2030), which highlight how the term 'sustainable' – often used only in reference to the environmental sphere – is deeply linked to social and economic dynamics. *Sustainable Development Goals*, United Nations, https://www.un.org/sustainabledevelopment/sustainable-development-goals/. Originally published in the first edition of this book, Il Cibo Perfetto, published in Italian in 2022.

Box 3.1   Food sustainability around the world[6]

The Food Sustainability Index (FSI), now in its fourth iteration, has been developed by Economist Impact with the support of the Barilla Center for Food and Nutrition (BCFN) Foundation. The first edition of the FSI was published in 2016 and ranked the food sustainability of 25 countries. The revision of 2021 examines the food systems of 78 countries, using 95 individual metrics across three key pillars: food loss and waste, sustainable agriculture and nutritional challenges. The Index now covers more than 92% of global GDP and 92% of the global population (Table 3.1).

Table 3.1 Food Sustainability Index 2021

	Overall food	Sustainable agriculture	Nutritional rating	Waste challenges
Argentina	3	3	2	2
Australia	4	2	4	4
Brazil	1	1	2	2
Canada	4	4	4	4
China	2	2	1	3
France	4	3	3	4
Germany	4	4	4	3

(Continued)

Table 3.1 (Continued)

	Overall food	Sustainable agriculture	Nutritional rating	Waste challenges
India	1	2	1	1
Indonesia	1	1	1	1
Italy	3	4	2	2
Japan	4	4	4	4
Mexico	1	1	3	1
Russia	2	2	1	2
Saudi Arabia	1	1	1	1
South Africa	2	2	3	1
South Korea	3	2	1	2
Turkey	2	1	2	3
UK	3	3	3	1
US	2	4	1	2

1: Worst quartile   2: Third quartile   3: Second quartile   4: First quartile

Source: Food Sustainability Index, Economist Intelligence Unit, https://impact.economist.com/projects/foodsustainability/.

As the world moves to act on pressing climate targets and embrace a food systems agenda, the results of the FSI highlight common lessons on how best to tackle key food systems' challenges faced by countries around the world. The correlation analysis shows that efforts to tackle food sustainability sit alongside efforts to address key social and economic objectives such as human development, sustainable development, gender equality, health spending and support for innovation.

Box 3.2   The personas behind eco-conscious consumers: the case of Italy

The eco-aware (17%). Members of this group tend to be female, well-educated, open-minded and progressive, with a deep understanding of the issues. They are aware that complexity can only be managed through knowledge and careful and conscious consumption choices. For the eco-aware, the ideal supermarket is the protagonist of important decisions: a supporter of local and national produce and, in parallel, a scientific laboratory for the protection of the planet's resources.

The eco-techs (22%). For this group, technology is the panacea for all evils. They believe human beings are a minor presence in an ever-evolving cosmos that will go on regardless of us. Only great effort to develop new technologies can save us. Their dream is a futuristic, hyper-technological, sustainable supermarket that embodies these qualities in its structure, logistics, production and waste-recycling system. In short, a concrete and brave example of a circular economy.

The veg-centric (17%). Traditionalists in their feelings and expectations, members of this group are reassured by the values of the past and protected from the dangers of the future. They imagine a sustainable supermarket that simply offers local produce and shows customers the secrets and benefits of cultivation according to traditional, natural methods.

The eco-narcissists (26%). Human are seen to be at the centre of the environmental emergency, and personal well-being and prosperity matter above all else. They demand help from science: just like 'it saved us from Covid-19, now it must make us happy and carefree once again'. Applied to the world of food, a sustainable supermarket must commit most of all to researching safe, healthy products.

The eco-thrifty (18%). Staying at the margins of culture and social change and disconnected from the issue of sustainability in its wider sense, this group focuses on the importance of 'savings'. They believe sustainable shopping is based on the hunt for the lowest price, and that a sustainable supermarket is one that offers opportunities for all-around cost-effectiveness, starting with plastic reduction which also has an impact on price.

Source: Osservatorio consumi sostenibili COOP – Roma Tre University – Sita Ricerca

---

Box 3.3   Market influence: the case of Australia and New Zealand

How sustainability is perceived by both consumers and businesses is significantly shaped by context, such as the country's demographics and their natural landscape. Australia and New Zealand have populations of 25 and 5 million respectively. They each have their population concentrated in four major cities (Australia 60% and New Zealand 50%). Australia is about the size of North America and only 25% smaller than the entirety of Europe. The economy is about $1,750 billion in Australia and $213 billion in New Zealand, with a food export of about $50 billion for both countries.

In Australia, with a large land mass and a concentrated population, logistics play an important role in determining food distribution. In New Zealand, exports are the focus of food supply chains given the abundance of production and natural resources. Farm production is generally privately owned and fresh produce is either distributed for local consumption or shipped for export.

The agricultural sector is currently trying to adapt and cope with the challenges of climate change, including extended droughts and extreme weather events. One of the starkest examples of change is in the wine industry, where vintage has advanced in some regions by about four to six weeks in the past 70 years. There are many examples of the agricultural sector adopting to more sustainable farming practices.

Processed food production is generally situated closer to the population base and can be in a single location to lower manufacturing costs. Finished goods require distribution countrywide. All major global food and beverage players are present including Fonterra (the largest dairy company in the world, headquartered in New Zealand), Mars, Coca-Cola, Unilever, McCains, Simplot, Mondelez, Asahi, etc. In addition, there are local manufacturers many of whom are owned by overseas companies.

The road to market for food produce in Australia and New Zealand is principally through major retailers, which are incredibly influential in the supply chain – Woolworths, Coles, Aldi and Metcash. Coles and Woolworth manage 55–60% of the total fresh food and grocery spend. These major retailers are integrated across the retail marketplace, owning alcohol retailers, petrol stations, clubs and gambling (poker machines). More recently, they have moved into the retail insurance market.

The sustainability agenda is being driven by multiple forces in Australia and New Zealand. Country commitments to greenhouse gas (GHG) reductions are driving the energy sector to transition to renewables. Rather than legislate and mandate recycling rates, both governments tend to offer capital incentives, although the slow progress in this area would seem to indicate that enforcement could be approaching.

The largest driver of change may be the retailers themselves, who have all published ambitious goals around recycled content of packaging, zero waste to landfill and the transition to green energy. These commitments are directly driving change in the industry, although the complete supply chain is yet to be aligned. There have been recent examples where government-initiated container deposit schemes have driven waste collectors, processors and companies to joint venture to build large facilities.

Box 3.4   Business perspectives on sustainability: the case of Pulmuone in South Korea

Pulmuone was founded as a food company in 1984. Its turnover is about $2.5 billion, and its main market is South Korea. Products are typical of the Korean culture such as tofu, bean sprouts and kimchi. The company's mission is to create a healthy tomorrow for the people and planet with wholesome foods. When Pulmuone started its business in the 1980s, food standards in Korea weren't stringent, making it difficult to trust a wide range of things such as manufacturing process and the use of raw materials.

Pulmuone began to inform consumers about the need for wholesome foods and started offering pesticide- and growth regulator-free bean sprouts and well-packaged tofu. This initiated the company's pursuit of sustainable values which continues to this day.

To better understand how sustainability is understood by a company such as Pulmuone, it is important to understand Koreans have historically had a mainly vegetarian diet, with meat consumption becoming common only in recent years. Since one of the company's main aims is to tackle the climate crisis, Pulmuone has set itself the target of achieving 50% of sales from plant-based foods.

This action raises dilemmas, one of which relates to one of the preferred Korean foods – ramen. Almost all of domestic ramen is fried in oil, the recipe itself is not vegan and is not particularly good for your health. The company has tried to make healthy ramen with raw noodles which are not fried in oil. The business of 'healthy ramen' is not thriving and the company is losing money in that product segment, but production continues as they are still committed to make ramen healthier in Korea.

Other trade-offs Pulmuone has faced include cases where they insisted on using organic agricultural raw materials and domestic products, resulting in missed opportunities to lead the market for certain products. The sesame oil business, for example, tried using domestic sesame seeds, with a price about five times that of Chinese products. While insisting on Korean sesame seeds, it missed an opportunity to be a market leader in the sesame oil market through being more competitive.

Sustainability for Pulmuone has a wide scope beyond food production and diet. In addition to food products, the company is expanding into a variety of businesses where consumers can enjoy a healthy experience such as houseware (induction instead of gas burners, air purifiers, etc.) restaurants/ service and skincare.

3.2.2   The rising demand for sustainable products

The market for sustainable products has been growing significantly over the last decades. The global ethical food market size will grow from $145.8 billion expected in 2023 to $280 billion by 2032.[7] In 2021, sustainability-marketed products delivered approximately one-third of all Consumer Packaged Goods (CPG) growth, despite representing 17% of the market share. Interestingly, products marketed as sustainable grew 2.7× faster than products not marketed as sustainable.[8] In addition, the 15 leading countries based on the Sustainable Competitiveness ranking (2017) are European.[9]

What is driving this growth is however complex and unclear, with drivers ranging from consumer beliefs and values, to education level, income level, demographics and environmental concerns. There is also a gap between consumer-stated preferences and their purchasing decisions, especially when sustainable products compel a price premium. Companies therefore looking to attract green consumers will need to understand deeply their motivations to purchase sustainable products, creating a tailored strategy to reach each segment of groups that includes specific personality traits, environmental concerns and the ability to buy, among others.

3.3   Defining a strategic approach

An effective strategy for a sustainable transition must shift both supply (how products are produced and made) and demand (what consumers want and purchase). It needs to leverage the uniqueness of the company, including its skillset and capabilities, to deliver impact while being commercially viable.

To build an effective sustainable transition, each individual company must look at its context to understand and define what sustainability means to it and its stakeholders (Figure 3.6). This has a significant advantage as each organisation can develop its own unique response, tailored to its strengths and opportunities as well as the specific customer demands it faces. Every company has unique organisational capabilities and a culture on which it can build: whether a strong charismatic leadership (e.g. Unilever's Paul Pollman or Danone's Emmanuel Faber), a good brand and marketing team (e.g. Nike's 'just do it' or Patagonia) or a technical, scientifically minded workforce (e.g. L'Oréal). This unique set of strengths is often a reflection of the company's positioning in the market, and it determines where they will be the most impactful when it comes to environmental and social sustainability.

To design reliable and efficient programmes and to set meaningful targets towards change a company must also listen to its stakeholders, especially consumers. The timeframe for implementing an integrated roadmap must embrace long-term planning and involve the entire business and key stakeholders, such as suppliers.

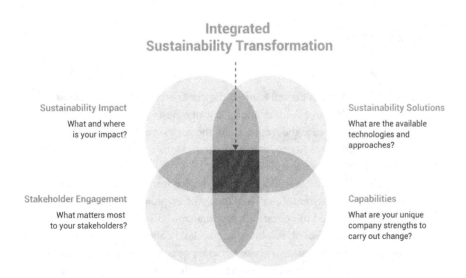

Figure 3.6 Integrated sustainability strategy. Authors' elaboration.

As a business embarks on its sustainability transformation, it can be useful to ask the following questions, which we explore in depth in the following chapters:

1 **What is your impact?** Reflecting on your holistic impact and how this can be measured. Chapter 4 explores what social and environmental impacts are and how these can be measured using different tools.
2 **Where is your impact?** This involves conducting risk assessments and calculations to understand and identify hot spots along the value chain and provide an order of magnitude on what is most important for a specific value chain. This is challenging in the food industry due to the many trade-offs and complexities, as explained in Chapter 5.
3 **What matters most to your stakeholders?** Identifying the topics and values that are most important to your stakeholder groups, and how to engage them – be they customers, investors, employees and others – is fundamental to shaping your strategy as it will influence the ability to enact change. This may involve carrying out a materiality assessment, customer listening or other stakeholder engagement and communication activities. This is expanded on in Chapter 6.
4 **What solutions are available to achieve your goals?** Approaches and technologies are constantly evolving to support changes, such as decarbonising your business and adopting circular economy or regenerative agriculture techniques. These are discussed in Chapter 7.
5 **What are your unique strengths to develop your strategy and carry out change?** As a company, there will be characteristics unique to you – such as your market, capabilities and company culture – which have a material impact on your strategy design and implementation approach. We discuss this in Chapter 8.

Chapter 3 Summary

Key takeaways

- Sustainability is now a central issue to the commercial viability of businesses, rather than solely an ethical or moral priority. Businesses need to factor in sustainability to secure their operations and appeal to their customers. It is essential for sustainability to be fully integrated into core business decisions, including core product and service design.
- Sustainability is a multi-faceted concept, ranging from economic, social and environmental considerations. The Doughnut economic model exemplifies how businesses need to operate within planetary boundaries, whilst enabling a minimum level of social well-being and societal cohesion.
- It is no longer enough to 'do no harm' or mitigate risks – innovative businesses nowadays actively strive to regenerate – such as regenerating ecosystems and communities.

- Sustainability can add significant commercial value, whether it is helping improve top-line factors (innovation, brand equity) or reduce bottom-line factors (reduce risk, costs).
- In order for a sustainability strategy to be successful, it must take into consideration a variety of market forces, such as business interests and consumer needs. These will be different depending on the market segment, as well as the country and profile of consumers.
- A path towards sustainability is bespoke for each company: it must leverage what is most material to the organisation's stakeholders as well as the company's unique strengths, internally as well as in relation to the company's role in the value chain and wider market.
- There are processes one can go through to build an integrated approach to a sustainability transformation: such as understanding what and where is your impact, listening and engaging your stakeholders, exploring existing solutions and tailoring your implementation approach to your company's unique capabilities.

Key questions for reflection

- Taking models such as the Planetary Boundaries or the SDGs, how do these influence your company's operations and how can your company contribute to the attainment of these goals?
- What value can be driven by sustainability initiatives within your organisation? Use the Sustainability Value Drivers framework for inspiration.
- How do customers in your markets perceive and understand sustainability? What values and motivations underpin their preferences?

Notes

1 I. Pratesi, M. Galaverni, M. Antonelli, *Pandemie, l'effetto boomerang della distruzione degli ecosistemi. Tutelare la salute umana consrvando la biodiversità*, WWF Italia, 2020, chrome-extension://efaidnbmnnnibpcajpcglclefindmkaj/https://d24qi7hsckwe9l. cloudfront.net/downloads/pandemie_e_distruzione_degli_ecosistemi.pdf.
2 J. Elkington, *Enter the Triple Bottom Line*, August 2004, https://www.johnelkington. com/archive/TBL-elkington-chapter.pdf.
3 K. Raworth, *Doughnut Economics: Seven Ways to Think Like a 21st Century Economist*, Random House Business Books, London, 2018.
4 The Non-Financial Reporting Directive (2014/95/EU, 'NFRD') introduced the requirement for some large companies to include a non-financial declaration in their annual report. In particular, the companies that fall within the remit of the NFRD are large public interest entities whose average number of employees during the financial year is found, at the end of the reporting period, to be at least 500.
5 V. Walt, A Top CEO Was Ousted After Making His Company More Environmentally Conscious. Now He's Speaking Out, *Time*, November 2021, https://time.com/6121684/ emmanuel-faber-danone-interview/.

6 *Economic Impact*, https://impact.economist.com/projects/foodsustainability/.
7 *Ethical Food Global Market Report*, The Business Research Company, 2023, https://www.thebusinessresearchcompany.com/report/ethical-food-global-market-report.
8 *Sustainable Market Share Index*, Sacco&Whelan, 2021, chrome-extension://efaidn-bmnnnibpcajpcglclefindmkaj/https://www.stern.nyu.edu/sites/default/files/assets/documents/FINAL%202021%20CSB%20Practice%20Forum%20website_0.pdf
9 *Statista*, 2021, https://www.statista.com.

4 Uncovering social and environmental impacts

To reduce the negative environmental impacts of food, effectively measuring and understanding these impacts is a crucial first step. To do this, we must define what we will measure, and why and how we will measure it. This chapter explores key concepts involved in measuring impact and how to apply key evaluation tools, based on the purpose of the evaluation.

4.1 Defining environmental impact

The term environmental impact is often used interchangeably to describe two distinct phenomena – cause and effect. To aid understanding, we need to distinguish between environmental aspects and impacts.

An environmental aspect is an '*element of an organisation's activities or products and services that interacts, or can interact with, the environment*'.

An environmental impact is the '*change to the environment, whether adverse or beneficial, wholly or partially resulting from an organisation's environmental aspects*'.[1]

If a company releases hot water into a river, for example, the waterway will see an increase in temperature that could result in damage to plants and animals. The industrial discharge is the aspect, and the heating of the river water is the impact. The distinction between cause and effect might seem academic, but it is useful to understand what is happening. We also must appreciate that the relationship between the environmental aspect and impact is not always obvious and can be influenced by a multitude of issues (Figure 4.1).

One such issue is time. Under certain conditions, the environment can overcome the effects of damage and return, in time, to its initial state. However, this natural resilience[2] has its limits. When an environmental aspect is too severe, the ability to self-repair fails and the environment is permanently damaged. Going back to the case of the hot water discharge, if the water is released too often or at too high a temperature, the river heats up (impact) to a point at which it will negatively impact aquatic life (damage).

The local conditions in which environmental aspect takes place (context) are also crucial for quantifying damage. The relative impact of 10 gram of pollutant

DOI: 10.4324/9781003449744-4

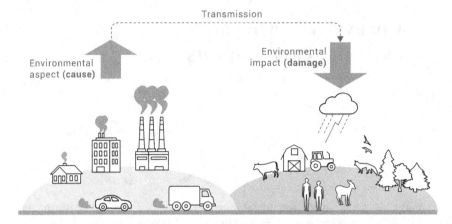

Figure 4.1 Environmental aspects are the cause, environmental impacts the effect (the damage). Authors' elaboration.

will be vastly different for a small mountain lake compared with the middle of the Atlantic Ocean. The same is true for freshwater consumption; using 1,000 litres of water in Sweden will have a different environmental impact compared with extracting the same volume of water in Israel.

An environmental aspect can also have different impacts and damages at different scales. Deforestation, for example, impacts climate change globally and biodiversity and habitats locally. These complexities require us to move beyond first impressions when analysing a system or comparing two food products to uncover hidden impacts that are beneath the surface. In doing so, we may find that a system that releases more pollutants is actually less damaging than one that releases a smaller volume, due to the context in which it happens.

4.1.1   *Global to local impact*

Space is an important variable; an environmental aspect may cause environmental damage in the locality where it occurred, or it may have global repercussions. For instance, a production plant with noisy machinery is a nuisance to local people and the wildlife immediately surrounding it. On the other hand, a company that burns a natural resource like petroleum causes damage that directly or indirectly affects the entire global population. The former has a local impact while the latter has a global impact.

Of course, the reality is more complex. If we consider a car driving through a city, we find a bit of everything. Its global impacts (energy use, carbon emissions) can be quantified relatively easily while its local impacts (particulates, noise, occupied space) require more complex techniques and models, relating to pollutant dynamics that take account of local conditions such as prevailing wind, presence of buildings, etc.

Going beyond academic definitions, analysing the impact of an aspect can lead to opposing results depending on whether we consider it locally or globally. This can be problematic when attempting to find simple solutions to complex problems. Can we confidently say that electric cars, hydropower or wood-burning fireplaces are more sustainable than their alternatives? Not in absolute terms: it depends on the parameters we consider, the context, etc. What we can do is define a set of objective data that are useful in supporting decisions made after due consideration and understanding the pros and cons for each alternative.

The complexities surrounding renewable energy and electric cars provide useful examples of the dilemmas that can arise in tackling complex environmental impacts.

4.1.1.1   Dilemmas in the production of renewable energy

The growing focus on the impacts of energy production has led to increased deployment of renewable sources: hydro, wind, solar and biomass power. Aside from biomass, which merits a separate discussion,[3] these energy sources are considered clean because their production happens without combustion, and no pollutants are emitted, avoiding the main problem with traditional fossil fuels (gas, oil, coal; Figure 4.2).

Another advantage of these systems is that they are renewable in the sense that nature provides a virtually inexhaustible source of energy. These considerations might lead us to conclude that the production of renewable energy is sustainable

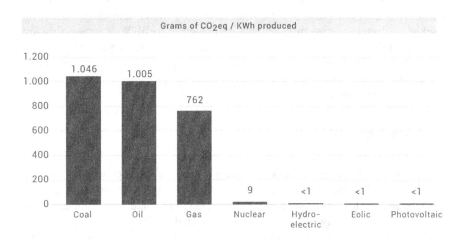

Figure 4.2 CO_2 equivalent emissions to generate electricity from different energy sources. The data account for both the energy conversion process and all the stages of fuel production and power plant construction and maintenance. Authors' elaboration. Data processed from Ecoinvent 3.6 database (2019). Originally published in the first edition of this book, *Il Cibo Perfetto*, published in Italian in 2022.

because it has no negative effects on the environment. However, on closer inspection we see this is true only for global impacts, such as CO_2 emissions.

Hydropower, by way of an example, is a widely used energy source which scores high in sustainability rankings based on avoiding CO_2 emissions. However, including local social and environmental impacts in the analysis can lead to different outcomes. The energy that powers hydroelectric plants comes from falling water or water moving near-horizontally. In both cases, there is a need to significantly alter the local physical conditions, either by building artificial mountain lakes or by diverting waterways from their natural course. If we focus on these local aspects, there are contexts in which hydropower may be less sustainable, especially for those living in affected areas.

4.1.1.2   *Dilemmas in the use of electric cars*

Air pollution is a serious problem in many cities, driving governments to introduce traffic restrictions. One solution could be to transition to hybrid (electric/fuel) or fully electric cars. But assuming that the use of an electric car is economically sustainable for everyone, this is still not a straightforward solution.

From a local perspective, there is a benefit to electric cars because their motors do not generate emissions which improve air quality in cities. But if the electricity that powers the cars comes from fossil fuels, then CO_2 emissions are generated that have a global impact, contributing to climate change in a similar way to traditional petrol engines. Hence, if the main goal is to decrease pollution in cities, electric (or hybrid) cars are beneficial. And if the main focus is on reducing emissions, then wider variables in the system must be analysed. Delving deeper into the problem, the focus should shift onto the function (mobility) rather than the means (car), working to create systems that are more sustainable overall. With remarkably low utilisation rates for the average car – for instance, in the UK, cars are parked 96%[4] of the time – optimising mobility using public transport systems, car-sharing programmes, cycling infrastructure, etc., could reduce the number of cars on the road and decrease air pollution.

4.2   Defining social impact

When discussing sustainability impacts in the food industry, social impacts are as relevant as environmental ones. However, they are often conceptualised and quantified in different ways and require a different approach to manage them. Historically, the topics of social and environmental sustainability were discussed in parallel without many overlaps. They were treated as different areas of expertise and often dealt with by different teams within an organisation, the social component being managed in an ethical trade team, or legal and HR, and the environmental one covered by the sustainability team.

In recent decades, strategic conversations about sustainability have driven a more joined-up approach. The use of ESG (environmental, social and governance) has grown as a synonym for sustainability. When upholding sustainability across the value chain, certifications are increasingly concerned with both social and environmental components, although to varying levels. In innovative approaches to conservation, social and environmental sustainability have even been recognised to be interdependent, where one is the precondition for the other – for example, when relying on local communities to protect areas of high conservation value such as forests.

Box 4.1   The inter-dependence between social and environmental sustainability: community and wildlife interactions by Kiran Mohan, Fauna & Flora International

Trade and economic development are portrayed as a leading cause of environmental degradation in many narratives. However, businesses with genuine interest in sustainability and opportunities to have tangible nature-positive impacts can play a crucial role in conserving natural habitats and biodiversity and meaningfully improving the lives of indigenous communities.

The 2022 WWF Living Planet Report[5] highlighted that the current bio-diversity crisis is accelerating, with 69% of animal populations wiped out since 1970 and up to a million species at risk of extinction.[6] Our global food system is the primary driver of biodiversity loss, with agriculture being the identified threat to 24,000 of the 28,000 (86%) species at risk of extinction.[7]

Conserving forest resources is a social imperative; 70% of the world's poor are directly dependent on wild flora and fauna and one in five people rely on forest resources for their food and income. For many indigenous and local communities, uses of wild species are embedded in and maintained through local knowledge, practices and spirituality. At the current rate of biodiversity loss, local livelihoods, food security and cultural identity of communities are at risk.

The traditional response to biodiversity challenges focused on 'fortress' conservation approaches, for example, setting up a protected area such as a national park. However, these often exclude local communities and can deny them their generational/traditional rights to forest resources. This margin-alisation often turned the long-term local stewards of forests to work against conservation.

Fauna & Flora International (FFI), the world's first international con-servation charity, works to develop an approach to conservation where local people economically benefit from forest preservation through the sustainable commercialisation of forest products. Like-minded private sector partners set up nature-positive small to medium enterprises at a community level that provide clear economic incentives for sustainable use of natural resources. These enterprises are linked to in-country traders to access niche markets in the food and cosmetic sectors that value biodiversity and social impact. Such sustainable supply chain models have been attempted in more than ten countries globally, supporting the sustainable management of more than 100,000 hectares of forest and seascape globally and economically benefiting more than 20,000 local community members.

The approach worked particularly well in Northern Albertine Rift Uganda, home to the last remaining 5,000 endangered eastern chimpanzees. Crop-raiding by the primates, and associated human-wildlife conflict, is a significant threat to biodiversity. This is further aggravated by local community groups growing sugar, amongst other crops, outside protected area and wildlife corridors, which attract chimpanzees to farmlands. To address the challenge, FFI partnered with organic in-country companies exporting herbs to develop a farmer association to introduce and market new crops, such as ginger, that are not palatable for chimps and deter them from entering farmlands. Farmers generate a better income with access to organic markets and, realising the importance of biodiversity conservation, set aside 5% of profits for conservation efforts.

In coastal Tanzania, Pemba Islands, FFI and the Mwambao Coastal Community Network (MCCC) work with the local community to promote the sustainable use of marine resources. With the growing population relying on fishing for their basic livelihood, pressures on the marine ecosystem are high. In consultation with the local community, it was agreed that part of a fishing area would be temporarily closed for part of the year. FFI and MCCC facilitated a meeting with octopus exporters, fishers, government and other key market actors to ensure the community were incentivised to respect the closure agreement. During the meeting, it became clear that overfishing resulted in a high proportion of small octopuses in the catch. This was decreasing the economic value generated as only the larger octopus (above the legal-size limit) can be sold for export. International exporters had been unaware of the conservation measures, which they recognised as well-aligned with their business interest of procuring large, export quality octopus. The community took the opportunity to successfully negotiate a better price for an opening day's catch and buyers agreed to make a financial contribution to the costs of conservation efforts. This secured a protected marine environment for part of the year and increased the economic value of trade through more sustainable production of octopus.

The value we place as a society on human life and well-being has evolved over the last century, ultimately developing legislation that has better defined human rights within our personal and civic life – the UN Declaration of Human Rights in 1948 being a significant milestone for humanity.[8] Governments have increasingly recognised the role organisations have to play in upholding human rights in the workplace by turning these standards into legislation. The International Labour Organization raised the profile of human rights in the workplace by establishing International Labour Standards to be ratified by individual countries. The 1998 Declaration of Fundamental Principles and Rights at Work[9] describes five fundamental principles that are considered paramount for all parties to respect, even when national governments are not signatories to the relevant conventions:

- freedom of association and the effective recognition of the right to collective bargaining
- the elimination of all forms of forced or compulsory labour
- the effective abolition of child labour
- the elimination of discrimination with respect to employment and occupation
- a safe and healthy work environment

To a certain extent, therefore, social sustainability is concerned with compliance with national and international law. There are times, however, when there is a gap between the ethical standards expected by society and the reality in the workplace. This is where a conscious effort is made (and expected by customers) to voluntarily improve the social impacts an organisation has on its employees and broader stakeholders.

This movement has given rise to two important concepts: those of **shared value** and **social impact**. Shared value was defined as practices that 'enhance the competitiveness of a company while simultaneously advancing the economic and social conditions in the communities in which it operates'.[10] The concept was adopted by multinational firms, such as Unilever and Danone, who repositioned themselves as companies who provide nutrition and health through their product range, whilst delivering social value. This notion of shared value includes direct customers of companies and also the communities they come into contact with through their business ecosystem. Unilever, for example, set up one of the largest-scale sustainable sourcing networks in the world, developing a decade-long partnership with Save the Children and Symrise to support the communities of vanilla farmers in Madagascar.[11] Unilever wanted the communities who were related to their vanilla production, even if they were only the neighbours of vanilla farmers, to feel they had benefited in some way. The rise of social impact, or social entrepreneurship, takes this to its extreme, where businesses are set up to purposefully target the creation of significant or positive change that solves, or at least addresses, social injustice and challenges.[12]

4.2.1 *Addressing social sustainability*

The food industry impacts across the full spectrum of social sustainability. Upholding the International Labour Organization (ILO)'s fundamental labour rights is of paramount importance when complex global value chains make it challenging to provide transparency and enforcement of ethical standards. Downward pressure on prices and complex geopolitical landscapes create unequal value being shared along the value chain. This inequality gives rise to movements such as fair trade, which demand the redistribution of economic profit to guarantee that the poorest receive fair remuneration for their work.

So where should companies start? The first task is to set the standard of social sustainability or shared value a company wishes to achieve through its business eco-system. This can be done by developing a code of ethics to address what is important

Social Sustainability Focus Areas	Description	Hotspots
Good working conditions	The provision of good working conditions at all levels of the value chain requires companies to ensure the safety and fair treatment of workers on a number of topics, from physical safety from accidents and abuse, to working hours, fair pay, freedom of assembly and the expression of grievances. These are well represented in the Ethical Trade Initiative Base Code and ILO standards. There are a number of certifications that can provide this level of trust, such as Sedex's SMETA audit (ethics) or ISO 45001 (safety).	Low-skilled food processing and manufacturing globally, particularly food primary food ingredients and animal products.
Modern slavery	Modern slavery is the recruitment, transport, receipt and harbouring of people to exploit their labour, and it affects almost all parts of the world. Globally, it's estimated that there are over 40 million men, women and children in situations of modern-day slavery today. Legislation is being pioneered in the UK, California, and NSW in Australia. These are often characterised by low-pay and poor working conditions, passport retention and forms of bonded labour. These especially affect seasonal workers and migrant labour who are unable to negotiate or influence the terms under which they work.	Low-skilled food farming, production, processing and packaging of food products globally; fisheries; goods such as crustacea, corn, palm oil, poultry, rice, sesame, wheat, sugarcane, cattle, beans, coffee and cocoa beans, seafood, nuts and tea.
Child Labour	Child labour, as degined by the International Labour Organization, is work that deprives children of their childhood, their potential and their dignity, and that is harmful to physical and mental development. It is therefore important to remember that not all work done by children is considered child labour or should be eliminated. Child labour therefore is work that is mentally, physically, socially or morally dangerous and harmful to children; and/or interferes with their schooling by depriving them of the opportunity to attend school with excessively long and heavy work. Child labour is often correlated with a country's socio-economic development. For more information visit the UNICEF-ILO child labour 2020 report, and the IPEC (International Programme on the Elimination of Child Labour) focused on Agriculture.	Manually labour-intense food commodities, such as cocoa; farming, including seed production; fishing and aquaculture; forestry; livestock production
Fair pricing	It is important that prices are paid that are commensurate with the work effort, fairly remunerating workers for their labour. Due to the fierce pressure on food pricing, agricultural commodities often are priced very low, which does not permit an adequate remuneration of workers. Efforts to evaluate a fair price are attempted in various forms. The Fair Trade Foundation sets a certification and recommends price adjustments compared to the market price. The Living Wage Foundation helps calculate a living wage, based on the cost of living in a given area. Fair pricing experts can support companies to ensure that prices paid adequately cover costs and wages involved for the most vulnerable along the value chain.	Bananas, tea, coffee, sugar, cocoa, flowers, sugar, cotton, quinoa, rice, fruit, nuts, herbs

Figure 4.3 Key hotspots in the industry. Authors' elaboration.

Social Sustainability Focus Areas	Description	Hotspots
Responsible marketing	Responsible marketing concerns the content and accuracy of communication within the food industry, both amongst businesses and to customers, all along the value chain. Responsible marketing supports a transition to sustainable food systems, covering both healthy diets as well as sustainable production systems. This includes, for example, the marketing of goods to children and adolescents.	Sustainability claims of products; health claims of products; marketing strategy of unhealthy products (e.g. with excessive sugar, fat, salt)
Food affordability	Food affordability concerns the access and availability of a healthy sustainable diet at an affordable cost for all. According to the WBCSD, 3.1bn people cannot afford a healthy diet65, defined as a diverse range of nutritious foods that meet energy requirements and provide all the essential micronutrients in the right amounts. Food affordability is measured as the ratio between food prices and wages. The average cost of a healthy diet globally in 2020 was USD 3.54 per person per day.	N/A
Gender	This topic concerns the gendered division of labour and income in the agriculture sector, exploring how income is distributed in the family and how topics such as the possession of formal identity cards, bank accounts and land rights influence the income, freedom to work and economic development of women and families across different geographies. At times, women are performing most of the agricultural work, though they are not recipients of the income of their labour and are limited in their ability to prosper due to systemic obstacles to owning land or opening bank accounts.	Many agriculture products in smallholder farming communities: e.g. Cocoa production in West Africa67.

Figure 4.3 Key hotspots in the industry. Authors' elaboration.

across the value chain. International bodies have drawn on ILO guidance to set standards for industry. For example, the UN Guiding Principles (UNGP) Reporting Framework encourages companies to report on how they uphold human rights.[13] The UNGP is supported by centres of excellence, such as Shift, which actively work with financial institutions, governments and companies to instigate change.

The Ethical Trade Initiative (ETI) has created a seminal ETI Base Code. It summarises the most important workers' rights to guarantee within the value chain along with a mechanism of reporting and continuous improvement for the industry. The ETI was set up at the turn of the century in the UK to create an impartial and accountable system of monitoring companies' compliance with a code of ethical trade, as a reaction to human rights abuses taking place in manufacturing apparel in Asia. This was subsequently extended to other industries. Food is a key component, and the majority of the UK food retail market members are members of the ETI.[14]

The food industry has specific social sustainability concerns that can be directly addressed within a company's value chain (Figure 4.3).

4.2.2 *Quantifying social outcomes at the business level*

While businesses aspire to act purposefully, the increase in use of the term impact has contributed to the widespread risk of 'impact washing'. The issue stems from confusion around how impact is defined and measured. At the time of writing in

February 2023, the field of social impact measurement is developing at pace at all levels.

From an investor perspective, the EU (European Union) Taxonomy has been created as part of the EU's Sustainable Finance Action Plan to help investors understand whether a particular economic activity is environmentally sustainable. The Environmental Taxonomy clearly defines all activities which fall into eight specific environmental buckets. The success of the Environmental Taxonomy has raised expectations of a Social Taxonomy to shed light on definitions and KPIs for activities deemed sustainable from a social perspective. The aim is to improve comparability between market players and reduce greenwashing by financial institutions claiming socially sustainable objectives as the goal of their funds. It will improve the parameters of how financial market participants measure and communicate their pursuit of a social impact by standardising the mandatory disclosures.

The Final Report on Social Taxonomy was published in February 2022,[15] covering questions and challenges that have arisen during the creation of the taxonomy. The Report[16] mentions a survey which showcases the four main problems with measuring social sustainability:

i   the social measurement evaluates what is most convenient, not what is most meaningful
ii current approaches are not likely yielding the information needed to identify social leaders
iii lack of consistency creates confusing 'noisiness' across the ESG industry
iv existing measurement does not equip investment to respond to the demand for socially responsible investment strategies

Compared to environmental impact measurement, where, generally, there are clear globally utilised units of measurement, social impact measurement is a broad and fragmented area of study. Units of measurement often depend on context as well as the products and services provided. In addition, companies may communicate the absence of social sustainability issues, through *zero incidence* or *low risk*, rather than reporting on a quantified impact. Impact metrics generally focus on generic global metrics or on specific, bespoke pilot projects in highly controlled and measured circumstances. It is, therefore, easier to speak of zero incidence and risk, rather than choose an ambiguous metric to disclose the impact of a firm's operations (Figure 4.4).

Despite the final report publication in 2022, and demand for a Social Taxonomy by stakeholders, the European Commission has prioritised other more pressing global developments such as the war in Ukraine and its fallout. This has left those waiting for the publication of a Social Taxonomy to consider the current regulatory landscape and what social metrics are already being mandated. Many have turned to regulations published within the EU's Sustainable Finance Action Plan, such as the Sustainable Finance Disclosure Regulation (SFDR) and the social metric disclosures required for each entity in scope. Financial market participants must disclose a mandatory list of indicators covering nine environmental metrics and five

Level of communication	Description	Examples
Zero Incidence	This is often the case where there is a degree of vertical integration in the supply chain and the company has direct access to information and can control the outcomes of its own operations and processes.	0 Fatalities / 0 injuries on a food processing site
Risk Level (e.g. Low or High)	A company is working across its value chain to assess and reduce the risk of a specific human rights violation. The level of risk is often measured internally, though not publicly reported externally, as it is used by companies to mitigate risk. It may be that a company chooses to outwardly discuss areas of high-risk to collaborate cross-industry.	Child labour, modern slavery
Quantified Social Impact	This is the best-case scenario of measuring social impact. Metrics measure outcomes, rather than actions. In a sustainable sourcing context, this is a move away from a measure of number of farmers trained in sustainable farming practices, towards number of famers (or volume of trade) who have achieved sustainability certification of their produce.	Actions: # of meals provided # of school books purchased Outcomes: # of people are no longer food insecure # of children passing their school exams
Reporting & Process Adherence	Where there is insufficient visibility across the value chain and complexity is such that it is hard to measure specific outcomes, a company can be evaluated against its compliance with process through rigorous reporting.	Ethical Trade Initiative Membership & Yearly Reporting, UN Guiding Principles Reporting Framework
Certification	Given that a minimum level of human rights in the workplace are guaranteed through legislation, certifications can provide the level of credibility and accountability required by companies along the value chain.	SMETA (by Sedex) Ecocert ISO 26000

Figure 4.4 Examples of generic social impact measurement and reporting. Authors' elaboration.

social metrics: violations of UN Global Compact Principles and OECD guidelines; lack of processes and compliance mechanisms to monitor United Nations Global Compact and OECD guidelines; unadjusted gender pay gap; board gender diversity and exposure to controversial weapons. However, these basic accounting metrics are not necessarily disclosing a quantifiable social impact for the firm, but more so, just a social input.

4.2.3   *Measuring social impact*

So how can we universally measure social impact? At the global level, the Global Impact Investing Network (GIIN) has created a solution to assist investors with identifying appropriate impact metrics, called IRIS+.[17] The IRIS+ team has developed a free online database which defines specific impact metrics for each of the UN SDGs and spans 17 thematic areas.

It uses the widely known framework of the five dimensions of impact: what is the goal? who is affected? how much change is happening? what is the contribution? what is the risk? Almost 19,000 organisations disclose impact using these metrics globally.[18]

The database of impact metrics suggested for those falling within the *agricultural* thematic umbrella can be filtered into strategic goals of impact, including *food security, smallholder agriculture* and *sustainable agriculture.* Analysing the *sustainable agriculture* goal further, the IRIS+ tool narrows the goal based on a list of options including *improving social equity and justice through agriculture.* Once this option has been chosen, an excel is available to download which includes a list of social impact metrics broken into the previously stated five dimensions of impact. These quantifiable impact metrics are backed up with guidance documents on *how to* collect data. Despite having free, accessible tools like IRIS+, the lack of global regulation for a standardised social impact metrics means data remains largely incomparable.

4.4   Key tools for assessing impact

The evaluation of sustainability indicators can be approached using assessment tools that have been introduced by the food sector. This adaptation, which is undoubtedly advantageous, is affected by two limitations that must be considered when analysing results: conceptual limitations and operational limitations.

The first aspect relates to complexity and uncertainty. Agricultural and animal husbandry systems are simple only on the surface. Compared with other industries, they are influenced by many more variables that make management – and precise measurement of impacts – much more complicated. These variables include climate and weather, crop varieties, disease, pests and previous harvests. If a major hailstorm hits an apple orchard while it is in flower, the harvest will suffer greatly, and the yield will be lower. In this case, farming practices should not be judged to be less sustainable because impact calculated per apple is greater than it would have been if all blossoms had fruited.

Another conceptual limitation concerns the so-called functional unit. When assessing the production of an object, the usual approach is to calculate environmental impact per production unit: for instance, emissions per kilogram of steel. When the same assessment is applied to the food system, interpretive difficulties may arise. Intensive farming, for example, tends to have smaller impacts per unit produced in the short term, hence the success of the Green Revolution that greatly increased yields with intensive production. But, in the long term, this can cause significant local and global impact. Intensive farming practices such as tilling, deforestation, monocropping and overgrazing may not lead to immediately measurable soil degradation, but large amounts of soil can be lost due to wind and water erosion over time[19] and impacts on productivity of depleted fertility may not be felt for some seasons. Assessments of food supply chains should account for this by giving greater weight to local impacts compared to those of other industries. Assessing topics such as biodiversity, ecosystem services and soil carbon sequestration enables a deeper view of systems and contributes to enhanced improvement actions.

The fact that the impacts of farming are affected by what happens over multiple years should shift analysts' focus from the impact of 1 kg of product to the impact of a hectare of land, or even the impact of a hectare of land over time, for example, four or ten years, including all cultivation systems involved.

Another variable that should be considered is the nutritional quality of the final product. For example, starting from the assumption that high-quality pasta is made from durum wheat that contains higher protein content than standard wheat varieties, it is likely that varieties with lower yield rates were used, and that more fertilisers were required in their production. How does this fit into the sustainability debate? One option is to interpret the available data very cautiously. In the case of wheat, for example, it might make sense to normalise a certain protein content to obtain comparable data.

Finally, an operational limitation. Agricultural production is widely distributed, with a particular food type being grown on hundreds, or even thousands, of farms scattered throughout a given territory. Data collection technology provides capabilities to achieve almost total coverage of primary data, allowing analysts to precisely understand the on-the-ground impacts of complex supply chains.

In order to assess the sustainability of an entire food system, we must combine methodologies to evaluate global impacts [such as life cycle assessment (LCA)] and local assessment (such as natural capital evaluation). In some cases, a deep assessment of specific topics such as animal welfare could be added to the scorecard.

4.4.1   Analysing complex systems: Life Cycle Assessment

The environmental impacts of a product, including food, can be calculated using the LCA method. This evaluates all stages of the production system throughout the supply chain, from sourcing raw materials to consumption of the product and disposal of waste. Today, the approach, which was introduced in the late 1990s, is widespread.

In practice, LCA requires the collection of production data from every single stage in the chain, which is converted into concise indicators using specific computing software. The indicators provide useful information that can inform business and advertising strategies. To calculate the impact of pasta production, for example, data is collected on what happens in the field, at the mill, during production and so on (Figure 4.5). The information that can be collected is effectively infinite, and analysts' expertise and the use of databases make it possible to focus on the most important and distinctive aspects of the system being assessed.

Almost all organisations use LCA to measure performance and corroborate, at least in part, their advertising activities. The computing rules, data, instruments and everything needed to perform the assessment are now consolidated and sufficiently mainstream.

There is often confusion over the use of information gained from an LCA analysis. A first potential use, simple and intuitive, is to improve understanding of what aspects can be worked on to improve sustainability performance. An assessment of the impacts of durum wheat pasta, for example, reveals that the main carbon footprint occurs during the agricultural and home cooking phases (Figure 4.6).

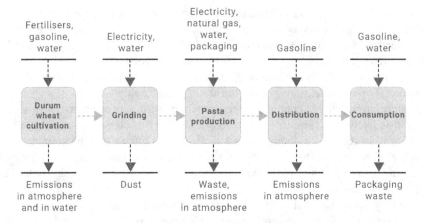

Figure 4.5 The life cycle of pasta requires the collection of data on what happens during farming, at the mill, during processing, and so on until the pasta is distributed to the consumer. Authors' elaboration.

Box 4.2   Where do we find food impact data?

LCA requires primary data, specially collected and representative of the processes involved, and secondary data, derived from publications in scientific journals, technical reports and support databases. The most notable scientific journals include the International Journal of Life Cycle Assessment, *the* Journal of Food Engineering *and the* Journal of Cleaner Production.

Since 2010, the Barilla Center for Food & Nutrition Foundation has undertaken an important project – known as Doppia Piramide (Double Pyramid) – to collate the information in many of these publications into a database containing over 1,500 sources of data grouped into different food categories. The International EPD® (Environmental Product Declaration) System could be considered another database available at www.environdec. com. In this case, the data relates not to generic products but to specific references by specific producers.

The sources most widely used by those involved in assessing the sustainability of food are the various internationally recognised professional databases, including:

Ecoinvent. *Recognised as the largest database on the market. Its data covers the majority of industrial sectors and is well-documented and transparently presented. Ecoinvent was created by a non-profit organisation of the same name, founded by several Swiss public institutions (including ETH Zurich, EPF Lausanne, and Agroscope, the Swiss Centre of Excellence for Agricultural Research). https://www.ecoinvent.org/*

Agri-footprint. Dedicated entirely to the agri-food sector, this database offers a range of alternative models for each reference (allocation methods) and a high level of detail in relation to fertilisers and the impact of land use. The database is a project by Blonk Consultants, a leading Dutch consultancy in the environmental, food, and health sectors. https://www.agri-footprint.com/

Agribalyse. A database wholly dedicated to the agri-food sector and born out of a broad partnership between French public and private research institutes, coordinated by ADEME (Environment and Energy Agency) and INRAE (National Institute of Agronomy Research). https://www.ademe.fr/en/agribalyse-program

GFLI. Created by its namesake institution (the Global Feed LCA Institute), this free database was launched to provide instruments to support the accurate assessment of the impact of animal feed production. The projects (and the database) are promoted by several feed producer associations/federations (Europe, US, Canada and the international federation) and international corporations in the sector.

Eaternity. This database is the largest and most comprehensive database for carrying out meal and product calculations. It is curated by scientists from Zurich University of Applied Science (ZHAW), University of Zürich (UZH), Swiss Federal Institute of Technology in Zurich (ETHZ), Research Institute of Organic Agriculture (FiBL), Quantis and others.

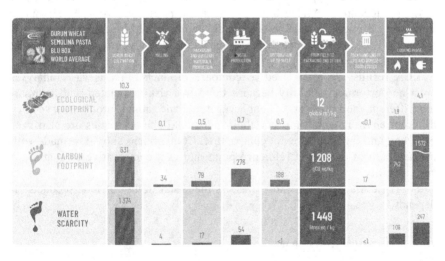

Figure 4.6 Environmental impacts of durum wheat pasta production by Barilla. Cooking environmental performances are calculated considering pasta cooking in local and export markets (in this case the most representative country, in terms of distributed volumes, is considered). *Durum Wheat Semolina Pasta in Paperboard Box – Environmental Product Declaration Pasta Barilla*, https://www.environ-dec.com/library/epd1563. Originally published in the first edition of this book, *Il Cibo Perfetto*, published in Italian in 2022.

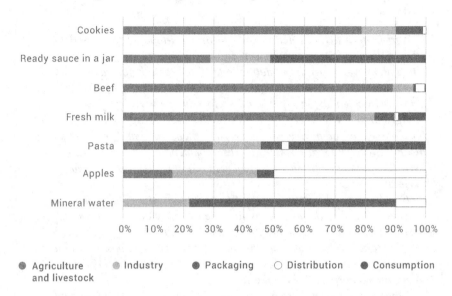

Figure 4.7 Distribution of impacts in the main life cycle stages of selected food products. Authors' elaboration. Data processed from certified and public Environmental Product Declarations.

These analyses often lead to counterintuitive results that challenge consumer perceptions. For example, not everyone is aware that the main impacts of most food products are generated by the agricultural phase (Figure 4.7). Of course, there are exceptions, such as bottled water where the bottle accounts for approximately 50% of impacts since the beverage itself does not contain any cultivated ingredients.

LCA results are often used to compare products. In this case, analyses must be performed carefully because there is a risk associated with comparing different food products. Though vegetable and animal products have very different environmental impacts, their nutritional characteristics are also very different, and thus they are not comparable. Comparisons should be made with the sole aim of creating a reference point and as a comparative estimation of sustainability.

So, is LCA a perfect method to assess the sustainability of food products? It depends.

4.4.2   Assessing ecosystem services

The need to simplify messages regarding environmental impacts while maintaining scientific rigour is no simple matter. This is especially true when global and local indicators have to be compared because, in many cases, the concerns raised are of a contrasting nature. Widespread attempts to find aggregate indicators that simplify communications by using a single value are ongoing.

One of the most interesting methods to emerge is that of ecosystem services, developed in 1997 by economist Robert Costanza. Drawing on the field of environmental economics, ecosystem services are 'services' that are generated by natural systems and beneficial to humans. They can be grouped into three main categories: regulating services (climate, water, atmospheric gases, erosion, pollination, habitats for biodiversity and prevention of hydrogeological instability), provisional services (food, resources, freshwater, biological variability) and cultural services (aesthetic, recreational, educational, spiritual, artistic and identity values).[20]

The assessment of ecosystem services aims to transform impacts, both local and global, into an aggregate economic value that represents the environmental cost of the process. From a methodological perspective, the value of impacts is calculated by assuming a replacement cost for natural capital. This is achieved by considering, for example, the market value of carbon credits in the case of GHG (greenhouse gas) emissions, the cost of treatment to remove chemicals that contribute to eutrophication and the average supply cost of water used on farms. Depending on the organisational conditions of a certain sector, other methods for estimating environmental costs may be applied. Monetising impacts in this way can make it possible to treat the cost as a budget item, work to reduce it, decide to include it in corporate costs and – once it has been reduced to a minimum – decide whether to launch local offset actions.

4.4.3 Measuring animal welfare

The perception of animal well-being is ambiguous and characterised by strong subjectivity, linked to ethical considerations and individual perceptions. The general public considers animal welfare as 'adequate' based on the perception of the animal and the perspective adopted. In contrast, decades of research have led the scientific

---

Box 4.3 The five freedoms[21]

FROM HUNGER, THIRST AND BAD NUTRITION by guaranteeing the animal access to fresh water and a diet that keeps it in full health

TO HAVE AN APPROPRIATE PHYSICAL ENVIRONMENT by giving the animal an environment that includes shelter and a comfortable resting area

FROM PAIN, WOUNDS, DISEASES by preventing them or quickly diagnosing and treating them

TO DISPLAY THEIR SPECIES-SPECIFIC BEHAVIOURAL CHARACTERISTICS by providing the animal with sufficient space, adequate facilities and the company of animals of its own species

FROM FEAR AND DISCOMFORT ensuring the animal conditions and care that do not involve psychological suffering.

community to converge on shared definitions and measurement methodologies. The 'five freedoms' were institutionalised in 1979 by the Farm Animal Welfare Council (FAWC) and are still the basis of international legislation on animal welfare today. These freedoms should be protected to guarantee the animal a state of well-being, in terms of both the absence of pathologies and overall health (physical and mental).

Adaptation to these factors can vary intensely on a case-by-case basis: an animal can be, for example, at a good level of welfare with respect to factors such as the rearing structure, but a poor level for others, such as health status. In other words, we must speak of well-being in terms of not only presence/absence of a freedom but also intensity.

In the case of livestock, the five freedoms should be guaranteed by focusing attention mainly on the farming phase, but without disregarding transport and slaughtering. In this regard, the type of farming is not the only criterion on which to measure animal welfare. An intensive farming system, with high densities but managed efficiently and with innovative housing systems, often offers better welfare conditions than a more traditional system, with lower densities but managed with less care.

In the EU, there has been legislative intervention to regulate these aspects, establishing minimum thresholds to be respected to guarantee an acceptable state of animal welfare. The intervention of the legislator has been accompanied by the considerable growth of standards and voluntary initiatives, brands and certifications. This is the case, for example, of animal-welfare awards and animal-farming standards proposed by non-governmental organisations such as Compassion in World Farming and the RSPCA.

4.5   Sustainability indicators: from global to local

Sustainability assessment generates a lot of data that, to be interpreted effectively, must be summarised using indicators that are representative of the system being assessed. This process is complicated by the need to balance simplification, which is useful in communicating complex ideas, and scientific rigour. In many cases, considerations associated with a process in relation to different environmental impacts can lead to controversial results.

In theory, agri-food supply chains generate considerable environmental impacts, and a scientifically robust analysis ought to compare an array of different indicators. Instead, only a few indicators are often focused on to simplify communication. GHG emissions, land use and water use are the most common, usually represented by their so-called footprints. Despite their limitations, the combination of these indicators represents a balanced dataset, in terms of both simplicity and scientific rigour – at least as far as global impacts are concerned (Figure 4.8).

The analysis of these indicators is discussed in more depth below, with more attention on the application of carbon footprints, given the current focus of institutions, the media and consumers on the climate crisis.

Indicator		Aim	Scale
	Carbon footprint	Reduction	Global
	Water use	Lower the local pressure during the usage Reduction of the pollution	Local
	Land use	Reduction	Local
	Deforestation	Reduction	Local / Global
	Biodiversity loss	Preservation	Local / Global
	Eutrophication	Reduction	Local
	Resource use	Use of renewable Recycle	Global
	Air pollution	Reduction	Regional / Local

Figure 4.8 The main environment topics in the agri-food sector. Authors' elaboration. Originally published in the first edition of this book, *Il Cibo Perfetto*, published in Italian in 2022.

4.5.1 *Measuring carbon footprints*

The carbon footprint comprises the emission of GHGs associated with a company, process or product. It is one of the most widely used indicators because it is correlated to climate change and because it indirectly includes the consumption of energy from fossil fuels, which is undoubtedly one of the least sustainable human activities. In this book, we use the carbon footprint to simplify certain topics. However, it should be noted that viewing environmental questions through a single lens can generate paradoxical results, such as making nuclear energy appear sustainable because its CO_2 impact is essentially zero. Given the widespread interest in this indicator, it is worth delving into some of its features to help aid the interpretation of results.

4.5.1.1 *Emissions data trends*

The first key aspect is the geographical scale of the problem. Given that CO_2 emissions have a global impact, it can be misleading to analyse and attribute them to different regions of the world. Consider any commodity – an item of clothing, a smartphone or a computer. In most cases, its emissions are attributed to the geographical region where it was manufactured (China, for example), even though it may be purchased and used elsewhere.

For a correct interpretation, data related to GHG emissions should be managed using two complementary approaches. A macroscopic approach starts from global, absolute data (yearly emissions) and serves to understand the general dynamics, as in the case of macroeconomic analysis. For example, what is the carbon footprint benefit of investing in renewable energy? And what is the impact of deforestation? These are typical examples of macroscopic analyses, useful in assessing the carbon footprint of an entire production sector.

From this perspective, it is still difficult to find a correlation between sectors, such as between the consumption of a specific foodstuff and deforestation. Another approach, which we might call analytical, focuses on products by adopting a perspective that is typical (but not exclusive) of LCA. This data is useful for identifying problems at specific points in the production chain and maximising efficiency to reduce impacts. Given the high level of detail, deriving global-scale conclusions from this approach is a much more complex and delicate issue.

According to data sourced from Our World in Data, annual global GHG emissions increased from 35 to 50 billion tonnes (+40%) between 1990 and 2019 (Figure 4.9). Narrowing in on agriculture, forestry and land use change – which are the most connected with the food production – are responsible for 18% of global GHG emissions (Figure 4.10).

All sectors have seen emissions increase, with the largest upswings in industry, aviation and energy transformation, although growth in the latter sector has

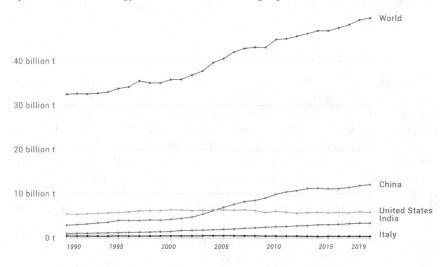

Figure 4.9 Global GHG emissions. H. Ritchie, M. Roser and P. Rosado, *CO₂ and Greenhouse Gas Emissions*, published online in 2020 at Our World in Data, https://ourworldin-data.org/co2-and-other-greenhouse-gas-emissions. Originally published in the first edition of this book, *Il Cibo Perfetto*, published in Italian in 2022.

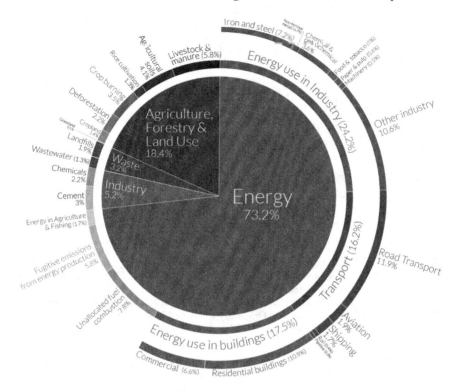

Figure 4.10 Global GHG emissions per sector. The energy production and transport sectors are responsible for the highest levels of GHG emissions. H. Ritchie, M. Roser and P. Rosado, *CO_2 and Greenhouse Gas Emissions*, published online in 2020 at Our World in Data, https://ourworldindata.org/emissions-by-sector.

slowed thanks to investment in renewables. Agricultural emissions are estimated at 6 billion tonnes per year, amounting to approximately 12% of the total. If we add the 3 billion tonnes associated with deforestation, this rises to approximately 15% of total emissions (Figure 4.11).

It is also interesting to look at emission trends in relation to population growth. The data in Figure 4.12 clearly shows that the agricultural sector is the only one where per-capita emissions have decreased over time.

FAO data also confirms a trend of improved performance by the agricultural sector. Since 1960, emissions intensity – i.e. kilograms of CO_2 equivalent per kilogram of food – has gradually decreased, with ever-greater efficiency (Figure 4.13).

Upon closer inspection, this is especially true of the animal husbandry sector. Cereal production, meanwhile, has followed a different trend. The explanation is not simple but one possible factor could be the introduction of agrochemical inputs (primarily through synthetic fertilisers) which led to an initial environmental inefficiency (excess nitrogen use, thinking it could all be stored) which was followed by a trend reversal, with impact reduction consistent with that in other sectors.

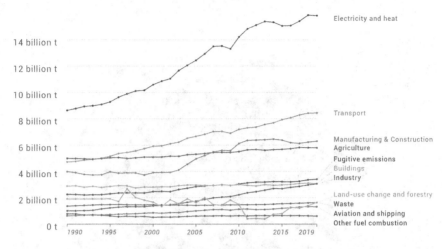

Figure 4.11 Variation in global GHG emissions per sector. Farming is among the sectors
with the lowest growth in GHG emissions. H. Ritchie, M. Roser and P. Rosado,
CO₂ and Greenhouse Gas Emissions, published online in 2020 at Our World in
Data, https://ourworldindata.org/emissions-by-sector#by-country-greenhouse-
gas-emissions-by-sector. Originally published in the first edition of this book,
Il Cibo Perfetto, published in Italian in 2022.

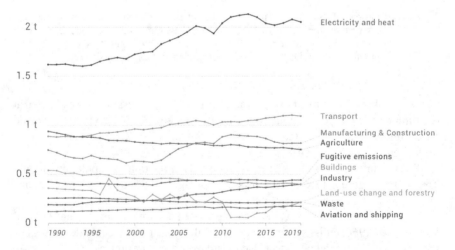

Figure 4.12 Per-capita GHG emissions in various industrial sectors. Emissions in the agricultural sector are decreasing. H. Ritchie, M. Roser and P. Rosado, *CO₂ and
Greenhouse Gas Emissions*, published online in 2020 at Our World in Data,
https://ourworldindata.org/emissions-by-sector#by-country-greenhouse-gas-
emissions-by-sector. Originally published in the first edition of this book, *Il
Cibo Perfetto*, published in Italian in 2022.

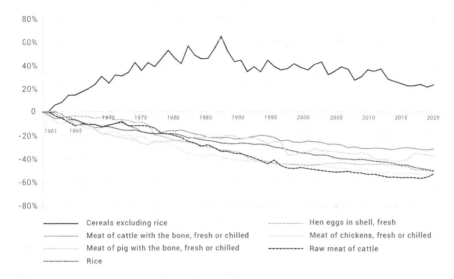

Figure 4.13 GHGs per tonne of food produced. The data refer to the period 1960–2020 and
the trends are shown as variations (positive or negative) compared to 1960.
Emission Intensities, FAOSTAT, https://www.fao.org/faostat/en/#data/EI.

4.5.1.2   What greenhouse gases?

The three most impactful GHGs are carbon dioxide (CO_2 – generated by the use
of fossil fuels), methane (CH_4 – generated through enteric fermentation in bovine
digestion and the management of manure), nitrous oxide (N_2O – linked to the over-
use and mismanagement of natural or synthetic nitrogen-based fertilisers).

These three substances contribute to climate change in different ways due to the
variations in their chemical-physical behaviour, which is constantly monitored by
the Intergovernmental Panel on Climate Change (IPCC). Research has shown that
the emissions factors for methane and nitrous oxide are 28 and 265 times higher
than for CO_2 respectively. In other words, emitting 1 gram of methane is like emitting almost 30 grams of CO_2, whereas releasing 1 gram of N_2O corresponds to the
emissions of 265 grams of CO_2.

Nitrous oxide is one of the most problematic substances. Even though emission
volumes are relatively low, its per-unit impact massively increases its significance
in terms of overall impact. This substance is created by the action of soil bacteria during the process of fertiliser absorption by plants and occurs regardless of
whether the fertiliser is chemical or natural (manure). In many cases, improper
management or excessive use of manure can lead to high levels of nitrous oxide
emissions, with a heavy impact on climate change.

Despite the very high per-unit impact of N_2O, CO_2 emissions remain the greatest problem in absolute terms, with emissions steadily rising while the others stay
fairly constant (Figure 4.14).

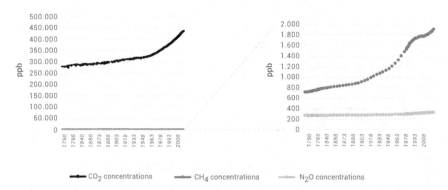

Figure 4.14 Atmospheric concentration of methane, nitrous oxide and carbon dioxide over time. The concentration of the gas is expressed in parts per billion. H. Ritchie, M. Roser and P. Rosado, CO_2 *and Greenhouse Gas Emissions*, published online in 2020 at Our World in Data, https://ourworldindata.org/atmospheric-concentrations.

Box 4.4 *Balancing emissions and removals: the case of methane*

The international community recognises that methane has important consequences on climate change. It is essential to understand the behaviour of this molecule to quantify its impacts and implement effective strategies for reducing its emissions. **Two crucial aspects are still too often overlooked:** *the balance between emissions and removals. This is the model with which the presence of methane in the atmosphere is converted into its relative contribution to climate change.*

The most recent version of the Global Methane Budget shows that human methane emissions derive essentially from three sources: fossil fuel production and use; agriculture and waste; and biomass and biofuel burning. These amount to approximately 576 million tonnes/year (in Figure 4.15, 576 teragrams). While there is clarity on emissions, the aspect of **methane removal processes** *(above all through the oxidation of CH_4 into CO_2 directly in the atmosphere, but also through storage in the soil by, for example, methanotrophic bacteria) is often overlooked. These removals are estimated at about 556 million tonnes per year. In brief, the net contribution of methane to global warming must be calculated as the difference between the two values, resulting in a significantly lower contribution than is commonly communicated.*

The second key aspect to be taken into consideration is the mathematical model with which methane (and other GHG) emissions are converted into impacts. The currently used metric is the Global Warming Potential (GWP) referred to an observation interval of 100 years (GWP_{100}), which indicates an effect of CH_4 28 times more powerful than that of CO_2.

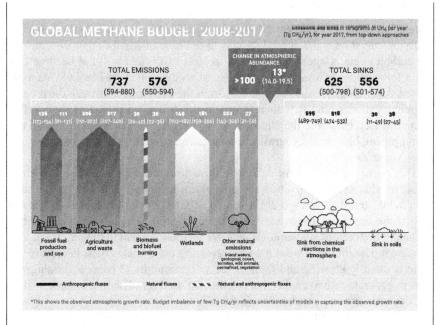

Figure 4.15 Global methane budget, 2008–2017. The project includes the quantification of global budgets for the three dominant GHGs (CO_2, CH_4 and N_2O). *Global Carbon Project*, July 2020, https://www.globalcarbonproject.org/methanebudget/.

*However, this metric has the limitation of not considering the short life of methane in the atmosphere. To go beyond this uncertainty, a team of Oxford researchers has developed a calculation method named the Global Warming Potential Star (**GWP***) model, capable of taking into account how increasing, constant or decreasing emissions of methane would affect global warming. The results indicate that, in a scenario with constant emissions, the GWP_{100} metric returns an impact four times higher than that obtained with the updated method (GWP*). In addition, the conventional metric neglects the beneficial consequences on the climate when methane emissions cease to be constant and start to decrease.*

This new approach is arousing the attention of the scientific community, in terms of both the theory's validity and the potential consequences of its eventual adoption. It has been mentioned in the new version of the IPCC report, which admits the limit of the system currently used. While awaiting a formal position from the international community, the best approach remains that of maximum transparency, taking into account both emission and absorption sources and calculating the impacts both with the GWP* and with the current metric GWP_{100}.

4.5.1.3   Nature's contribution: biogenic emissions

When measuring the GHG emissions of an agri-food system, the issue of biogenic emissions must be confronted. Whereas in the case of fossil fuels it is clear that the carbon cycle is open (burning coal releases CO_2 that will not become coal again for millions of years), the agricultural production cycle is somewhat more closed. As crops grow, they absorb CO_2 from the atmosphere through the process of photosynthesis, and it is then stored in the soil for a period of time before being released back into the atmosphere. The release of emissions from soil and decomposing biomass (e.g. grass clippings, crop residues) are referred to as *biogenic emissions*.[22]

This opens up avenues for collaboration between experts in different fields to assess to what extent agriculture and animal husbandry are a problem and a solution. While farming systems are a source of GHGs, their processes can absorb part of the emissions generated through a cyclical flow regulated by a constant exchange between plants, animals and the surrounding environment. Thus, they hold great potential to be a solution for reversing the climate crisis. Interest in this topic is steadily growing and farmers see an opportunity to harness certain practices to generate carbon credits that can then be used for offsetting schemes within and beyond their value chain (Figure 4.16).

Let's try to understand the factors which are responsible for the complexity of this topic. The first is that the time delay between the moment of atmospheric emission and the complete reabsorption of CO_2. The problem here is that the time

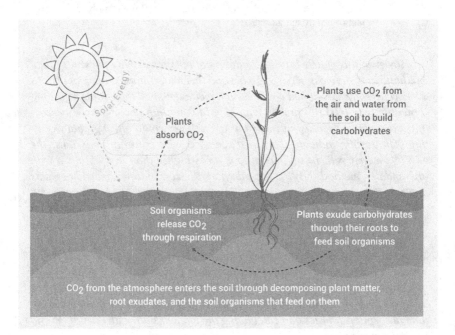

Figure 4.16 The closed biogenic carbon cycle. Widespread representation.

required for creation of new fossil fuel stocks (millions of years) is much longer than the time GHGs spend in the atmosphere (years), making it unfeasible within a realistic timeframe comparable to human life on Earth. It is therefore important that, in order to achieve carbon neutrality, the emission-absorption cycle must be as balanced as possible in the same time period. The possibility of storing carbon in the soil, effectively slowing the flow of emissions, plays a crucial role in this balancing equation. As we will see in the following chapters, this factor is closely dependent on the agricultural practices that are adopted.

A second complication arises when considering how long gases remain in the atmosphere, a variable that is regulated by complex chemical-physical exchanges. Normally, the greenhouse effect is measured according to a 100-year timeframe (a molecule emitted today has an effect for 100 years), even though the behaviour of different substances can vary. CO_2, for example, can persist in the atmosphere and continue to have an effect on the climate for thousands of years after it is released. Conversely, the atmospheric lifespan of methane is around ten years, but its impact is 28 times higher than CO_2 and it must be monitored very closely.

It is clear that there is still much research to be done in this field. As we await more definitive considerations and measurement conventions, we must be aware of two key issues:

- it is important to keep biogenic emissions separate from fossil-based emissions in the measurement and reporting of emissions
- agricultural processes can be a (partial) solution only insofar as it can be proven that the absorption-emission cycle is regulated according to a timeframe that allows us to consider it balanced

4.5.2   *Water use*

Even if the planet has plenty of water on its surface overall, we must focus on fresh water as a critical resource for the global population. Use of water by the agri-food sector has two key impacts: water quality is impacted by pollution and water availability is impacted by its extraction and use. These aspects, which should be analysed together, are monitored and measured using different assessment parameters. Historically, water quality has been subject to greater monitoring to limit damage to the local environment. More recently, the focus on the amount of water being used has come to the fore, especially as pressure on water resources increases and climate change adds to the challenge.

The need to communicate concise and intelligible information to stakeholders has driven the creation methods and protocols to calculate aggregate indicators. At times, these have led to the use of sensationalised data that may have been incorrect from a scientific standpoint.

Because water consumption has a local or regional impact, volume used should always be stated in relation to local availability. Is it more damaging to use 500 litres in Saudi Arabia or 1,000 litres in Sweden? To answer this question, different methods are used to address the twin concepts of water scarcity and water availability. Water scarcity refers to a condition where water demand is greater than supply. It intensifies as demand increases and/or as water supply is affected by decreasing quantity or quality. Water availability is the true availability of water that is accessible, both qualitatively and quantitatively. The ISO 14046 standard defines water scarcity as the impossibility of having adequate quantities of water to meet needs. In other words, water consumption is weighed up against the real availability of water in the place of production. Unlike when we calculate impact on climate change, local characteristics do matter here!

In the past, a very widespread model to quantify water scarcity was ***Water Resource Depletion***. It was developed in 2010 by the Joint Research Center (JRC) of the European Commission and promoted by the same as part of the initiatives for the calculation of the environmental footprint of products (PEF, Product Environmental Footprint) and organisations (OEF, Organisation Environmental Footprint). This metric was replaced in 2018 by the ***AWARE*** (Available WAter REmaining)[23] model, which was also based on the concept of water scarcity. This new impact indicator measures the potential for water deprivation, both for humans and for ecosystems, assuming that the less water remains available per area, the greater the likelihood that another user in the same area will be deprived of it (Figure 4.17).[24,25] The AWARE model is still used today within the European certification schemes such as the PEF and the OEF. It is also adopted by the International EPD System®

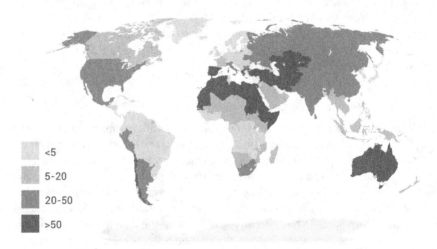

<5

5-20

20-50

>50

Figure 4.17 AWARE model: a simplified map of characterisation factors for agricultural uses (12-month average). The lowest values are observed for tropical rainforests (Amazon area and Central America, Central Africa, Southeast Asia), areas characterised by both intense rainfall and not very high water demand. A.M. Boulay, J. Bare, L. Benini, M. Berger, M.J. Lathuillière, A. Manzardo, M. Margni, M. Motoshita, M. Núñez, A.V. Pastor, B. Ridoutt, T. Oki, S. Worbe, S. Pfister, The WULCA Consensus Characterization Model for Water Scarcity Footprints: Assessing Impacts of Water Consumption Based on Available Water Remaining (AWARE), in *The International Journal of Life Cycle Assessment*, Vol 23, pp. 368–378, June 2017.

and can be used to calculate the water scarcity footprint as defined in the standard ISO 14046.

Among the most widespread calculation methods, the Water Resource Depletion metric, developed by the European Commission's Joint Research Centre (JRC), aims to assess how much the use of water in a certain geographical area effectively influences the depletion of water resources in that region.[26] Incidentally, this method is promoted by the European Commission in the context of initiatives to calculate the PEF and OEF. The metric is based on the factors provided by the Ecological Scarcity method, which involves multiplying the water consumption of the process by a characterisation factor[27] derived from the ratio between total consumption and availability in the reference region (low, medium or high). The impact is expressed in water volume equivalent and transforms the data regarding the extraction of water into information that is more closely linked to the damage actually being caused to the environment.

Box 4.5   Water footprint analysis

Most of the data and literature communicated today on the water footprint of food and other products are based on the method developed by the Water Footprint Network[28] (WFN) or other methods developed by researchers based on the WFN. Until the publication of the ISO 14046 standard and the introduction of the Water Scarcity concept, the WFN was the most widely used protocol for calculating the water footprint of products and processes. It breaks down the water footprint into three components: green, blue and grey.

The 'green water' footprint is a feature of agricultural or forestry products and represents the amount of rainwater used for crop production. This comprises the amount of water lost through evapotranspiration – water passing from the soil to the air due to evaporation from wet soil and transpiration (natural water movement through plants), which leads water to be stored in the surface layer of soil. Not all rainwater is used, for reasons linked to the peculiarity of the soil, the needs of plants and the features of root systems. Therefore, the green water footprint comprises exclusively the rainwater that is retained by the soil and available to meet the needs of crops, calculated as a function of the type of crop, the weather and climate in a given region and average yearly precipitation.

'Blue water' is the amount of water extracted from waterbodies (rivers, lakes, groundwater reservoirs) that is effectively used in the production process and is not returned to the source from which it was drawn. If water is extracted and used in a cooling system, for example, and then fed back into the water body it was drawn from, the blue water footprint comprises solely the portion of water that evaporated during the process.

> *Finally, 'grey water' is defined as the amount of water theoretically needed to dilute contaminants in the water leaving the system (such as water leaching from a crop field or the output of an industrial process) if the aim is to bring the water back to its original quality. In practice, the higher the level of pollution generated, the higher the grey water footprint.*
>
> *An issue that has been fixed by the new measurement methods is the evaluation of water lost by plants through evapotranspiration (known as green water), which used to always account for over 90% of impacts. This quantity used to be disconnected from the measurement of direct indicators and improved through the introduction of methods for calculating the differential between evapotranspiration on farmland and the natural level in the same area.*
>
> *If we look more closely, we can see that the quantity that has been consumed or polluted directly consists of the blue component (necessary as an input to the process) and the grey component (necessary to reduce the output load of pollutants). On the contrary, the green component is simply water that completes its natural hydrogeological cycle, continuously passing from the atmosphere to the ground and to the waters (surface and groundwater). This component represents over 80% of the total water footprint of all agro-zootechnical systems calculated according to the WFN.*

The newer net water footprint (WFP_{NET})[29] model aims to improve this aspect of the calculation by quantifying the difference between the evapotranspiration of the crop under investigation and the evapotranspiration of a natural reference situation (e.g. forest) for the geographical area in question. In other words, the model assumes that if there were no crops in the fields for the production of feed for livestock, the area in question would still have a vegetation cover with relative evapotranspiration. The value obtained is the difference between the water consumed by the crop and that which would have been consumed in a situation of natural cover. This value is then added to the drinking water.

Using the method suggested by the JRC[30] to weigh the direct water consumption figures, it is possible to estimate virtual water consumption by correlating actual direct consumption with water availability in the areas in which consumption occurs.[31] The assessment should be understood as preliminary because it is based on the hypothesis that the entire supply chain (cultivation, farming and processing) is located in the region in question, and that all water used for the final product is consumed in the same country (Figure 4.18).

Factoring in these limitations shows how, in regions experiencing water scarcity such as India, meat production supply chains have a greater weighted water footprint than the base value. Instead, when the production chain is located in regions with greater water availability, the environmental damage is lessened: as is the case in Argentina or Ireland, for example.

4.5.3   *The water footprint of beef*

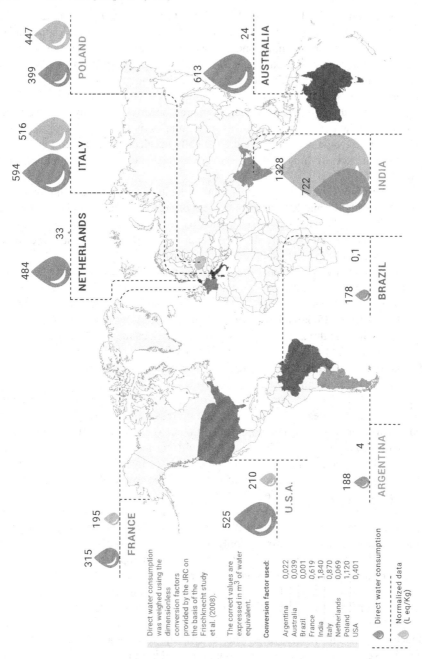

Figure 4.18 The water footprint of beef (using the water scarcity index). E. Bernardi,
E. Capri, G. Pulina, *La sostenibilità delle carni e dei salumi in Italia*, Fran-
coAngeli, Roma, 2018. Originally published in the first edition of this book, *Il
Cibo Perfetto*, published in Italian in 2022.

4.5.4   *Water quality and eutrophication*[32]

Eutrophication is a leading cause of impairment of freshwater and coastal marine ecosystems. The consequences include tainted drinking water supplies, degradation of recreational opportunities and damage to aquatic ecosystems that negatively affect wildlife. Eutrophication is characterised by excessive plant and algal growth due to the increased availability of one or more limiting growth factors needed for photosynthesis, such as sunlight, CO_2 and nutrients.

Over the course of history, this phenomenon occurred naturally as lakes aged and filled in with sediments. However, human activities such as agriculture, industry and sewage disposal have dramatically accelerated its rate and extent by releasing an excess of nutrients (especially nitrogen and phosphorus) into aquatic ecosystems.

Algal blooms limit sunlight penetration, reducing growth and causing plants in littoral zones to die and lowering the success of predators that need light to pursue and catch prey. When these dense algal blooms eventually die, microbial decomposition severely depletes dissolved oxygen, creating a hypoxic or anoxic 'dead zone' lacking sufficient oxygen to support most organisms.

Today, such hypoxic events are found in many freshwater lakes. They are particularly common in marine coastal environments surrounding large, nutrient-rich rivers (e.g. Mississippi River and the Gulf of Mexico) and have been shown to affect more than 245,000 km² in over 400 near-shore systems. Some algal blooms pose an additional threat because they produce noxious toxins. Over the past century, harmful algal blooms have been linked with degradation of water quality, destruction of economically important fisheries and public health risks.

Keeping the problem under control is complex and challenging as it is predicted that climate change and human population growth will exacerbate water quality and scarcity issues further. In agricultural areas, nutrients reach water bodies from non-point sources and can be difficult and expensive to control. To manage eutrophication, scientists, policymakers and citizens need to reduce nutrient inputs and develop effective, long-term techniques for removing algal blooms without putting humans, livestock and wildlife at risk. The eventual goal should be to restore the aquatic communities affected.

The first point can be achieved by combining implementation of bottom-up controls of point-source industrial discharges with awareness campaigns/training courses for farmers to effectively apply and manage fertilisers and manure. With regard to the second point, a promising option is biomanipulation which increases selected generalist herbivorous species to control phytoplankton.

Methods of measuring and monitoring eutrophication vary regionally, preventing a straightforward interpretation of eutrophication symptoms. Results are interpreted depending on the characteristics and current knowledge of the waterbody under study and difficulties arise when attempting to compare the eutrophication state between two rivers. This problem was tackled in Europe by adopting eutrophication indicators and a common monitoring and interpretation approach to ensure fair comparisons under the Marine Strategy Framework Directive (2008/56/EC).[33] Harmonisation between EU member states in the measurement and reporting, although still ongoing, represents a great step forward.

4.5.5   Land use

Applying a simple economic analogy helps to explain the use of the ecological footprint as a means for understanding land use. Consider a family with €100,000 in capital and a yearly income of €30,000. If expenditure is below or equal to €30,000 per year, the family capital is not affected: this can be considered sustainable economic management. If instead, annual expenditure is €40,000, capital would decrease by €10,000 per year, leading the family to poverty in the space of ten years.

The ecological footprint is an indicator that allows us to estimate how many resources (natural capital) are used, compared to what is available. Its representation enables us to quantify the surface area of terrestrial and marine ecosystems needed to provide the necessary resources and absorb any emissions generated.[34] Using conversion factors and specific equivalencies, this composite indicator measures the different ways natural resources are used through a single, standardised unit of measurement: the global hectare (gha), based on world average productivity. One of its components, known as energy land, is measured as the surface area required to absorb the CO_2 emissions generated by the system in question. Because this is a virtual metric, the land requirement is much greater than what is actually available, proving that humanity is consuming more resources than are available to us. Hence, we are eroding the natural capital. This is clearly illustrated by the Earth Overshoot Day concept (Figure 4.19).

Box 4.6   Earth overshoot day

For many years, the Global Footprint Network has calculated and revealed the date of Earth Overshoot Day, which is the day each year when humanity's resource consumption surpasses what the Earth can regenerate annually. In 2022, humanity used up its ecological budget for the year by 28 July. This means that, in approximately seven months, we consumed more renewable resources and carbon sequestration capacity than the planet is able to sustainably provide for the entire year. For the entire rest of the year, the resources we consumed depleted our 'share capital'. In the case of environmental resources, this means extracting stored resource stocks and accumulating CO_2 in the atmosphere. Interestingly, in 2020 – the year of the pandemic, the situation marginally improved, with Overshoot Day falling in August.

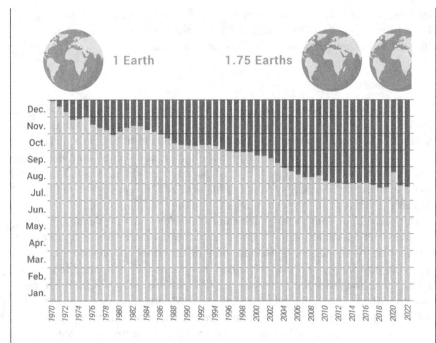

Figure 4.19 Earth Overshoot Day, 1971–2022. *Earth Overshoot Day 1971–2022, Earth Overshoot Day,* https://www.overshootday.org/.

4.5.6   *Deforestation*

The topic of deforestation has received increased attention in recent years, including among the public and consumers. Causes which contribute to deforestation include the expansion of agriculture production and livestock grazing, resource extraction and growth of the world's urban centres. Deforestation contributes to biodiversity loss and climate change: forests that are felled and burned emit CO_2 instead of absorbing it, contributing approximately 15% of global GHG emissions.[35]

Some of the world's most biodiverse forests are rapidly being destroyed – approximately 1 million square kilometres of Amazon rainforest have been destroyed since 1978.[36] The leading causes of tropical rainforest deforestation are industrial agriculture activities to grow crops and create areas for cattle to graze. The cultivation of soy – one of the main sources of food for humans and animals – is an especially critical issue. The expansion of soy plantations is widespread in South America at the expense of forests, with deforestation causing incalculable damage to biodiversity and the environment (Figure 4.20).

The FAO is responsible for monitoring forest data. Its latest available report shows that between 1990 and 2020, forest cover decreased by over 80 million hectares and is now at 31% of the world's total land area. Most of the losses happened in countries in the Global South – Sub-Saharan Africa, South America and

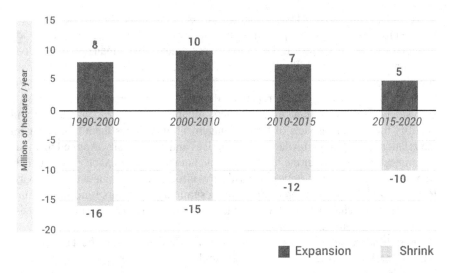

Figure 4.20 Global deforestation. Authors' elaboration. Data processed from FAO, UNEP, *The State of the World's Forests. Forests, Biodiversity and People*, Rome, 2020, https://bit.ly/3JUmGNp.

Southeast Asia – where, as the population increases, forests are felled to make space for human activities like animal farming, crop production and the extraction of natural resources. In some parts of the world – such as Asia, North America and Europe – forest cover has increased. This is partially thanks to conservation programmes and the abandonment of low-productivity farmland, which is gradually reforested.

It is worth noting that tree planting actions cannot be considered sustainable unless they meet stringent biodiversity criteria that ensure that the ecosystem being created is resilient and stable. Also, the development of policies to promote renewable energy production have encouraged some farmers to convert their land into power plants, with large expanses of solar panels, or to grow crops to be used as bioenergy feedstock. Such policy incentives motivate further conversion of forests to cultivated land that can earn farmers increased financial rewards.

4.5.7 *Biodiversity*[37]

In recent decades, the major focus for agricultural systems was to grow raw materials for the production of food, textiles and fuel, with little attention given to environmental and social functions. This led to the creation of highly simplified intensive agroecosystems that, faced with today's environmental challenges, suffer heavy damage. The dominant model in the 20th century essentially disregarded the concept of biodiversity, which is a vital prerequisite for resilience to climate change, supporting the balanced provision of ecosystem services and increasing habitat connectivity.[38]

To address this lapse, EU member states offered incentives to farmers to protect biodiversity. These include agro-environmental and climate measures that provide financial support to farmers if they implement predetermined management actions (e.g. mowing after a specific date, reducing fertiliser use and planting wildflower corridors).

The effectiveness of these practices depends on the presence of a suitable assessment framework that gives farmers reliable information to monitor and quantify the various aspects of farm management and allows them to understand the relationship between management practices and biodiversity. Applied methods and indicators must cover the largest possible number of factors, be easy to understand and find a balance between feasibility, informational value and sensitivity. Biodiversity is a complex topic and defining summary indicators is no simple matter. Thus, researchers are working to find useful solutions that can provide measurement instruments and guidance.[39]

Most biodiversity indicators used today are limited to specific taxa (plants, grasshoppers, butterflies or birds, for example), specific habitats or habitat quality. Their assessment and interpretation often require specialist knowledge. The most common indicator is plant species abundance, which provides an insight into environmental conditions regarding soil, topography and climate. This indicator is responsive to human factors, such as land use, and is significantly correlated with overall biodiversity. However, plant species richness surveys are often limited to regionally developed lists of indicator species and handled only by experts. This limitation must be overcome so that the use of such indicators can be brought closer to farmers. An interesting effort came from a 2019 study[40] involving 114 experts and stakeholders in four European countries, which resulted in the definition of an aggregated biodiversity index comprising four indicators – flower colour index, butterfly abundance, landscape structuring degree and patch diversity index.[41] A further example is a set of indicators based on the degree of naturalness, distance to natural habitat and the composite distance to nature index, whose goal is to measure and describe the anthropic influence on ecosystems and habitats due to land use.[42]

To sum up, it is difficult to find a single, universally applicable indicator for biodiversity. Nonetheless, methods chosen must be consistent with conditions in the system in question and, most importantly, those who design indicators should aim for simplicity so that their use is not limited to researchers and scientists.

4.5.8   *Measuring local impacts*

Beside the global indicators discussed, the nuances of food production impacts should also be measured at the local level for specific aspects, such as use of antibiotics in livestock rearing. Antibiotics are molecules originating from fungal species and synthetic processes which are used to treat infections caused by microorganisms, including fungi and protozoa (by killing them or inhibiting their growth).

The advantages of antibiotics are innumerable: many bacterial infections that could kill a person up to 50 years ago, such as pneumonia, are much less of a danger today. In animal farming, antibiotics represent a powerful tool for the control of infectious diseases, contributing to the improvement of animal welfare and the safety of food products.

However, when the use of these antibiotics is excessive or poorly controlled, it can lead to increased resistance of bacteria to these substances, both in treated animals and in people consuming animal products (such as meat, milk and eggs). The crucial importance of this problem has been underlined by the World Health Organization (WHO) which has stated that, to prevent and control the spread of antibiotic resistance, the agriculture sector should:

• give antibiotics only to animals under veterinary supervision
• not use antibiotics for growth promotion or to prevent diseases in healthy animals
• vaccinate animals to reduce the need for antibiotics and use alternatives to antibiotics when available
• promote and apply good practices at all steps of production and processing of foods from animal and plant sources
• improve biosecurity on farms and prevent infections through improved hygiene and animal welfare

Increased awareness of the problem has seen a progressive reduction in farmed animals treated with antibiotics. The World Organisation for Animal Health confirmed that the use of these drugs decreased by 27% worldwide between 2016 and 2018.

In the EU, permitted drugs are authorised by the health authorities and it is required by law that foodstuffs such as meat, milk or eggs must not contain residue levels of veterinary medicines or biocidal products that might represent a hazard to the health of the consumer. Specific rules and procedures establish the Maximum Residue Limits (Regulation (EC) No 470/2009) as well as the withdrawal period[43] (Regulation (EU) 2019/6), with the latter being part of the marketing authorisation procedure for each individual veterinary product. In some member states, the use of antibiotics is subject to compliance with even more stringent rules. With regard to the use of hormones, the EU has prohibited the use of substances having a hormonal action for growth promotion in farm animals since 1981.

As far as we know, no country is currently monitoring the administration of antibiotics to farmed animals on an ongoing basis. This is due to the fact that not all the medicines prescribed by the vet (and for which there is therefore a traceable medical prescription) are ultimately purchased by the farmer. And not all drugs purchased are actually used. When they are used, they are also not administered equally to all farm animals but only to animals that need pharmacological treatment.

Key takeaways

- An evaluation of sustainable impact should be based on the whole value chain, taking a product life cycle approach.
- LCA is one of the most used methodologies for calculating environmental impact across a product life cycle. However, it is suitable for calculating indicators with an aggregate global impact, such as CO_2. Additional analysis of local impacts such biodiversity, water use, local pollution, etc., are often necessary for a deeper evaluation.
- The short-hand sustainability = environment = carbon footprint is a shallow interpretation of sustainability of a product or value chain. An understanding of sustainability of food chains needs to include many other aspects such as animal welfare, social conditions, the safety and the nutritional value of the food and food security.
- Food waste is one of the most important issues of the food economy. Prevention of food waste is necessary and must be tackled at both the policy and the industry level.
- Sustainability evaluation shall be based on the whole supply chain. Even if LCA is one of the most used methodologies, it is necessary to remember that it is suitable for the calculation of global indicators such as CO_2. Often the study of local conditions such biodiversity, water use, local pollution, etc., is necessary for a deep evaluation.
- Sustainability = environment = carbon footprint is a poor approach to the topic. The study of food chains needs to include many other aspects such as animal welfare, the social condition, safety and nutritional value of the food and food security.
- Food waste is one of the most important issues of the food economy. The prevention of food waste is mandatory for policymakers and industries.

Key questions for reflection

- What are the environmental indicators most relevant to your business and your positioning in the value chain?
- What is the level of ambition you aim to achieve on social sustainability, from compliance to social impact? Consequently, what is the monitoring and evaluation system that you wish to adopt? Do you need to build bespoke social impact metrics?
- What are the priority products where the application of LCA can be instrumental in your business?
- Are other sustainability measurement tools relevant in your context, taking into account your ambition and what you wish to achieve?

Notes

1 ISO 14001:2015 Environmental Management Systems. Requirements with Guidance for Use, https://www.iso.org/standard/60857.html?browse=tc

2 C.S. Holling, Resilience and Stability of Ecological Systems, in *Annual Review of Ecology and Systematics*, Vol 4, pp. 1–23, 1973.

3 The combustion of biomass does generate atmospheric emissions, but its advantage is that the energy source used (primarily wood) is renewable.

4 *Spaced Out: Perspectives on Parking Policy*, July 2012, https://www.racfoundation.org/research/mobility/spaced-out-perspectives-on-parking.

5 *Living Planet Report 2022. Building a Nature-Positive Society*, WWF, 2022, https://livingplanet.panda.org/en-GB/.

6 *A Warning Sign from Our Planet: Nature Needs Life Support*, WWF, https://www.wwf.org.uk/updates/living-planet-report-2018.

7 T.G. Benton, C. Bieg, H. Harwatt, R. Pudasaini, L. Wellesley, Food System Impacts on Biodiversity Loss. Three Levers for Food System Transformation in Support of Nature, Chatham House, London, 2021.

8 *Universal Declaration of Human Rights*, https://www.un.org/sites/un2.un.org/files/2021/03/udhr.pdf.

9 *ILO Declaration on Fundamental Principles and Rights at Work and Its Follow-Up*, International Labour Organization, 2022, https://www.ilo.org/declaration/lang--en/index.htmm.

10 M.E. Porter, M.R. Kramer, Creating Shared Valute. How to Reinvent Capitalism and Unleash a Wave of Innovation and Growth, *Harvard Business Review*, January–February 2011, https://hbr.org/2011/01/the-big-idea-creating-shared-value.

11 *Vanilla for Change*, Unilever, July 2019, https://www.unilever.com/news/news-search/2019/vanilla-for-change/.

12 N. Mitchell, *Social Impact: Definition and Why Is Social Impact Important*, Duke, September 2021, https://careerhub.students.duke.edu/blog/2021/09/03/social-impact-definition-and-why-is-social-impact-important/#:~:text=In%20essence%2C%20the%20definition%20of,in%20their%20operations%20and%20administrations.

13 UN Guiding Principles (UNGP) Reporting Framework, https://www.ungpreporting.org/.

14 *Annual Review*, 2016–2017, Ethical Trading Initiative, https://www.ethicaltrade.org/sites/default/files/shared_resources/eti_annual_review_2016_17_reference.pdf.

15 *Final Report on Social Taxonomy. Platform on Sustainable Finance*, Platform on Sustainable Finance, 2022, https://commission.europa.eu/system/files/2022–03/280222-sustainable-finance-platform-finance-report-social-taxonomy.pdf

16 Ibid.

17 IRIS+, https://iris.thegiin.org/.

18 Ibid.

19 T. Begum, *Soil Degradation: The Problems and How to Fix Them*, Natural History Museum, April 2021, https://www.nhm.ac.uk/discover/soil-degradation.html.

20 Definition provided by the UK Natural Capital Committee in 2013, *Natural Capital Committee*, https://bit.ly/3GskqLj.

21 *Farm Animal Welfare in Great Britain: Past, Present, Future*, Farm Animal Welfare Council, 2009, chrome-extension://efaidnbmnnnibpcajpcglclefindmkaj/https://assets.publishing.service.gov.uk/government/uploads/system/uploads/attachment_data/file/319292/Farm_Animal_Welfare_in_Great_Britain_-_Past__Present_and_Future.pdf.

22 *Biogenic Emissions, SIMAP*, https://unhsimap.org/cmap/resources/biogenic#:~:text=What%20are%20biogenic%20emissions%3F,2%20due%20to%20degradation%20processes.

23 Method implemented by the WULCA (Water Use in LCA) working group with the sponsorship of UNEP-SETAC Life Cycle Initiative. *WULCA*, https://wulca-waterlca.org/.

24   A.M. Boulay, J. Bare, L. Benini, M. Berger, M.J. Lathuillière, A. Manzardo, M. Margni, M. Motoshita, M. Núñez, A.V. Pastor, B. Ridoutt, T. Oki, S. Worbe, S. Pfister, The WULCA Consensus Characterization Model for Water Scarcity Footprints: Assessing Impacts of Water Consumption Based on Available Water Remaining (AWARE), in *The International Journal of Life Cycle Assessment*, Vol 23, pp. 368–378, June 2017.
25   Global Guidance for Life Cycle Impact Assessment Indicators (Vol 1), UNEP-SETAC Life Cycle Initiative, 2016.
26   Further detail on this measurement method is available at European Commission, Institute for Environment and Sustainability, *Characterization Factors of the ILCD Recommended Life Cycle Impact Assessment Methods. Database and Supporting Information*, Joint Research Centre, 2012.
27   This factor is stated under Water Resource Depletion within the ILCD 2011 Midpoint+ V1.07 measurement method, included in the SimaPro® software.
28   *Water Footprint Network*, www.waterfootprint.org.
29   A.S. Atzori, C. Canalis, A.H. Dia Francesconi, G. Pulina, A Preliminary Study on a New Approach to Estimate Water Resources Allocation: The Net Water Footprint Applied to Animal Products, in *Agriculture and Agricultural Science Procedia*, Vol 8, pp. 50–57, 2016.
30   This is the ILCD 2011 Midpoint+ V1.07 measurement method, included in the SimaPro® software. Nation-specific measurement factors are stated under Water Resource Depletion.
31   Other comparable methods exist, including the one proposed by Pfister, Koehler and Hellweg (S. Pfister, A. Koelher, S. Hellweg, Assessing the Environmental Impacts of Freshwater Consumption in LCA, in *Environmental Science & Technology*, Vol 43, pp. 4098–4104, April 2009), which uses a Water Scarcity Indicator (WSI) whose measurement requires a system of characterisation factors based on the ratio of water consumption and availability in different countries.
32   M.F. Chislock, E. Doster, R.A. Zitomer, A.E. Wilson, Eutrophication: Causes, Consequences, and Controls in Aquatic Ecosystems, in *Nature Education Knowledge*, Vol 4, pp. 1–8, 2013.
33   All the qualitative descriptors, criteria and methodological standards for the determination of GES (Good Environmental Status) are described in the 2008/56/EC Directive itself and in the Commission Decisions (EU) 2017/8481. Eutrophication is among these descriptors and its assessment implies the monitoring of a set of eight individual criteria which are integrated to describe the overall eutrophication status of an area. Some of these criteria are considered 'primary' and their use is mandatory (except under justified circumstances) whilst others are 'secondary'. Source: R. Araujo, S.T. Boschetti, *Marine Strategy Framework Directive, Review and Analysis of EU Member States, 2018 Reports, Descriptor 5: Eutrophication, Assessment (Art.8) and Good Environmental Status (Art. 9)*, EUR 30677 EN, Publications Office of the European Union, Luxemburg, 2021, doi:10.2760/180642, JRC124915.
34   *Global Footprint Network*, www.footprintnetwork.org.
35   Deforestation and Forest Degradation, WWF, https://wwf.to/3nbekak.
36   R.A. Butler, Amazon Destruction, *Mongabay*, November 2021, https://rainforests.mongabay.com/amazon/amazon_destruction.html.
37   In cooperation with Cristiana Peano, Dipartimento di Scienze Agrarie, Forestali e Alimentari Università degli Studi di Torino.
38   C. Kremen, A.M. Merenlender, Landscapes That Work for Biodiversity and People, in *Science*, Vol 362, Issue 6412, October 2018.
39   Some examples are available in work published by certain international institutions: EEA – European Environment Agency, *Halting the Loss of Biodiversity by 2010: Proposal for a First Set of Indicators to Monitor Progress in Europe*, Copenhagen, 2007; UNCED – Division for Sustainable Development, *Indicators of Sustainable*

Development, Guidelines and Methodologies, United Nations, New York, 2007; ISPRA, *Indicatori di Biodiversità per la sostenibilità in Agricoltura*, Rome, 2008.

40 E. Tasser, J. Rüdisser, M. Plaikner, A. Wezel, S. Stöckli, A. Vincent, H. Nitsch, M. Dubbert, V. moos, J. Walde, D. Bogner, A Simple Biodiversity Assessment Scheme Supporting Nature-Friendly Farm Management, in *Ecological Indicators*, Vol 107, Issue 105649, December 2019.

41 Shannon Diversity Index, SHDI.

42 J. Rüdisser, E. Tasser, U. Tappeiner, Distance to Nature – A New Biodiversity Relevant Environmental Indicator Set at the Landscape Level, in *Ecological Indicators*, Vol 15, Issue 1, pp. 208–216, April 2012.

43 The withdrawal period is the time period required after cessation of treatment to assure that drug residues in meat (or in other animal-derived products for food) are below the Maximum Residue Limit. It is different for each veterinary medicinal product, animal species and food type, meaning there are different withdrawal periods for meat (slaughter), fish, eggs, milk and honey.

5   Analysing impact across the value chain

The sustainability of the food sector can be improved only by understanding the structure of the value chain, from farm to fork and beyond. Many variables influence the life cycle of food products and measuring total impact is a complex challenge. To drive progress and understanding, we must identify the most important factors and prioritise assessing their relevance and effects on the final product.

In addition to methodological limitations, the outcomes of quantitative analyses can often be counterintuitive. For example, the farming phase of the value chain (upstream of the supply chain) often has the greatest environmental impact relative to other phases further downstream (e.g. processing). And the production of food products differs from the production of non-food goods made with technical (non-biological) materials, because raw ingredients are produced directly in nature and are therefore significantly impacted by climate, pests, diseases and many other variables.

Compared with other industrial sectors, the food value chain integrates complex production and processing chains operating in highly interconnected systems. For example, farms often use natural fertilisers (manure) sourced from animal husbandry processes, which in turn source animal feed from agricultural residues and the by-products of industrial processing. Because different farming systems can be heavily interlinked, we cannot disregard the assessment of the entire system when assessing the sustainability of a particular foodstuff.

In this chapter, we discuss the environmental matters and impacts related to the different phases of the agri-food value chain. To illustrate the journey, we focus primarily on the carbon footprint, while acknowledging that other impacts can, at times, be more significant. While carbon is the focus, it is important to maintain a multi-faceted lens which accounts for impacts beyond carbon, both to avoid the risk of 'carbon tunnel visioning'[1] and to give a full view of potential sustainability solutions.

5.1   Crop farming

The farming phase is the most challenging of the entire food value chain in terms of its environmental impacts because of the prevalence of conventional agricultural practices involving misuse of fertilisers and agrochemicals and poor land use and land management.

DOI: 10.4324/9781003449744-5

Box 5.1   The stages of food production

Primary production – *The farming stage involves the production of the raw ingredients through arable, livestock and dairy farming. For arable crops, the major environmental impacts are caused by mismanagement of fertilisers, agrochemicals, land use and management (e.g. high tilling, monocropping, no rotations), fossil fuels used for farming activities and water used for irrigation. Livestock impacts relate primarily to the agricultural production of feed and herd management, including those generated by the animals' waste. In conventional systems, where externally produced feed is used, animal husbandry is an intermediate stage of the value chain that sits between agricultural production and industrial processing.*

Industrial processing – *Raw ingredients undergo processing to transform and combine them into products that are distributed to consumers. Some foodstuffs, such as eggs, seafood and aquacultural products, reach consumers with barely any processing. The environmental impacts of this stage are typical of industrial production: energy and water use, waste, air and water pollution and by-product streams.*

Packaging – *Product packaging is crucial to facilitate distribution, avoid food waste and increase the safety and shelf life of food products. Paper, cardboard, plastic, aluminium and glass are the main materials used. Careful design of packaging and delivery systems makes it possible to minimise impacts in both the production and end-of-life stages.*

Distribution – *Food products are transported from production plants to distribution points such as retailers and food service providers where they are sold to consumers. Intermediate steps of aggregation and re-distribution often take place en route to the final distribution outlet. In addition to transport-related impacts, impacts related to food preservation (such as cold chain shipping) and transport can be significant.*

Preparation and consumption – *Food is prepared by cooking at home or in out-of-home kitchens of eateries, restaurants and cafeterias. Environmental impacts are primarily driven by energy and water used for cooking as well as by-product and waste management.*

Box 5.2   Managing risk

After decades of viewing sustainability as an add-on, businesses have woken up to the need to manage and communicate their approach to managing sustainability risks across the value chain. This is crucial to avoid reputational risks and greenwashing, as we discuss further in Chapter 6.

> *Risk assessment is an important lever for the transition to a more sustainable food system. There are two main risks in the food sector:*
>
> *Weak attention to the market – Food companies are closely connected to consumers, who have the power to alter purchasing decisions and shine a spotlight on issues in the supply chain. Examples include the attention placed by consumers on products with palm oil and animal-based ingredients. Despite the realities of the actual sustainability impact, if the market closes the door on a product, it can be very difficult for companies to maintain market share.*
>
> *Weak attention to the supply chain – Most food products are based on raw materials that come from agriculture and/or animal breeding. Climate change will modify the scenario under which they are produced and resources, such as fresh water, could become less available in some regions. How will a milk producer who needs a lot of maize deal with water scarcity?*
>
> *Risk assessment is the right approach for companies that want to deal with sustainability with a medium- to long-term approach.*

Crop farming techniques can have a considerable effect on the environment – both negative and positive. Fortunately, the use of technology is prominent in the field today, and digital support systems that guide farmers in their daily choices are becoming increasingly widespread. This means that the ability to use fertilisers based on the real needs of plants, even differentially within the same field, is becoming the norm rather than the exception.

Unlike what happens in other industrial sectors, beneficial agricultural outcomes are not immediately visible. Farmers must wait for at least one crop cycle, and in some cases several years, before they see a change. Crop rotation practices are a classic example, as are the benefits of organic farming which may not be evident for up to ten years. This is because soil fertility takes time to build and changes are often invisible to the naked eye, taking effect underground. In contrast, changes to an industrial processing system have immediately visible benefits. This underlines the importance of having a long-term vision when designing and monitoring changes to agricultural practices.

5.1.1   *The misuse of fertilisers and agrochemicals*

The careful use of fertilisers is a core aspect of sustainable agriculture. Fertilisers provide nitrogen, phosphorus and potassium to the soil – crucial nutrients that plants need to grow. However, they are one of the main sources of agricultural pollution because of their direct environmental impact when overused and mismanaged. The processes involved in synthetic fertiliser production also have an impact; for example, the production of synthetic fertilisers entails significant burning of fossil fuels to fix nitrogen from the atmosphere to make ammonia. It also requires extracting finite resources, such as mining phosphorus, which can contribute to deforestation and biodiversity loss.

Of the three nutrients commonly supplied by fertilisers at the farm level, the greatest environmental impact comes from nitrogen. This is due to its direct effects and the biochemical reactions that happen in the soil to transform part of it into nitrous oxide (N_2O) – a substance that has a considerable impact on climate change (an impact almost 300 times higher than CO_2). In the US, agricultural emissions account for nearly 80% of anthropogenic N_2O emissions, 74% of which is from cultivated soils and 5% from manure management.[2]

Synthetic fertilisers release nitrogen faster than natural ones, often overdosing the plants with nutrients beyond their needs. The excess nitrogen turns into food for soil microbes, which release N_2O. Furthermore, when excessive amounts of fertiliser are used, rain washes away unused fertilisers and the runoff can contaminate waterways and groundwater reservoirs. This leads to an abnormal rise in nitrogen concentrations, promoting exaggerated plant growth through a process known as eutrophication (see Section 4.4). The environmental impact of fertilisers can be both global (the impact of nitrous oxide on climate change) and local (effects on waterbodies and ecosystems).

Natural fertilisers, which are widely used in organic farming, lessen the impacts at the production phase, but not those linked to their use. When mismanaged, the biochemical reactions that promote plant growth are liable to cause the same damage as with the use of synthetic fertilisers. Paradoxically, synthetic fertilisers sometimes allow for preventative measures that are not possible with their natural counterparts. For example, slow-release fertilisers make it possible to dispense nitrogen gradually over time in a way that is better suited to a plant's nutritional requirements.

Box 5.3 Manure: waste or resource?

Over the course of a year, a pig can produce 1,500 kg of manure and a cow might generate 12,000 kg. Given a single farm can have hundreds of animals, manure is a serious issue to be managed. In some cases, it can also be an opportunity to develop a valuable resource supply.

Manure contains nutrients (nitrogen, phosphorus and potassium) and organic matter (carbon) that can be used to fertilise crops and build soil organic matter. This closes a natural cycle: livestock produce manure, manure is used as a crop fertiliser, and crops are used as ingredients for human consumption or, in the case of conventional livestock production, fed to livestock for meat or dairy production. This can all go smoothly when the enabling conditions are set, and large swaths of land are available on which manure can be spread without the risk of pollution.

In some place, the ratio of livestock numbers to available land is set by law. In Italy, for example, limited space means farms can face a twofold problem: the need to purchase feed externally because space limitations prevent livestock from continuously grazing, and the concentrated accumulation of manure which is challenging to spread due to lack of space and thus becomes 'waste'.

Manure is used most effectively when it is spread over fields and ploughed into the soil before sowing. To optimise and reduce fertiliser use, modern agriculture suggests administering fertilisers even during the subsequent phases of crop production, providing nutrition to plants when they need it – sometimes not long before harvesting. In these cases, it is very difficult – if not impossible – to use manure due to technical problems (spreading it over a field of almost mature wheat would cause the stalks to collapse) and for hygiene and health reasons: who would buy a tomato covered in manure?

So, while manure is undoubtedly an excellent resource for farms, it cannot completely replace synthetic fertilisers if the right management infrastructure and logistics are not in place. Managed grazing approaches integrate livestock with grasslands and food production areas so that their manure is actively applied to the soil. A contrasting example is Terrgar'eau,[3] a project initiated by Danone in 2014 with local farmers in Plateau de Gavot, Switzerland. It uses the natural process of methanisation to transform manure into a natural fertiliser and biogas. The fertiliser is spread in a balanced way over 65% of the agricultural area so that it does not pose a risk to the water resources, while the biogas is sold back to the national grid to heat 900 houses. Revenue from gas sales covers the manure collection and operating costs and provides an extra revenue stream for farmers.

In addition to nutrients, plants need to be protected from disease, insects and weeds. Plant diseases have negative implications for plant health and crop yields, as well as food safety. Diseases can be managed by administering chemical (or, in some cases, natural) substances to plants, either preventatively or as treatment, during various growth phases. The intelligent management of crop fields can be adopted; for example, a disease of durum wheat – known as *fusarium* – occurs more frequently on land that was previously used to grow corn. Taking this into account and planning crop rotation intelligently can help reduce the use of agrochemicals and bring down costs for farmers.

Weeds are plants that serve no agricultural purpose but that compete with crop plants for nutrients and can leave unwanted residues (grasses among salad leaves, for example). To combat this, farmers can use substances that serve to selectively eliminate plants that are not useful.

Using agrochemicals generates a dual impact and environmental risk. On the one hand, there is the risk of pollution from substances that are not present in nature (local environmental impact) and, on the other, food production may be at risk of contamination (risk for humans). For instance, glyphosate came onto the market in 1974 and went on to become the world's most widely used herbicide.

It has recently been banned in at least ten countries following studies showing that it damages wild bee colonies[4] and is linked with health problems including cancer, reproductive problems, neurological diseases like amyotrophic lateral sclerosis (ALS), endocrine disruption and birth defects.[5]

Because of these risks, use of these substances must be minimal, with necessary precautions to ensure no more than the dosage needed to ensure plant health and food safety. Beyond minimising the dosage to treat weeds and diseases, farmers can apply techniques to prevent these threats in the first place, such as intercropping specific crops which cover plants that can be used to usurp resources used by weeds or suppress weed growth through natural allelopathy.[6]

One of the most serious and topical problems caused by the use of some agrochemicals is linked to the health of bees. Bees are a cornerstone of biodiversity and have been severely compromised by years of careless management of agrochemicals. Fortunately, a growing interest in these issues is leading to greater caution in the use of chemicals in agriculture. In Section 7.2, we explore regenerative agriculture which uses farming techniques that help reduce or eliminate the need for external agrochemicals and synthetic fertilisers.

5.1.2   Protecting crops from disease[7]

There are a growing number of alternative solutions to avoid the widespread and unsustainable use of agrochemicals to protect and treat crop plants. These approaches can be grouped into three main categories – organic techniques, genetic techniques and precision agriculture.

Organic techniques include activities that function by triggering natural phenomena whose purpose is to treat disease or prevent disease from developing. Examples include:

- use of natural compounds suited to both organic and conventional farming
- pheromone-based traps to capture and monitor insect pests or sterilised insects to confuse species that are harmful to crop plants
- use of traps to capture spores and minimise the impact of fungal attacks, also through the creation of mathematical models that help prevent the issue
- release of insects that prey on pest species, such as ladybirds to combat aphids
- long-term crop rotation with certain fields dedicated to nectar-rich wildflowers that serve to attract pollinators
- use of biostimulants to make plants stronger, more resistant to stress and parasites and more competitive against weeds – for example, nitrogen-fixing bacteria that decrease the need for chemical fertilisers

Modern genetic and molecular biology techniques select plant varieties (genotypes) that are better adapted to respond more effectively to specific problems such as disease, parasites, drought or climate change. Precision agriculture applies mathematical models to data, Decision Support Systems (DSS) and aerial imaging from satellites or drones to predict the risk of infestations in crop fields or orchards.

An example which is widely applicable in vegetable farming is the implementation of hydroponic and aeroponic techniques that enable vertical farming in enclosed spaces, with specialised LED lighting to minimise energy and water use and the risk of parasite infestation.

5.1.3   *Field management*

Other agricultural practices, such as irrigation and the use of machinery, are responsible for environmental impacts. One of the most topical issues is water use in agriculture. Water is a vital resource for the growth and development of plants, and it is becoming scarcer as a result of climate change and other pressures. Sustainable progress must focus on water conservation and water quality, including avoiding the dispersal of chemicals that cause pollution.

The evolution of irrigation techniques has led to positive steps in water conservation. There are a variety of opportunities available to farmers depending on the type of crop and the water source. A first loose grouping of water sources might distinguish between water sourced from underground wells and water extracted from shared irrigation canals. In Italy, one of the most important examples of water infrastructure is the *Canale Emiliano-Romagnolo* (Emilia-Romagna Canal[8]), which draws water from the Po River and supplies water to a vast portion of Emilia-Romagna. The region lacks surface water but features heavy agricultural activity and widespread urban and industrial settlements. Where suitable, modern high-efficiency irrigation techniques are used in areas experiencing water scarcity. For example, drip irrigation makes it possible to deliver water in a highly localised way, directly into the soil surrounding a plant's roots. This system minimises wastage and is especially well-suited to orchards and to vegetables such as tomatoes.

Many agricultural operations are carried out using tractor-drawn machinery. This is a major contributor to emissions due to fuel use; tractors can use up to 30–40 litres of diesel per hour. One way to reduce the impacts and costs of crop farming is to limit the number of fuel-intensive activities, avoiding superfluous tillage – as in the case of annual crops, like wheat – and fertilisation or agrochemical treatment. Farm management strategies are crucial to avoid unnecessary practices and to ensure proper consideration of the characteristics of the soil.

5.1.4   *Organic farming*[9]

Organic farming is central to the debate about food and sustainability. A range of organic certifications exist globally, each with their own criteria. In general, they push for the use of natural substances to be applied to agricultural products (such as fruit and vegetables) and the production of dairy or meat.

With regard to the agricultural stage, the basic rule is that the use of synthetic substances (fertiliser, herbicide, fungicide, insecticide and pesticides, more generally) is strictly prohibited. To protect crops, prevention strategies must be implemented such as the selection of species suited to the growing conditions, crop rotation and land management practices that promote biodiversity. For example, hedgerows and trees promote the presence of natural predators (primarily birds and insects, such as ladybirds) and create a physical barrier against potential exter nal pollution. Nutritional substances are provided using natural fertilisers, such as manure and other appropriately composted organic matter (cuttings, etc.) and green manures – fast-growing plants that cover bare soil and can improve soil fertility.

Organic farming in the animal husbandry sector uses animal feed grown under organic conditions and farming practices which are closely connected to the land and allow animals the lifestyle and space they need to express their natural behaviour. A further consideration relates to breed selection. In addition to prohibiting genetic manipulation, organic certification promotes the use of native breeds that are adapted to local environmental conditions, resistant to disease and suited to open pasture.

Aside from what is stated in production regulations, organic farming works only if the agrosystem is managed according to the precise dictates of agroecology – the practice of farming by harnessing the forces of nature. Essentially, this means activating the set of biogenic cycles that make it possible to achieve good outputs without large amounts of inputs. This type of regenerative organic farming is something humans started doing from the dawn of the agricultural age (some 10,000–12,000 years ago) and continued until the green revolution of the 1960s. We used to implement these practices because there was effectively no alternative; there were no chemicals that could counteract biotic challenges, nor were there low-cost synthetic fertilisers.

After the end of World War II, new means of chemical synthesis developed as a result of the immense technical progress the war effort facilitated, leading to the creation of low-cost fertilisers and pesticides. Agriculture was transformed. Paradoxically, this new type of agriculture – which was only established itself in the last 60 years – is commonly known as conventional farming (synonymous with traditional) while organic farming, with its millennia-old traditions, is labelled non-traditional.

The risk that is currently being faced by the organic production sector is that it could fall back into the same destructive patterns as industrial production. The fact that a means of production is natural (i.e. not synthetic) does not necessarily mean that it has a smaller impact on people or the environment. For example, rotenone is a natural product, but its elevated toxicity is vastly greater than any other pesticide on the global market today. Untreated manure, or fresh poultry manure, does not always equal better environmental outcomes due to issues during the use in the field (it is not always possible to use precision farming, for example). In fact, when mismanaged, their groundwater contamination potential is undoubtedly greater than that of synthetic urea.

This is the risk associated with so-called input substitution, which is when farmers decide to transition to an organic farming system by simply replacing chemical inputs with non-synthetic, natural inputs. An initial phase of input substitution is understandable and acceptable, especially when farmers come from decades of industrial agriculture. However, it must be followed by progressive business management based on principles leading to a preventative approach to adversity management.

In late May 2020, the European Commission published the long-awaited farm to fork (F2F) strategy, a vital component of the European Green Deal. It sets out a ten-year plan designed to guide the transition towards a just, healthy and environmentally friendly food system. Organic farming will play a key role in achieving its goals, with the policy aiming to increase the proportion of certified organic farmland from 9% (the current level) to 25%.

This is an ambitious target, and it is not clear how it will be met. Actions must focus on improving knowledge, investing in training and rethinking economic support mechanisms while ensuring the necessary framework conditions to support a radical change in the agri-food production system.

5.1.5   *Agriculture and genetics*

Ever since humans learned how to raise animals and grow crops, our evolution has been accompanied by the steady and careful selection of animal and plant species to find the breeds and varieties most suited to the production of foodstuffs and to meet higher-order needs – as in the case of ornamental plants and pets. This kind of selection started thousands of years ago and was often driven by unwitting interventions, as in the case of farmers in Mesopotamia who preferred wheat varieties with ears that facilitated the dispersal of seeds.

One of the most interesting of the many available examples is the humble tomato.[10] In the mid 20th century, genetic selection enabled the distinction between industrial tomatoes, generally used in sauces, and those for direct consumption, in salads, for example. The two types have different end-uses and different production requirements. In the case of industrial tomatoes, cultivars (varieties) were selected to improve mechanical picking and processing. This led to tomatoes that reached maturity simultaneously, had stems that remained attached to the plant and not the fruit and were sturdier overall with thicker skin. Genetic selection is one of the factors that, between 1920 and 1990, increased the average productivity of industrial cultivars in the US from 10 to 70 tonnes per hectare.

Today, genetic improvement in the agricultural sector uses methods that, for the sake of convenience, can be grouped into three major categories – conventional crossbreeding, consolidated genetic modification and new crossbreeding techniques.

Conventional crossbreeding techniques are generally used by farmers and seed producers. They include natural crosses between seeds of the same species or seeds of different species, followed by the selection of individuals (plants) with desired characteristics, such as higher productivity, resistance to pathogens or abiotic stresses, etc. In the US, chefs, farmers and breeders have collaborated on a project called Row 7[11] which is breeding organic non-GMO (genetically modified organism) varieties of produce by combining traditional breeding techniques and a flavour-first approach, helping to promote agro-biodiversity while discovering new ingredients.

New crossbreeding techniques intervene in a cultivar's DNA, changing it by adding genes from a sexually compatible member of the same species, effectively accelerating something that could feasibly happen naturally.

Consolidated genetic modification techniques rearrange nucleic acids (DNA and RNA) and insert a genetic sequence into a target plant, regardless of sexual compatibility with the donor organism, which can belong to a different species. The resulting plants are known as genetically modified organisms (GMOs). The use of GMOs is one of the most controversial and frequently recurring aspects in the realm of genetic selection, which is often accused of not being sustainable.

GMO refers to any organism in which the genetic material (DNA) has been altered in a way that does not occur naturally by mating and/or natural recombination.[12] While genetic selection is a millennia-old practice, the GMO techniques developed over the past 40 years make it possible to alter features of living beings in the lab. Genetic engineering can be used to insert a foreign gene (transgenesis) into an organism's genome, for example, to increase a plant's resistance to pesticides or parasites and improve its nutritional profile or ability to adapt to adverse climate conditions such as through drought resistance.

Plant cultivars on the market today have been created to optimise resistance to parasitising insects, herbicide tolerance, resistance to viruses and more. In the near future, the primary driver of trade will be primarily tied to parasite and herbicide resistance, even though there has long been a need to design plant varieties that can adapt to adverse environmental and climate conditions. Research is ongoing to develop plants that can adapt to drought conditions and shifts in temperature, or that can grow in soil that is rich in certain minerals or metals. Scientists have also come up with techniques to move beyond transgenic GMOs and achieve superior organisms using the genetic library of the species to be improved. The CRISPR Cas9 technique, whose discoverers won the Nobel Prize, is the most promising of these and will soon make it possible to design cultivars based on the various targets being pursued in the genetic improvement of plants.

The WHO has asserted that GMOs currently on the market pose no risk to human health.[13] In 2018, humans cultivated 192 million hectares of genetically modified crops. The 26 countries involved mostly produced corn, soy, cotton and rapeseed followed by sugar beet, papaya, courgette and tomato.[14] To help the average consumer navigate the tangle of scientific evidence, preconceptions, and ideology, the FAO has provided an easy-to-understand summary of the potential positive and negative repercussions of GMO crops, with a brief analysis of their verifiability. Environmental and ethical issues are undoubtedly among the most important. One of the matters that draws the greatest attention is crop specialisation, which is linked to monoculture and increased risk of biodiversity loss. The current food system is non-diverse, with 75% of the world's calories coming from 12 plants and 5 animal species.[15] This leaves the food system more vulnerable to shocks. Patent management is also a serious ethical concern because of its potential implications for the international seed market (Figure 5.1).

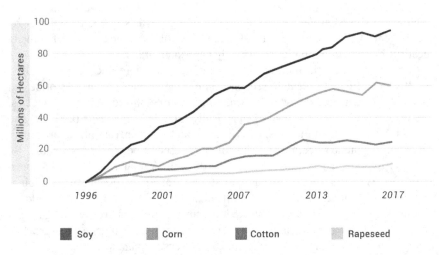

Figure 5.1 Land area used for GMO crops globally. *Brief 53: Global Status of Commercialized Biotech/GM Crops*, 2017, ISAA, https://www.isaaa.org/resources/publications/briefs/53/. Originally published in the first edition of this book, *Il Cibo Perfetto*, published in Italian in 2022.

5.2   Animal husbandry

Debate around the sustainability of animal farming is often influenced by ethical considerations. Vegetarianism and veganism involve the partial or total avoidance of animal products for a wide variety of reasons. With due respect to those who decide to exclude animal products from their diet for ethical reasons, in this book we limit our discussion to technical matters, being aware that our limited scope cannot adequately address ethical matters concerning animal welfare.

Animal husbandry and farming practices are widespread and closely inter-linked with other agri-food production systems, so much so that few foods are not directly or indirectly influenced by these farming practices. For example, agricultural production and organic farming use manure from animal farming as fertiliser and to increase soil organic matter content. The use of by-products of animal farming – such as leather, wool or bovine products used for medical applications – extends well beyond the agri-food sector. Animals also provide valuable services that are beneficial for farms. For instance, duck-rice farming is an integrated organic farming system found in Asian countries. The ducks live amongst rice paddies, feeding off the weeds and fertilising the soil with their droppings. Studies have found integrating ducks can increase yields by 20% and lead to a 50% increase in net return.[16]

The assessment of animal farms must consider all by-products and benefits generated to measure the total impact of a product. If we take a dairy cow, for example, and set the value of its total environmental impact throughout its lifetime at 100 (including the production of its feed, the management of its excreta, etc.), then we need to consider the impact of its meat, its leather and its milk. The hypotheses and

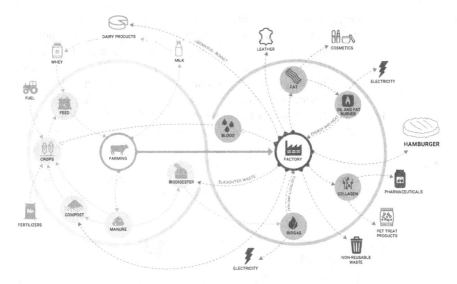

Figure 5.2 One of the most practical examples of circularity in the agri-food sector: the beef cattle value chain. E. Bernardi, E. Capri, G. Pulina, *La sostenibilità delle carni e dei salumi in Italia*, FrancoAngeli, Roma, 2018. Originally published in the first edition of this book, *Il Cibo Perfetto*, published in Italian in 2022.

calculation methods used to perform this allocation have a major influence on the final outcomes, so much so that the definition of shared rules is vital.

In this context and others (a mill faces the same problem between flour and chaff), transparent rules must be followed to ensure accuracy and comparability. These rules are known as Product Category Rules (PCR) (Figure 5.2).

5.2.1 *Animal feed*

Regardless of the type of farming – from the most intensive to the most artisanal – the environmental impacts of this activity occur mostly at the feed production stage and in the management of excreta.

The production of animal feed is the first phase of the conventional animal husbandry supply chain, where animals are primarily fed external feed rather than grazed on land. We must understand the characteristics, needs and advantages associated with the production of feed because, without it, industrial animal husbandry as it exists today would not be possible. We will explore sustainable livestock production systems that minimise external feed demand by grazing livestock in managed systems later on in the discussion.

The term 'feed' refers to any foodstuff or product used to provide nutrition to animals. This definition comprises a vast set of products, ranging from simple raw ingredients administered directly (such as hay) to composite feeds made up of various raw ingredients and additives. But why is feed necessary? There are many reasons, all of which can be traced back to three main factors.

The first factor is nutrition. As with humans, animals' diets must provide the right intake of macronutrients such as carbohydrates, proteins, fats and micronutrients like vitamins and minerals. Composite feeds ensure animals have a balanced diet throughout their lives without lacking any nutrients. The second factor relates to production efficiency. Bearing animal welfare in mind, it is important to maintain a highly efficient relationship between the products being created (in this case, meat, fish, eggs and milk) and the resources used. The third element concerns animal health. The primary goal of protecting animals' health and well-being is achieved through a balanced diet, designed to provide all necessary nutrients according to the species and phase of production.

Let's take a closer look at what animals eat. A first key point is to grasp the difference between nutrients and ingredients, because this allows us to understand

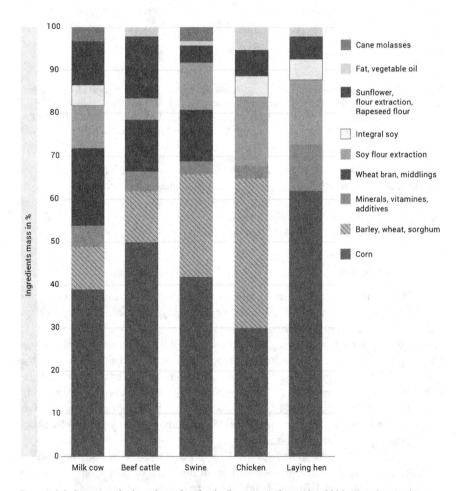

Figure 5.3 Some typical recipes for feed. *Report Ambientale*, 2020, Assalzoo, chrome-extension://efaidnbmnnnibpcajpcglclefindmkaj/https://www.assalzoo.it/wp-content/uploads/2021/06/ASSALZOO_Report_Ambientale_2020.pdf. Originally published in the first edition of this book, *Il Cibo Perfetto*, published in Italian in 2022.

the features of different feed formulas. The same concept applies to human nutrition; our recommended intake of vitamin C, for example, is expressed in mg per day and not in grams of lemon. Vitamin C is the nutrient, and lemon is the ingredient which provides the means of obtaining the nutrient. This difference allows nutritionists to optimise feed formulas by working directly with nutrients, often before considering ingredients. This also allows them to meet nutritional requirements effectively while reducing environmental impacts and minimising costs (Figure 5.3).

The nutrients required by livestock are analogous to those needed by humans: carbohydrates, proteins, fats and micronutrients like vitamins and minerals. Everything must be balanced based on the species and the different phases of growth such as weaning, growth, lactation, etc.

When it comes to ingredients, the main raw ingredients are cereals (corn, wheat, barley) and protein crops (soy, sunflower, rapeseed). This applies to all animal husbandry systems aside from fisheries, because the nutritional needs of fish are very different and require non-agricultural ingredients. This topic is treated in more depth in the relevant section.

Sometimes, raw ingredients are grown as part of the same farming business that manages the animal husbandry processes. In other cases, they are purchased on the market – such as is often the case with soy. Italy, for example, is not self-sufficient in soy and must import it from suppliers abroad. Beyond food safety, which is ensured via monitoring and traceability throughout the food value chain, sustainability improvement becomes more difficult when a company has to procure feed products from the market, because the products' impact cannot easily be controlled.

Box 5.4   The sustainability of feed production[17]

Animal feed producers play a strategic role in agri-food sustainability due to their ability to influence processes upstream and downstream in the value chain. Upstream, we find agricultural production and by-product creation, and downstream are animal husbandry systems, whose production efficiency may be affected. Analyses must be performed with care and should consider all stages to avoid mistakes, such as considering one type of feed more sustainable because it has a smaller impact than another, without taking the conversion ratio into account.

The feed production industry is working on three different fronts to help contribute to sustainability. First, there is processing. Feed production systems are characterised by simple processes which have limited environmental impacts. In the case of a bag of feed, the carbon footprint of the processing stage accounts for approximately 5% of the total, and the industry is focused on reducing energy use and using renewable energy where possible.

Procurement and supply constitute the second front. Feed producers rarely have direct control over what happens in the field, but they have more control over raw ingredient selection. Increasingly, procurement decisions are made in accordance with sustainability criteria. For example, in the case of soy there tends to be a preference for domestic (or EU-sourced) products. Where imports are unavoidable, they must often be certified as sustainable.[18] There is also the opportunity to use by-products of food production as animal feed to avoid having to grow crops solely for animal feed. Insects are increasingly used to rapidly valorise organic waste streams (e.g. food scraps, agricultural residues) and provide a sustainable feed source. In Kenya, companies like Insectipro use black soldier flies to treat organic waste streams and create organic fertiliser and then become insect meal, which serves as a highly nutritious alternative feed for livestock.[19]

The third and most important element is collaboration with farmers to carry out nutritional research and develop techniques to increase nutritional efficiency. Designers of feed formulas are highly specialised nutritionists who design balanced diets, taking into consideration the animals' needs and the raw ingredients at their disposal. In the case of ruminants, feed designers are trying to minimise enteric fermentation, which takes place in the digestive system of animals, to reduce GHG (greenhouse gas) emissions. Increased heat treatments for feed and use of natural-based additives have so far proven effective. For example, in the case of dairy cow nutrition, certain yeasts and enzymes can be integrated into the feed to reduce methane output.

On-farm, the application of precision feeding techniques which optimise animal nutrition in terms of both quantity and timing are becoming increasingly widespread. An example of this relates to feeding fish in aquaculture settings where it is impossible to see all the animals, making direct control of feeding difficult. Nutritional monitoring can be achieved thanks to underwater cameras that allow fish farmers to design nutritional plans that are consistent with the animals' needs and the growth requirements of production strategies. The growing focus on these topics has led to a considerable increase in production.

5.2.2   The perfect egg?

Eggs present a classic dilemma concerning the trade-off between environmental sustainability and animal welfare. If data from the literature is used to compare different farming systems, the results show that industrial, caged farms have a smaller carbon footprint. This can be easily understood if we consider that industrially farmed chickens have less freedom of movement and, if the chosen reference variable is the amount of feed consumed per egg produced, the system is clearly more efficient (Figure 5.4).

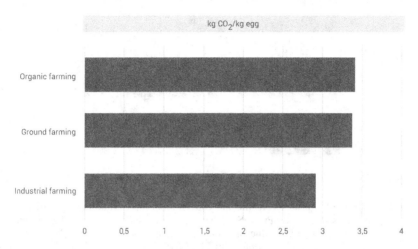

Figure 5.4 The carbon footprint of eggs from different farming systems. Authors' elaboration. Data processed from I. Leinonen, I. Kyriazakis, Quantifying the Environmental Impacts of UK Broiler and Egg Production Systems, in *Lohmann
Information*, Vol 48, Issue 2, pp. 45–50, October 2013. Originally published in
the first edition of this book, *Il Cibo Perfetto*, published in Italian in 2022.

This does not, however, mean that caged farming should be considered
sustainable. Driven by market demand, many companies have made a value-based
decision to stop using eggs from industrial chicken farms, prioritising animal welfare over environmental impact. There is also the widespread belief that animals
kept in worse conditions produce lower-quality eggs, in terms of both taste and
nutritional value.

5.2.3   Dairy farming

As a foodstuff, milk is associated with all the problems that are typical of conventional value chains. For the sake of simplicity, we focus solely on the carbon
footprint metric to show how almost half the emissions of the entire cycle – from
farm to glass – arise from the inevitable process of enteric fermentation in cattle.
These emissions are primarily made up of methane (CH_4) and have a considerable
climate-altering effect. The impact of domestic milk refrigeration is also extensive,
accounting for almost 10% of its total emissions. The assessment does not account
for the possible heating of the milk by the consumer, because this data can vary
greatly; the longer the milk is heated, the greater the GHG emissions.

The comparison between organic and conventional products again leads to a
dilemma associated with CO_2 emissions per kilogram of product. Due to the greater
efficiency of conventional production, emissions are greater in organic systems.
Does this mean we should conclude that conventional farming is more sustainable?
Perhaps, but only as it concerns this one aspect. A broader and more in-depth analysis might yield a different outcome (Figure 5.5). In some studies, regeneratively

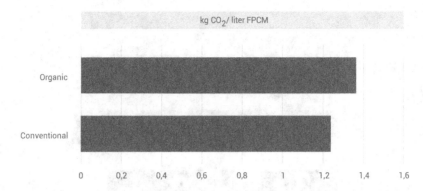

Figure 5.5 Carbon footprint of organic and conventional milk. Authors' elaboration. Data
processed from G. Pirlo, S. Lolli, Environmental Impact of Milk Production
from Samples of Organic and Conventional Farms in Lombardy (Italy), in *Journal of Cleaner Production*", Vol 211, pp. 962–971, February 2019. Originally
published in the first edition of this book, *Il Cibo Perfetto*, published in Italian
in 2022.

produced dairy (cows raised in managed intensive grazing (MIG) systems) can
yield 50% lower emissions than conventional dairy.[20] The key here is that cows
are integrated into grasslands and can support accelerated carbon sequestration in
a way that some organic cows raised on certified organic feed do not. Discussion
of organic agriculture is complicated as the benefits are not easily measured. The
organic content of the soil, improved soil texture and improved water management
are all points that should considered. For this reason, the CO_2 angle should be considered as just one facet of production impact. The best decisions cannot be made
on this basis alone.

The environmental impacts of cheese are even more difficult to measure due to
the complexity of the production process. In a dairy, milk is the input and there are
many outputs and by-products, with cheese being the main product. Measurement
requires the application of specific algorithms to partition the various impact flows,
which vary based on the fat and protein content of output products. In the simplest
terms, the impact of cheese is normally between five and ten times that of milk
(Figure 5.6).

5.2.4   *Meat production*

The meat production chain is also complex and its impacts – when compared with
the production of other foodstuffs by output weight – are among the highest. The
most simple and intuitive explanation is that, unlike plant-based products, conventional systems require a 'double step' process: first feed crops are produced
and then the protein conversion process takes place as the animals are farmed.
This process is not heavily dependent on systems such as MIG[21] and silvopasture[22]
where animals graze on pastures in a systematic way, and feed is used only when
needed as a supplement.

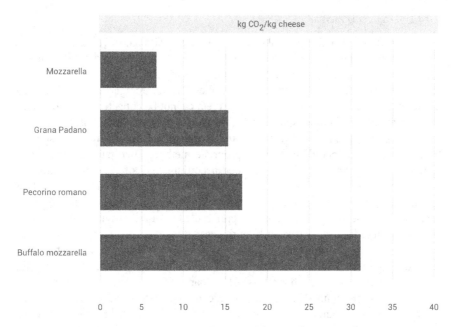

Figure 5.6 The carbon footprint of some of the most important Italian cheese. Authors'
elaboration. Data are processed from various bibliographical sources and must
be considered merely illustrative and approximate. Mozzarella: A. Dalla Riva,
J. Burek, D. Kim, G. Thoma, M. Cassandro, M. De Marchi, Environmental Life
Cycle Assessment of Italian Mozzarella Cheese: Hotspots and Improvement
Opportunities, in *Journal of Dairy Science*, Vol 100, Issue 10, pp. 7933–7952,
October 2017; Grana Padano: L. Bava, J. Bacenetti, G. Gislon, L. Pellegrino,
P. D'incecco, A. Sandrucci, A. Tamburini, M. Fiala, M. Zucali, Impact Assess-
ment of Traditional Food Manufacturing: The Case of Grana Padano Cheese, in
Science of the Total Environment, Vol 626, pp. 1200–1209, June 2018; Pecorino
Romano: E. Vagnoni, A. Franca, C. Porqueddu, P. Duce, *The Environmental Pro-
file of Pecorino Romano PDO. A Case Study, Proceedings of the XI Conference
of the Italian LCA Network*, 2019; Buffalo mozzarella: M. Berlese, M. Corazzin,
S. Bovolenta, Environmental Sustainability Assessment of Buffalo Mozzarella
Cheese Production Chain: A Scenario Analysis, in *Journal of Cleaner Production*, Vol 238, November 2019. Originally published in the first edition of this
book, *Il Cibo Perfetto*, published in Italian in 2022.

Nevertheless, it is important to remember that the impacts of food should not
be compared per kilogram of output. Nutritional (functional) properties must be
considered, and impacts must be measured based on actual food consumption in a
balanced diet.

As we have seen, the most high-impact stages are at the level of agricultural
production. But what are the most problematic aspects? In addition to the topic
of animal feed, the management of animal husbandry systems must be considered
with a particular focus on excreta, enteric fermentation and the age-old intensive
vs extensive debate.

5.2.4.1 Managing excreta

The impact of animal excreta is linked to atmospheric emissions of volatile substances (ammonia, methane and nitrous oxide) and release of nitrogen into the soil. In intensive farming systems, these environmental aspects are concentrated at two different stages of the overall management flow: the collection and storage phase and final disposal. In the case of free-range farming, excreta cannot be collected, and the impact depends on dispersal in fields, the control of which is virtually impossible.

After collection, excreta are stored so that treatment can occur at the most suitable time, location and according to the appropriate method. There are many different storage systems, but they can be grouped according to a key feature: whether or not they are covered. On intensive farms, absorbent material on the floor, such as straw, generates manure while a floor consisting of gratings generates manure slurry. Manure is almost solid, which makes it preferable because it provides more options for storage and disposal. Particularly in the case of slurry, open or closed tanks can have very different environmental impacts. Uncovered systems cause greater emissions due to direct release of volatile substances and the occurrence of spontaneous fermentation that causes further release of methane, CO_2 and other substances.

The emissions generated during storage can be estimated according to the Intergovernmental Panel on Climate Change (IPCC) guidelines for the three main compounds: methane, nitrous oxide and ammonia.[23] The IPCC presents three possible approaches based on expected precision and available data. Normally, the intermediate TIER 2 approach is used because it allows sufficient precision starting from generally known data. Emissions depend on the amount and type of excreta and storage methods – both the technology used and the geographical area. Climate can be extremely influential due to its effect on the biological degradation processes responsible for emissions.

After storage, the excreta must be disposed of. There are various options, based on the animal species that generated the excreta (chemical composition may differ) and the storage methods used (Figure 5.7). In principle, agricultural use of manure and slurry can be seen as closing the loop because nutrients (mainly nitrogen and phosphorus) and organic matter are restored to crops without having to use chemical fertilisers. However, correct management is vital because excessive use and mismanagement can lead to the uncontrolled release of pollutants – primarily nitrogen. For this assessment, in addition to quantity, it is important to consider the quality of the material, the properties of which can vary greatly. In the case of poultry manure, for example, its low moisture content (30% compared to 90% for cattle and pig manure) means nitrogen concentrations are elevated and land spreading must be performed with extreme caution.

Agricultural use of animal husbandry effluent is often regulated by specific rules, such as the Nitrates Directive in EU. These vary from region to region for the protection of areas vulnerable to agricultural nitrates. The basic principle is the need to have an area of land proportional to the heads of livestock farmed so that excreta can be managed directly within the same farm.

Managed grazing systems have been shown to help evenly distribute manure more effectively than continuous grazing systems,[24] which helps minimise risk

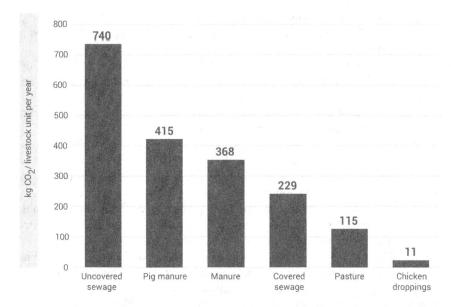

Figure 5.7 Estimated GHG emissions from manure storage in selected animal husbandry sectors. Adapted from E. Bernardi, E. Capri, G. Pulina, *La sostenibilità delle carni e dei salumi in Italia*, FrancoAngeli, Roma, 2018. Originally published in the first edition of this book, *Il Cibo Perfetto*, published in Italian in 2022.

of negative environmental consequences. Furthermore, diet and culture shift interventions can move towards a future where we eat 'less but better' animal products, decreasing instances of highly concentrated populations of animals generating large volumes of excreta. Ideally, the animals we eat are raised in integrated systems that reduce total impacts and realise the potential for animals' excreta to directly benefit soil fertility and crop production.

5.2.4.2   Enteric fermentation

Enteric fermentation is one of the outcomes of the digestion process in animals. It becomes particularly problematic in the case of ruminant herbivores (cattle, sheep, buffaloes, etc.) because it generates a considerable amount of methane (CH_4), which has a much higher climate-altering potential than CO_2. The amount of methane generated depends on the characteristics of the animal (breed, age and weight) and the type and quantity of food it is given.

The IPCC has performed in-depth measurements of enteric emissions, resulting in the definition of three approaches to estimate their scale, each with a different level of detail and precision.

- TIER 1 is the simplest and least precise method for estimating emissions based only on the type of animal (e.g. dairy cattle or beef cattle) and the geographical area in which it is found.

- TIER 2 involves a more complex measurement approach and a deeper knowledge of the farm. It should be used when the scale of emissions is considerable, as in the case of cattle.
- TIER 3 is the most precise method and requires thorough investigation of the farm to gather primary information such as ration composition, seasonal variations in animal populations, quality and quantity of feed provided to the livestock, and possible mitigation strategies for the emissions being generated. These data are often derived from direct testing.

TIER 2 is the most widely used approach. Feed formula analysis can show how emissions vary significantly with changes to animals' diets. This is due to the amount and type of feed. Without going into too much detail about the calculations, the interesting thing to observe is how the type of feed can have a considerable impact on enteric emissions. Nutritionists and feed producers are highly interested in researching the best alternatives for improving sustainability in this respect.

One of the measurement factors depends on the type of farming system. With cattle, the value suggested by the IPCC is twice as high for free-range livestock (or dairy cattle) than those of enclosed animals. At the same level of nutritional energy supply, the emissions of free-range cattle far exceed those of enclosed animals. However, the total quantity of feed supplied must also be considered. To illustrate the calculation method, we present a case in which we compare the diets of completely free-range cattle with those of cattle raised according to the Italian production system, which involves a combination of free-range and enclosed farming. The comparison is to be understood as preliminary because there are many different assumptions and implications. The first limitation, for example, comes from considering rations as constant throughout the animals' entire lifespan, which is never the case.

5.2.4.3   *Intensive vs extensive farming?*

Including water and energy use, the farming and transformation processes that start with slaughter and end at the point of consumption account for 10–20% of total impacts. As with other foodstuffs, this impact is calculated by correlating the use of raw materials, energy, water and other forms of pollution with the amount of meat produced. Considering the impact per kilogram of product, the lowest environmental impact is achieved when animals reach the target weight for slaughter in the shortest time possible, requiring the smallest amount of food and generating the least manure. This brings us to one of the greatest dilemmas in food production: is intensive or extensive farming – where animals spend their lives at pasture – more sustainable?

Before delving deeper, we need to clarify what is meant by 'intensive' farming. The intensiveness of a farm tends to be linked to the number of animals and the space they occupy per unit of area. However, this type of approach requires an upgrade. The intensiveness of a farm should be defined based on the ratio between the direct cost of labour and total costs: the lower the ratio – meaning that labour costs are a small fraction of the total – the more intensive or capital-intensive the system is. Conversely, when labour costs become a primary factor, the farming system can be considered extensive. This is usually applied to small, family-run businesses.

This definition allows us to move beyond the classic equation of 'lots of animals in a small space equals intensive farming'. There are livestock farms with thousands of heads of cattle or sheep where the animals have great swaths of land at their disposal (think of farms in Australia or Ireland), just as there are family-run

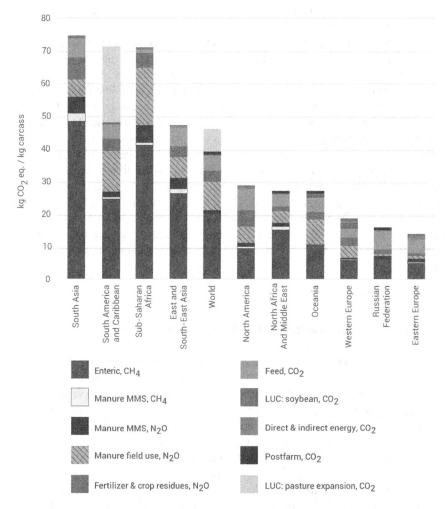

Figure 5.8 Comparison between different beef production scenarios. C. Opio, P. Gerber, A. Mottet, A. Falcucci, G. Tempio, M. MacLeod, T. Vellinga, B. Henderson, H. Steinfeld, *Greenhouse Gas Emissions from Ruminant Supply Chain. A Global Life Cycle Assessment*, FAO, Rome, 2013, chrome-extension://efaidnbmnnnib-pcajpcglclefindmkaj/https://www.fao.org/3/i3461e/i3461e.pdf.

farms with very few animals kept in very small spaces. This shift in perspective opens a new outlook in which judgement over the quality of a farm is not based on the concept of intensiveness or extensiveness, but rather on the objective characteristics which are a consequence of farmers' behaviour. Hence, the distinction between 'good' and 'bad' farmers is more appropriate.

If the focus is limited to environmental issues, intensification would lead to lower impacts per kilogram of product (global impact) but could cause excessive pressure on ecosystems (local impact). Once again, we are faced with a dilemma. In the case of livestock, matters such as animal welfare and veterinary pharmaceuticals remind us that sustainability must be sought as the correct balance between extreme models.

Considering GHG emissions per kilogram of meat produced provides an interesting comparison between different production systems across the world. The most high-impact regions in terms of emissions are South America and Southeast Asia, followed by Europe and North America. There is a notable difference in production between the different regions, in terms of both species farmed and farming systems; in South America, beef farming is prevalent, and it is mostly carried out via extensive systems; in Asia, production is mostly focused on dairy cattle and pigs; North America is a major producer of beef cattle in industrial systems; and production in Europe is semi-intensive, with a balanced distribution of species, pig farming being marginally prevalent. These variations in production inevitably correspond to differences in emissions. In countries where extensive farming is prevalent, emissions per unit produced are higher than in regions where the system is more industrialised. However, we must remember that the excessive pursuit of productive efficiency can conflict with product safety or animal welfare considerations (Figure 5.8).

Box 5.5   Focus on sustainability: international working groups

Founded in 2002, the global Sustainable Agriculture Initiative Platform brings together over 100 organisations operating in the agriculture and animal farming sector. To protect Earth's resources, the platform encourages the exchange of information and expertise among members, promoting the search for solutions to common problems and driving the development of sustainable agriculture in a pre-competitive environment. The platform is developing several measurement tools and operational protocols, with a particular focus on beef, dairy and crops.

The Spotlight collaboration tool is an aggregator that promotes dialogue among businesses. Farms input their key features (main product, country of origin and the topic to be explored) and are guided in a search for other companies that share the same interests/concerns before choosing whether or not to get in touch with them.

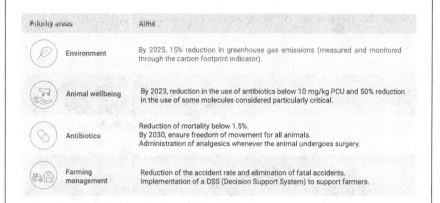

Priority areas		Aims
	Environment	By 2025, 15% reduction in greenhouse gas emissions (measured and monitored through the carbon footprint indicator).
	Animal wellbeing	By 2023, reduction in the use of antibiotics below 10 mg/kg PCU and 50% reduction in the use of some molecules considered particularly critical.
	Antibiotics	Reduction of mortality below 1.5%. By 2030, ensure freedom of movement for all animals. Administration of analgesics whenever the animal undergoes surgery.
	Farming management	Reduction of the accident rate and elimination of fatal accidents. Implementation of a DSS (Decision Support System) to support farmers.

Figure 5.9 The four priority focus areas at the European level identified by ERBS. Authors' elaboration. Originally published in the first edition of this book, *Il Cibo Perfetto*, published in Italian in 2022.

The European Roundtable for Beef Sustainability (ERBS), launched in 2018, aims to address key links in the beef value chain. It has identified four priority focus areas at the European level and set eight targets (Figure 5.9).

Each member country (Italy, France, Germany, Ireland, Poland and UK) has created its own national platform and is required to present a yearly report of actions implemented towards achieving the targets. As with SAI, the main function of the ERBS is to share information among participants, increasing the knowledge and expertise of all stakeholders in the sector.

5.2.5 *Fishing and fish farming*

Global fish consumption is steadily increasing. According to FAO data,[25] it rose from 9.9 kilograms a year per capita in the 1960s to 20.5 kilograms in 2018 (Figure 5.10).

Faced with growing demand, the fishing industry provided a fairly steady supply over the past 20 years – around 90–95 million tonnes per year – but this has caused mounting pressure on biodiversity. According to WWF estimates,[26] over 30% of global fish stocks are fished at unsustainable levels and approximately 60% are completely overfished, a fact that is aggravated by unsustainable or illegal fishing practices.

Sustainability problems with wild fisheries relate to the relationship with the natural environment rather than the technology used. This means that the environmental indicators typical of life cycle assessment (LCA) analyses are less relevant, whereas respect for natural resources is key. According to the WWF, the problem of overfishing affects not only the so-called target species, fished for their commercial value, but all the species that are accidentally captured by insufficiently selective fishing equipment, known as bycatch. In the Mediterranean, bycatch can

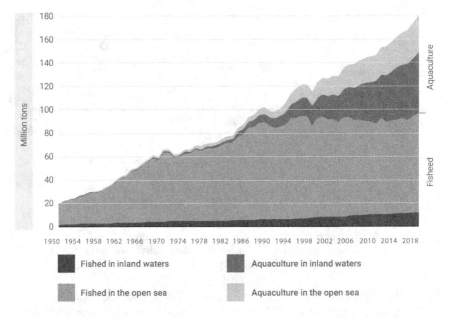

Figure 5.10 Global fish production from 1950 to 2018. Note: aquatic mammals, croco-
        diles, alligators, caimans, algae and other marine plants are not included. FAO,
        The State of World Fisheries and Aquaculture. Sustainability in Action, Rome,
        2020, https://bit.ly/3qh2XQa. Originally published in the first edition of this
        book, *Il Cibo Perfetto*, published in Italian in 2022.

account for up to 70% of fish caught and includes fish with no commercial value
and those under the required size.

Fishing is a hotly debated and controversial topic. The risk of ecosystem damage
must be considered alongside the needs of local economies that are based on fishing
practices. Consider, for example, fishing villages on coastlines and minor islands
where the problems are so widely known that local fishers approach the practice in
the most sustainable way possible.

Since the 1990s, global demand for fish has been met thanks to a major contribution from aquaculture – the farming of fish and shellfish. This practice has now
expanded to the point that it is the main source of fish for human consumption.
Aquaculture can involve species with a variety of nutritional and environmental
needs. Farmed fish can be carnivorous – like salmon, trout and seabass – or herbivorous, like tilapia and carp. Some species are marine, as in sea bream and amber-
jack, while others live in freshwaters, such as catfish and sturgeon. There are fish
that prefer cold waters, like turbot, and warm waters, like pangasius.

This diversity makes for fish farming systems that are highly varied, depending on the species farmed and the different technologies in use, including water
recirculation, land-based aquaculture, floating cages and natural reservoirs. The
concept of sustainability in aquaculture can relate to both methods and priorities,
which change with the region, species farmed and techniques used. A highly salient
issue in Europe, for example, where the most-farmed species are carnivorous, is

the matter of feed formulas. Fishmeal and fish oils – sourced from industrial wild catch – are among the main ingredients used to deliver protein and fats. Essentially, fish farming requires wild-caught fish. This issue is monitored through the FIFO (Fish In, Fish Out) indicator, which correlates kilograms of wild-caught fish used in the production of feed with kilograms of farmed fish for human consumption. Obviously, lower values are better, and the ideal target is for this ratio to be less than one, making aquaculture a net producer of fish. This has become the reality, with the FIFO ratio for aquaculture globally at 0.22 according to the International Fishmeal and Fish Oil Organisation (IFFO).[27] Even in the case of carnivorous fish, like salmon, the ratio remains below one (0.82 compared to close to 10 for its wild counterpart). In the wild, salmon is at a higher level on the food chain than herring (4.4 vs 3.4). Given that the conversion efficiency between trophic levels in nature is 10%, it follows that 1 kilogram of wild salmon requires 10 kilograms of herring.

The promotion of food industry co-products has made this progress possible. Over 30% of all fishmeal and fish oil on the global market comes from by-products of processing fish for human consumption, alongside by-products of meat processing and innovative ingredients such as insect-based flours. This achievement goes hand in hand with the increasing prominence of sustainability certification programmes for industrial fishing, such as Marin Trust and the Marine Stewardship Council.

However, simply altering feed formulas by reducing fishmeal and fish oil content in favour of alternative ingredients does not eliminate the problems. Some alternatives, such as soy and palm-based products, can present other sustainability-related problems. The most careful companies sign international memoranda of understanding aimed at minimising environmental impacts, as was hinted at in the section about the sustainability of soy.

The balance between raw materials that come from the sea (fishmeal) and their alternatives also affects the nutritional properties of fish products, in particular the level of omega-3 contained in the farmed fish fillet. These highly nutritional fatty acids can only be provided by the marine food chain. Sustainability must be sought in the balance between protecting biodiversity and maintaining adequate levels of the essential nutrients that make fish a unique food product. Algae are a promising renewable source of omega-3 fatty acids for feed production, alongside the repurposing of food industry by-products.

In parts of Africa and South America, the primary value of aquaculture is to provide low-cost animal protein, thanks to the greater efficiency with which fish convert nutritional inputs compared to other farmed animals. Fish achieve over 30% efficiency in terms of protein conversion, compared to 20% for poultry and just 6% for beef. The most-farmed species in these regions are herbivores, such as tilapia, which raises different problems to those discussed for carnivore species farmed in Europe. In this case, feed sustainability is not the primary concern (the FIFO index is always well below one) but problems arise due to the introduction of farmed species to areas where they were not originally present, causing a risk of biodiversity loss through competition with native species. This has been found in Madagascar, Kenya, Mexico and Nicaragua, for example. Chemical and organic water pollution due to irresponsible farming practices are also concerns.

Another oft-discussed case is that of prawns, farmed in Asia and South America to meet growing demand on the global market. This form of aquaculture has often been criticised for competing for space in areas of ecological importance, such as mangrove forests in Vietnam, Thailand, the Philippines, Bangladesh, Ecuador and Brazil. Managing these issues has been the focus of initiatives like the Aquaculture Stewardship Council (ASC). This organisation, coordinated by WWF, has developed shared standards for responsible farming of species, including tilapia and prawn, and a certification scheme that is gaining ground as a useful value enhancement tool for products. All stakeholders in the value chain were involved in the development of the standards, including fish farmers and environmental NGOs.

Marine systems offer production of ingredients yet to be widely used globally. Innovative organisations like Greenwave[28] are pioneering new vertical ocean farming techniques which are designed to tap into the 10,000 edible plants in the ocean and harvest 'ocean greens' which are rich in iron, calcium and other nutrients, while using zero inputs and restoring oceans in the process.

5.3   Industrial processing

Industrial processing is the stage of the value chain during which a raw agricultural material (such as wheat) or a semi-finished product (such as flour) is transformed into a product to be sold.

Common processes involved are cooking, pasteurisation, mixing ingredients, drying, refrigeration, washing and cleaning. The most significant environmental impacts are due to energy use (electricity and heat), water use and the generation of waste and by-products. In most cases, by-products are repurposed, such as for animal feed, compost, new ingredients or as feedstock for a biodigester to turn into fertiliser and bioenergy. Industrial facilities and production plants are often very large, using much more energy than domestic systems. This leads to the common misconception that they pollute a lot more than when food is prepared at home. There are two reasons why this is misleading.

The first is that the impact of these processes must be considered in relation to the amount of food produced, and not simply the absolute value. If energy use is divided by production volume (kWh of power per kilogram of biscuits, for example), it is easy to see that the efficiency of industrial processes is much higher and, therefore, environmental impacts are considerably smaller. The second reason is that impacts are concentrated in one location. Consider, for example, the peeling of vegetables in an industrial setting. All the waste is promptly and correctly dealt with (through composting or energy conversion, for example). Meanwhile, in most domestic cases, waste management is not completely sustainable, and this type of waste often ends up in a landfill, with a heavy environmental impact.

A key term in correctly interpreting impact is 'efficiency'. An industrial system is more efficient, meaning it can produce more using fewer resources. This statement is valid in a general sense, although it is worth noting that the economy of scale might also lead to inefficiencies due to the need to keep infrastructure active when it is not strictly required for production processes. For example, a facility with very large production lines is efficient when production takes place over three work shifts. But if volumes force one shift to be cancelled, for example, at night, there is a risk that inefficiencies could arise as certain machinery cannot easily be turned off. The larger a factory is, the more it will be focused on efficiency because reduced resource consumption, while maintaining production levels, allows for significant cost savings.

The use of industrial technologies can lead to further benefits beyond energy efficiency. In the case of marmalade, the cooking process in an industrial setting can happen under vacuum, making it possible to cook at lower temperatures and ensuring better quality control than in a domestic setting. Alongside the opportunities provided by technologies to organise processing, the food industry takes great care in the selection of ingredients based on flavour and nutritional qualities and the technological needs of production processes. Recipes are mostly created using the same ingredients as those used by consumers at home, with the addition of very limited amounts of additives, preservatives and flavourings.

The regulatory constraints that producers must respect in their use of ingredients and process management also act in favour of the industrial model. This is especially true when products are marketed under registered brands or trademarks and, even more so, when they must conform to specific protocols, such as with seasonal products.

5.3.1   *Fresh, packaged or frozen vegetables?*

The key message in the advertising of some industrial products is focused on the functional advantage of ready-to-eat products (i.e. more on the service than on the product itself). This is the case with washed and bagged salad, which competes on supermarket shelves with the classic head of fresh lettuce. Five groups categorise how 'ready-to-eat' a food product is: first-level (fresh produce); second-level (preserved produce); third-level (frozen produce); fourth-level (fresh; ready-to-eat produce) and fifth-level (cooked, ready-to-eat produce).

The production process for fourth- and fifth-level foodstuffs are more resource intensive than at lower levels because cleaning and packaging are required to make the product easily consumable, minimising at-home preparation and food waste (due to over-buying) for the consumer. Ready-to-eat foods can come with cost and benefit tensions, often revolving around the impact of waste and packaging. For instance, studies carried out on the supply chains of some of the main Italian producers of bagged salad show that, from an environmental perspective based primarily on water and energy use, loose produce has a lower environmental impact if waste from farm to fork is kept below 30% and collected separately and composted. The sustainability of loose fresh produce is thus dependent on effective waste collection systems in different localities, which is not widespread both within a country and across different countries.

The same considerations apply to frozen produce, which enables consumers to eat products out of season without their nutritional qualities suffering, thanks to low-temperature preservation processes and cooling technologies within distribution chains. In this case, the cost includes energy consumed in the cold chains and at-home freezers, and the benefits include increased shelf life and minimising waste at harvest time.

In addition to convenience and affordability, other benefits of processed foods include high standards of food safety, increased shelf life and availability around the world and throughout the year, food waste repurposed, for example, turning overripe fruit into dried products, increased dietary diversity and nutritional fortification.

Box 5.6   The benefits of freezing vegetables

Interview with Silver Giorgini – Quality Manager at Orogel, one of the biggest companies in Italy

Q. How are frozen vegetables made?
A. The quality of frozen vegetables starts in the field. It is important to carefully choose the right farmland and trust the expertise of agronomists who find the varieties most suitable for freezing. Sowing takes place at the best times for each vegetable and is staggered to ensure regular harvests and instant processing. Freezing vegetables immediately after they are harvested is crucial to obtain a high-quality product and retain nutritional and organoleptic characteristics. Frozen produce is one of the greatest evolutions in the food sector because it ensures access to high-quality, practical ingredients. To guarantee maximum efficiency, Orogel has set up three facilities located throughout Italy and close to agricultural areas to facilitate immediate processing and ensure a high quality of finished product. On average, 80% of the fresh produce we process reaches our facilities within two hours of harvest. Once it arrives, it is washed, sorted, blanched, deep-frozen and stored until – based on demand and distribution requirements – and is packaged and shipped to consumers.

Q. What are the differences between fresh and frozen vegetables? Is it true that frozen vegetables do not contain preservatives?
A. From a nutritional standpoint, frozen vegetables are comparable to fresh vegetables under normal consumption conditions. The most important nutrients in vegetables are fibre, minerals, vitamins and antioxidants. One of the major advantages of frozen produce is the possibility to overcome the seasonality of primary production. This is made possible by low-temperature technology and has been greatly advantageous to consumers who can now enjoy the health benefits of natural produce at any time of year.
Fresh vegetables often take several days to reach the point of sale and are sometimes left in the refrigerator for another few days before they are eaten. During that time, the vitamin and antioxidant contents suffer, meaning that frozen vegetables are often more nutrient-rich than their fresh counterparts.

Frozen produce is one of the major evolutions in the kitchen because it provides fresh, very high-quality and extremely practical raw ingredients, without detracting from the personal pleasure of cooking. Another important aspect is that the preservation of frozen vegetables is ensured by cold alone, without the addition of preservatives. Current legislation expressly prohibits the use of any additive in unaltered frozen produce. This includes all products such as vegetables, fish and meat that are frozen without having undergone processing steps like cooking or the addition of condiments.

Q. What is the difference between deep-freezing and freezing?
A. Industrial deep-freezing achieves temperatures well below −18°C in a very short time. The speed of the process enables the creation of minuscule ice crystals within the cellular tissue that does not damage the structure of the foodstuff. Orogel uses large deep freezers with good thermal insulation that, unlike home freezers, never experience temperature fluctuations, regardless of the season. Maintaining a constant temperature increases efficiency. In our cold-storage facilities, temperatures are generally kept at −30°C because the lower the temperature, the better the product is preserved. The home freezing process, meanwhile, happens more slowly. Consequently, larger ice crystals form that partially rupture a product's cells. When the product is defrosted, the cellular liquid leaks out, leading to a loss of nutrients and diminished

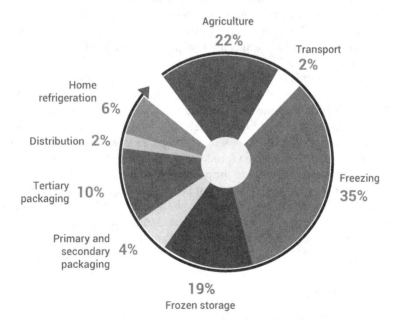

Figure 5.11 The impact of deep-freezing: which phases are most impactful? Authors' elaboration for an Orogel study. Originally published in the first edition of this book, *Il Cibo Perfetto*, published in Italian in 2022.

organoleptic properties. For this reason, freezing vegetables at home does not preserve the characteristics and quality of the product, whereas these are kept unaltered by industrial deep-freezing.

Q. What are the environmental impacts of the process?
A. Orogel decided to delve deeper into this issue, implementing an LCA to understand the percentage distribution of environmental impacts across the different phases, in terms of carbon footprint. The main impacts (approximately 80% of the total) are linked to three phases: farming vegetables (22%), industrial washing and deep-freezing (35%), and the cold storage of the finished product at our facilities (19%), before packaging and shipping (Figure 5.11).

5.4   Packaging

Food packaging is often necessary and important for distribution and to preserve the quality and safety of products for as long as possible. It is commonly thought that packaging is the main source of a product's environmental impact, but this is not always the case. In fact, in most cases, the impact of packaging is very low relative to the entire product life cycle.

Despite this, companies focus a lot of attention on packaging to manage costs and impacts, respond to consumer concerns around plastic pollution and communicate with consumers. In terms of marketing, it is important that packaging communicates the distinct sustainability properties of the food it contains to gain credibility amongst consumers.

The way a product is packaged, and the marketing that surrounds it, is one of the most important variables driving consumer choices. Marketing and brand creation has the power to deeply influence individual food choices and entire food cultures.

General packaging causes approximately 1.5–2.0% of the carbon footprint of a European consumer, with 0.7% caused by food packaging. On average, the carbon footprint of the packaged product (production and distribution) is around 30 times higher than the carbon footprint of the packaging itself.[29]

In other words, only about 3.0–3.5% of the climate impact of packaged food, on average, comes from the packaging (production and end of life). It also follows that if more than 3.5% of food waste is avoided due to the protective function of packaging, then the use of packaging has paid off from a climate protection perspective (Figures 5.12 and 5.13).

5.4.1   Packaging design

The materials most commonly used to make food packaging are paper, cardboard, glass, aluminium and plastic polymers. Plastic polymers present the greatest controversies. In some cases, the combination of different materials makes plastic packaging difficult to recycle (and thus less sustainable, but the in-depth study

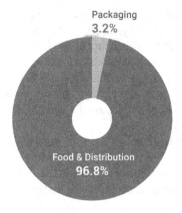

Figure 5.12 On average, only about 3.0–3.5% of the climate impact of packaged food is caused by the packaging process itself. In individual cases this proportion can of course be significantly higher, e.g. in the case of very heavy packaging or very small portion sizes. Authors' elaboration.

Share of emissions due to packagings, out of the total carbon footprint of packaged foods

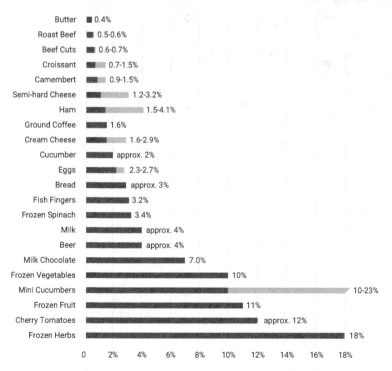

Figure 5.13 Weight of packaging in the environmental impact of selected foodstuffs. Food Packaging Sustainability. *A Guide for Packaging Manufacturers, Food Processors, Retailers, Political Institutions & NGOs*, Stop Waste – Save Food, 2020, chrome-extension://efaidnbmnnnibpcajpcglclefindmkaj/https://denkstatt.eu/wp-content/uploads/2020/08/guideline_stopwastesavefood_en_220520.pdf.

of technical properties makes it possible to achieve a highly specialised degree of protection that, among other things, increases the shelf life of products).

This is a crucial point in the debate about food sustainability. We must not consider the packaging as a product itself; the correct approach is to consider packaging as a part of the food product for the different functions (Figure 5.14). If the protection of the food helps to prevent food losses, the environmental impacts of the packaging could be accepted because the benefit of avoided food waste could be much higher (Figure 5.15).

In any case, the companies must work on the design to improve the performances and the sustainability of the packaging solutions. Some solutions are the reduction of the number and volume of materials used, the use of recycled and easily recyclable components and educating consumers on the correct disposal procedures.

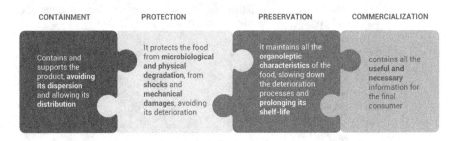

Figure 5.14 The main function of the packaging in the food distribution chain. Authors' elaboration.

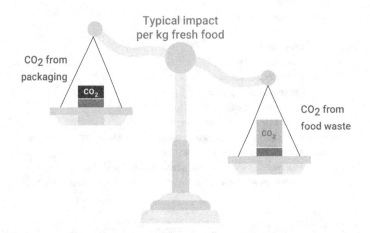

Figure 5.15 This is one of the typical dilemmas in food sustainability: it is not possible to discuss about the best packaging solution if the whole food chain is not considered. Authors' elaboration.

5.4.2   *The plastic debate*

While the goal should undoubtedly be to reduce plastic waste, especially those with a short lifetime such as single-use plastic, a rational understanding of the issue requires a holistic approach between innovation at the service of environmental sustainability and responsible attitudes from producers and consumers. To understand the complexities at hand, a thorough debate needs to be had regarding products that contain plastic, avoiding the pitfalls of vague generalisations. For example, there are clear differences between a plastic water bottle (fully recyclable via extremely efficient dedicated systems) and a single-portion, single-use plastic plate at a buffet.

The topic of plastic might be navigated by following two different but embeddable approaches. The first focuses on the type of object in question, distinguishing among:

- essentially useless products that should no longer be used, such as all overpackaging that has no protective function for the product
- useful but non-essential products, whose use must be reduced and, in any case, might be replaced using existing natural alternatives
- useful products (glasses, plates and cutlery, shopping bags) whose use could be responsibly reduced by adopting new modes of consumption, such as reusable bags
- essential and recyclable products
- non-recyclable products (medical products, for example) that must be disposed of correctly

The second approach requires delving deeper into the definition of plastic. It is undeniable that this material is one of the most interesting and complex components of packaging. Interesting because it offers designers highly specialised technical features, which can often be combined and are low-cost, light and flexible. However, plastic is complex because of the combination of the origin of its raw materials and limitations of end-of-life management. The combination of these two variables can guide choices between polymers that are compostable, biodegradable and made from natural raw materials, etc. (Figure 5.16).

Because the topic of plastic is so complex, it is impossible to reach definitive conclusions in the limited space we have here. The important thing is to always have an objective approach, based on three variables:

1 necessity, namely, whether its use function is truly essential
2 reducibility, namely, whether it is possible to reduce the amounts used
3 replaceability, namely, what more eco-friendly alternatives are available

Otherwise, the risk is that natural industry pressures could drive investment in alternative materials to plastic (point 3) that might not have a smaller impact, without adequately assessing whether there is a real need for the product (point 1) and if all the possible ways of reducing its use have been explored (point 2). It is worth noting that any material, even the most natural, can have negative environmental

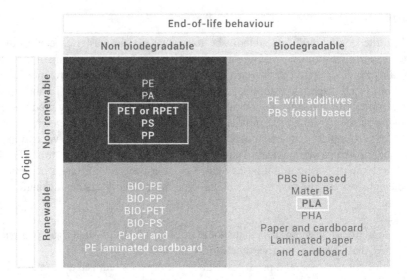

Figure 5.16 The many ways to produce plastic packaging: the different solutions aim to solve
different environmental issues. *Quando il packaging è sostenibile?*, Comieco,
Jul 2019. https://www.comieco.org/quando-il-packaging-e-sostenibile/.

impacts if large amounts of it are put on the market. An example of this could be
the trays for fresh fruit and vegetables that are typically made from plastic or paperboard (Figure 5.17).

5.4.3   Composite packaging

The concept of composite or multilayer packaging is an interesting technological
development because it allows different materials to be used simultaneously, each
conferring a particular property to the packaging product.

One of the most widespread examples involves drink cartons used in the preservation and distribution of liquid foodstuffs. Cardboard provides mechanical
resistance to the packaging, and thin layers of polythene make the material imper-
meable. Additionally, when products' nutritional and organoleptic properties need
to be preserved for a long time, as in the case of long-shelf-life products, a thin
layer of aluminium protects the foodstuff from the oxidising effects of light and air.

In addition to factors concerning packaging performance, one of the main environmental advantages of these systems is their reduced impact during production
and transport. For example, one litre of milk can be packaged in a 30-gram carton
or a 300-gram glass bottle, with significant repercussions for transport systems and
associated impact.

The main problem with multilayer materials concerns their post-use recovery.
When there is no prevalent material, or when components cannot be easily sepa-
rated from one another, the only solution is for the packaging to be sent to a landfill or to a waste-to-energy plant. In the case of drink cartons where the average

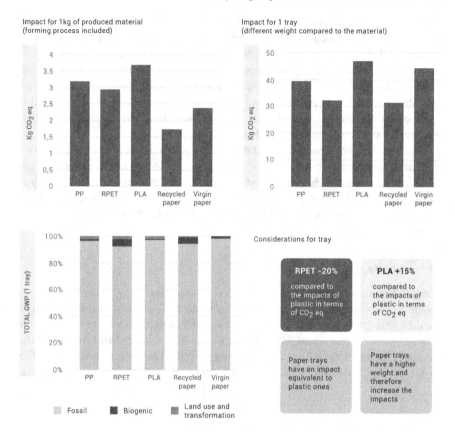

Figure 5.17 Carbon footprint of different trays for fresh fruit. If the assessment ends at the raw materials (carbon footprint of 1 kg of material), the paper has less emissions than the plastic. Since the plastic has better performances, it is possible to use less material to produce trays and it means that the overall carbon footprint of the trays is similar. Authors' elaboration.

cardboard content is in excess of 70%, collaboration between manufacturers and organisations in the cellulose-based packaging collection and recycling sector has made it possible to overcome this problem, significantly increasing the possibility of recycling for this type of packaging.

5.4.4 *Returnable packaging*

Container-deposit schemes have been developed as a way of managing packaging waste at business-to-business and business-to-consumer levels. In many cases, the optimisation of materials and logistics has enabled more efficient management of product distribution. These schemes can be grouped into two macro-categories: primary packaging and secondary packaging.

By way of an example, primary packaging includes glass bottles of water sold in restaurants. In most cases, water producers collect them and return them to production facilities, where they are repurposed. Secondary packaging might include crates (generally made of plastic) that producers use to transport products to distribution hubs and shops. In both cases, the recovery and refurbishment processes have their own impacts (transport, washing, etc.). Thus, a sustainability benefit is achieved only if the same container can go through multiple repeated use cycles (between five and ten, based on packaging type).

Food products are among the most demanding packaging-wise, in terms of quantity and unique types of packaging. As well as having a transport function common to all products, food packaging almost always serves a protective function, such as to prolong shelf life. This is often provided by complex technical properties. Such packaging is often made up of different materials that, when combined with one another, make recovery of waste more difficult.

5.4.5   *Loose food distribution*

The question of loose versus packaged food often comes up in the context of sustainability. Loose produce is generally regarded as more sustainable because it requires less packaging and generates less waste. Often, the more considerable impacts often lie elsewhere. Take fresh milk as an example. Most of its impacts arise during the animal husbandry phase and reducing packaging has a minor effect on the product's overall impact. In some cases, industrially packaged products

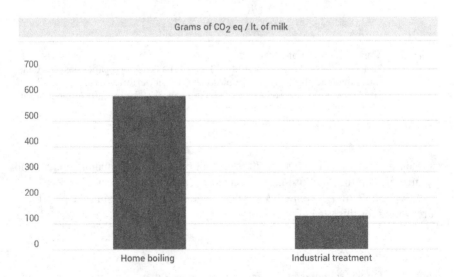

Figure 5.18 Milk: home boiling vs pasteurisation. The data illustrate the carbon footprint per litre of milk of home boiling (assuming 0.5 litres of milk heated on the hob for five minutes) and the entire industrial process, from the arrival of raw milk to the storage of packaged milk. Authors' elaboration. Originally published in the first edition of this book, *Il Cibo Perfetto*, published in Italian in 2022.

ensure a greater level of food safety than loose produce. Paradoxically, raw milk should only be consumed after it is boiled, and boiling milk at home requires much more energy per unit than the entire industrial system of pasteurisation, packaging and storage of packaged fresh milk (Figure 5.18).

In short, if packaging is the only variable being considered, then loose produce is the more sustainable option. However, if a product's entire life cycle is taken into account, the lack of packaging can increase perishability and compromise food safety without generating a major benefit for the product's overall environmental impact.

5.5   Transport and logistics

Food distribution involves both social aspects – protecting local economies and traditions – and environmental aspects related to emissions from transporting goods around the world. As with the other areas we have discussed, having a too-limited vision of the problem can lead to incorrect interpretations. If we focus solely on environmental matters such as the carbon footprint, it can easily appear that food distribution has only a major impact in a few cases.

Figure 5.19 shows the impact of transport for fruit, milk and meat. It is apparent from the data that the transport phase is only proportionally significant for low-impact foodstuffs and, even then, only when they travel beyond a certain distance. The case of air freight is different.

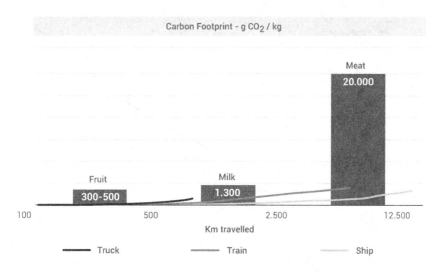

Figure 5.19 The impact of food transport: transport via road freight, train or ship: CO_2 emissions in the transport phase are always very low in proportion to those deriving from the production phase, except in the case of fruit where long-distance transport (5,000–10,000 km) can have a relatively large effect on the overall impact. Authors' elaboration. Originally published in the first edition of this book, *Il Cibo Perfetto*, published in Italian in 2022.

Given the relatively low impact of transport, it is not always true that local food has a smaller environmental impact than those with a greater distribution radius. It may even be the case that a remote system is more environmentally efficient – for climate reasons, for example – than a local one as transport-related emissions are fully offset by production efficiencies. This is the case with certain agricultural raw materials where farming is more efficient when they are grown in areas suited to their needs. However, this is not to say that local produce is only rarely the right option. The important thing to be aware of is that this choice does not necessarily guarantee environmental benefits, despite its positive cultural and economic impacts and promotion of the local region.

5.6   Cooking at home

Cooking food at home requires energy and generates CO_2 emissions and some foodstuffs can only be eaten once cooked (Figure 5.20). In many cases, the environmental impacts of the cooking phase are in the same order of magnitude, if not higher, than those generated during all stages of a product's journey from farm to shop.

Assessing the impacts of cooking must be based on approximate estimates, given the influence of the recipe, techniques used, consumer preferences (rare or well-done steak, for example) and the amount of food being prepared. The

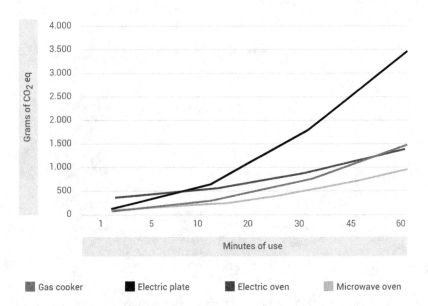

Figure 5.20 Estimate of CO_2 emissions associated with selected cooking systems. Emissions associated with the production of electricity were estimated based on Italy's energy mix. In the case of electric ovens, a 15-minute preheating phase was included. Authors' elaboration. Originally published in the first edition of this book, *Il Cibo Perfetto*, published in Italian in 2022.

simplest approach is to use cooking time and the instrument being used as part of the estimate.

Pasta provides an interesting example of consumers' influence on environmental impacts. Cooking water must be brought to a boil, and the more water there is, the more time will be required before it is ready for the pasta to be thrown in. Producers normally suggest using 1 litre of water per 100 grams of pasta and to cover the pan with a lid to speed up the boiling process and reduce energy use. If this advice is not followed, environmental impacts can increase by up to 10%.

Using a pressure cooker can save water and energy by reducing cooking times. Take rice as an example; if we assume that the cooking time goes down from 15 to 10 minutes and boiling the water has the same impact, cooking four portions in a pressure cooker can save at least 60 grams of CO_2. This corresponds to a reduction in emissions of approximately 200 grams per kilogram of rice compared to cooking on a gas hob.

Box 5.7   The best way to cook pasta

Research commissioned by Italian pasta makers has calculated the energy required to bring water to boil and to cook 200 grams of pasta (the average for a typical Italian family of 2.5 people). Three alternative cooking methods to the conventional one (with the pot uncovered and with the proportion of 1 litre of water for every 100 grams of pasta) were analysed: with a lid during the boiling phase, with 30% less water (700 ml for 100 g of pasta), and with passive cooking (after the first two minutes, the pasta cooks indirectly, with the heat off and with a lid on to conserve heat).

There was an increasing energy saving and reduced equivalent CO_2 emissions compared to conventional cooking: between 6% when cooking with lid; 13% when cooking with less water and 47% when using passive cooking. With an average consumption of 23 kg of pasta per capita, every Italian could save up to 44 kilowatt hours, 13 kg of CO_2 and almost 70 litres of water in a year.

5.7   Food waste

No matter how sustainable a food is, if it is not eaten then it is not a perfect food. Current global statistics paint a stark picture of food waste. While hunger and undernourishment have increased,[30] nearly a third of all the food that is produced is wasted – amounting to 1.3 billion tonnes annually. Beyond the ethical issues, this harms the environment and contributes 8% of GHG emissions, losing an estimated trillion dollars' worth of value.[31]

In Europe, 129 million tonnes of food were wasted out of a total 638 million tonnes available for consumption, representing approximately 20% (Figure 5.21).[32] Most of the food is wasted during the consumption phase (46%), followed by

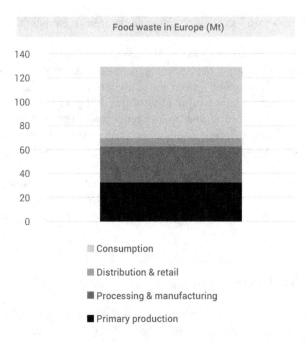

Figure 5.21 Food waste in Europe. Adapted from *The European Commission's Knowledge Centre for Bioeconomy*, European Commission, chrome-extension://efaidnbmnnnibpcajpcglclefindmkaj/https://food.ec.europa.eu/system/files/2021-04/fw_lib_stud-rep-pol_ec-know-cen_bioeconomy_2021.pdf.

primary production (25%), processing and manufacturing (24%) and distribution and retail (5%). However, the distribution of waste varies across global regions. A study supported[33] by FAO investigates the relationship between total food waste and its distribution across the value chain and the industrialisation of the region.

On a global level one-third of waste occurs during primary production, which represents the greatest amount of total food waste (Figure 5.22). Upstream waste volumes, including production, post-harvest handling and storage, represent 54% of total wastage. Downstream waste volumes include processing, distribution and consumption at 46%. On average, food wastage is balanced between the upstream and downstream of the supply chain. An analysis of the food supply chain phases by region (Figure 5.23) reveals that upstream losses occurring at the agricultural production phase appear homogenous across regions, representing about one-third of each region's food wastage. Downstream waste at the consumption level is much more variable, with waste in middle- and high-income regions at 31–39% and much lower in low-income regions, at 4–16%.

These data illustrate some fundamental characteristics of food waste, which arises at all stages of food supply chains for reasons that depend on local conditions. At the global level, a pattern is visible. In high-income regions, volumes of lost and wasted food are higher in downstream phases of the food chain, but the opposite is true in low-income regions where more food is lost and wasted in

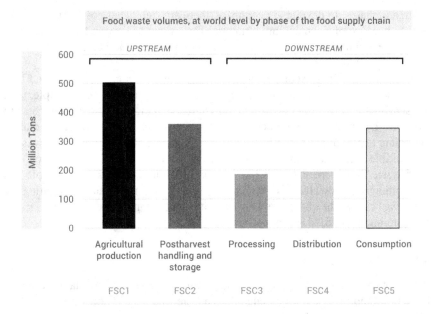

Figure 5.22 Food wastage volumes, at world level by phase of the food supply chain. *Food Wastage Footprint. Impact on Natural Resources. Summary Report*, FAO, 2013, chrome-extension://efaidnbmnnnibpcajpcglclefindmkaj/https://www.fao.org/3/i3347e/i3347e.pdf.

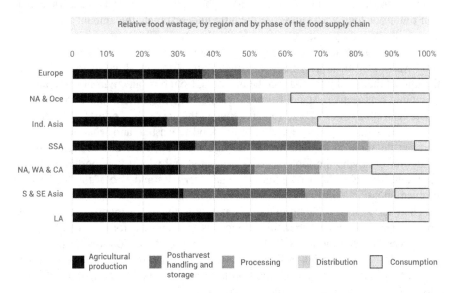

Figure 5.23 Relative food wastage, by region and by phase of the food supply chain. *Food Wastage Footprint. Impact on Natural Resources. Summary Report*, FAO, 2013, chrome-extension://efaidnbmnnnibpcajpcglclefindmkaj/https://www.fao.org/3/i3347e/i3347e.pdf.

upstream phases. In developing countries, there are significant post-harvest losses, mostly because of financial and structural limitations of harvest techniques, lack of storage and transport infrastructure such as cold chains and climatic conditions adding to the risk of food spoilage.

In the most affluent societies, a combination of consumer behaviour and lack of communication in the supply chain has the greatest impact. For example, with consumers there can be insufficient purchase planning or exaggerated concern over best-before dates. As for actors in the supply chain, overly restrictive quality according to size or aesthetics is responsible for a large amount of the food wasted.

Multiple actors and initiatives are working tirelessly to reduce the amount of food waste that is created. This has increased public awareness of the topic and is resulting in policy changes, supported by vast amounts of data highlighting the alarming scale of the challenge. However, it is so far hard to see how this is translating to impact in food waste metrics.

5.7.1   Monitoring waste

A lack of harmonised food waste metrics contributes towards uncertainty over the amount of food waste that is generated and the success of food waste reduction efforts. Organisations often measure food waste differently, and many do not monitor it at all. In the hospitality sector, it is estimated that less than 2% of restaurants of organisations measure food waste.

While improving and harmonising monitoring would be helpful at a country and global level, it is also essential at an organisational level, for several reasons. First, it reveals the true extent of the issue and impact on the business. Organisations that don't monitor food waste may significantly underestimate the amount they generate, as illustrated by research from the Pledge on Food Waste which shows that restaurants that do not monitor their food waste generate three to eight times more food waste than what they believe. Quantifying volumes allow us to understand the impact that food waste has on the business, from both an environmental and an economic perspective. Again, research from Pledge indicates that the cost of food waste can represent 6–14% of food revenue in the hospitality industry. Monitoring also helps to identify where and why the food is wasted, and what an organisation can do about it. In other words, monitoring food waste allows organisations to answer both why the food waste is generated and why it is important to act to reduce it. Therefore, understanding the characteristics and size of the food waste problem in an organisation is an essential first step.

There are several ongoing initiatives and tools aimed at supporting the consistent and harmonised measurement of food waste. In the UK, for example, Waste & Resources Action Programme (WRAP)'s Food Waste Reduction Roadmap[34] is supporting UK food and drink businesses to set targets, measure or monitor outcomes and act on results. Their latest report on progress indicated that one-third of UK's large food businesses are measuring performance.[35]

As the case for monitoring food waste is clear, the number of tools to support companies in measuring their food waste is multiplying. To our knowledge, most perform well the key function of quantifying food waste. A key difference often lies in the degree of automation of the weighing, identification of food types and waste types and data entry as well as the implementation costs. For example, some systems employ artificial intelligence for the recognition of food waste types, requiring dedicated IT hardware, while others rely on identification by employees and are compatible with tablets or smartphones, significantly reducing implementation costs. While different organisations might find different characteristics more convenient, when measurement is harmonised, all monitoring systems contribute to the goal of understanding food waste – both globally and locally – and tracking progress in its reduction.

5.7.2   *Defining a waste strategy*

While data is essential to understanding the impact of food waste and tracking progress, prioritising actions is also necessary. The European Commission's revised Waste Framework Directive[36] adopts a pyramid ranking for proposed strategies according to the value kept in the system (Figure 5.24).

Food waste prevention is the preferred strategy followed by reuse for human consumption. Other strategies follow, from reuse for animal feed and by-products to recycling of food waste, energy recovery and landfilling as the least preferred option.

Reducing food waste in an organisation, and sustaining the reduction through time, requires a deep process of change that goes beyond identifying a strategy and monitoring progress. It involves setting up new processes, engaging internal and external stakeholders, developing capabilities and, where necessary, changing culture and behaviours. To waste less food, food must be properly valued as the crucial resource that it is.

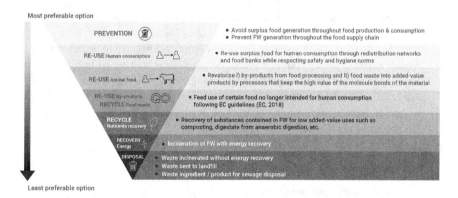

Figure 5.24 Hierarchy for the prioritisation of food waste strategies. Adapted from *The European Commission's Knowledge Centre for Bioeconomy*, European Commission, chrome-extension://efaidnbmnnnibpcajpcglclefindmkaj/https://food.ec.europa.eu/system/files/2021-04/fw_lib_stud-rep-pol_ec-know-cen_bioeconomy_2021.pdf.

Box 5.8   Reducing food waste through shelf-life extension

By Emma Cahill, Kerry Group

Kerry Group is an international leader in taste & nutrition innovation, headquartered in Ireland. Kerry's scientists create ingredients for products people enjoy & feel better consuming. Kerry has a unique position, standing at the intersection of taste, nutrition and sustainability, and in its role across the industry not only in providing food ingredients and finished food products, but also through food preservation and nutritional fortification solutions. Kerry aims to reach over 2 billion people with sustainable nutrition solutions by 2030. Below are some examples of how its solutions can improve both health and environmental impact.

Industry challenge – The time is now

Food waste is one of the greatest sources of inefficiency in our food system. There is a very disturbing global paradox between the increasing amount of edible food that is lost throughout the supply chain and the scarcity of food resulting in hundreds of millions of people suffering from malnutrition.

- *if food waste were a country, it would be the third largest contributor of GHG emissions[37]*
- *each year we waste 1.3 billion tonnes, the full financial cost of which amounts to $2.6 trillion annually, roughly twice the food expenditure of the US[38,39]*
- *in 2021, global hunger numbers rose to as many as 828 million people[40]*

How can we change this? We can use technology and ingredient solutions to ensure all food is produced to a maximum shelf life. This will feed more people as less food will go to waste. There is a huge opportunity to do more with already existing food produced today. Studies show that up to half of consumer food waste could be prevented through shelf-life extension (Martindale et al., WRAP UK). If we can act upon this, we will significantly reduce the environmental impact of food production and waste, feeding more people with the same resources.

Food preservation to prevent food waste

As food is a perishable item, the majority of food waste is driven by product spoilage before consumption, either because of storage along the value chain or at point of consumption. Extending product shelf life through ingredient solutions, such as preservation ingredients, is a viable and effective method to reduce food waste at the consumer level as well as further upstream in the supply chain.

For example, meat is currently the highest economic value and most carbon-intensive category of all food waste offenders. Currently over 73 billion kilograms of meat go to waste each year (UN FAO); that's a staggering 2 billion portions per day, which we estimate costs the industry $188 billion per year (Kerry Internal Estimations). Over 60% of food waste in the meat sector is attributable to consumers,[41] where the economic value is also at its highest. Comparatively, bread is a high-volume offender in packaged goods, but we estimate the cost to the industry at only $12.7 billion each year. In 2021, Kerry extended the shelf life of over 43.5 billion portions of meat through preservation ingredients. Continued development in effective preservation ingredients with a low environmental impact will unlock huge value in this area. However, while we scale these innovative solutions, the existing conventional and clean label preservation ingredients and processes do a great job of enabling the industry to reduce food waste today.

Preservation ingredients include organic acids and salts from a variety of sources that have an impact on bacterial growth, colour or flavour. These can act as antimicrobials or curing agents. They are most often used in processed meat that you would find at a deli counter or freshly packaged in a grocery store. Their role is most important in ready-to-eat products that won't be cooked before being eaten by a consumer. Some examples of conventional preservatives used in meat are acetates, lactates and nitrites while clean label alternatives may include kitchen cupboard ingredients like vinegar, cultured celery, cultured dextrose, lemon juice concentrate, smoke. These will be very different depending on the product category.

Translating into industry value

Recently, we partnered with the customer to create a turkey deli meat product that exceeded their current closed and open shelf-life goals, as well as cut their production costs and made their supply chain more sustainable. The customer was not willing to compromise on texture or taste, so we ensured the appearance of the turkey was not altered, with a completely nitrite-free solution (usually makes turkey appear pink and salty) and that a full sensory evaluation was done at the beginning and end of shelf life.

In this instance, the change to clean label ingredients (a patented combination of cultured dextrose and buffered vinegar) delivered a close to 75% cost saving versus the combined cost of the processing and transport involved in the previous preservation method. Once implemented, our customer was able to also quantify additional cost savings from open product not going to waste as often or at all in some cases because the secondary shelf life offered was sufficient to protect it so that it could all be eaten/used before the end of shelf life. In this instance, for this product, the shelf-life extension delivered by our solution has the potential to deliver a 24% waste reduction, which is a great indication of the value in investing in the reformulation, over and above the initial cost savings.

Education and empowerment will move the dial

Consumer behaviours are also a considerable contributor to food waste; 66% of total food waste (i.e. wastage related to retail, foodservice and consumer behaviour) occurs in developed markets (UN FAO) and the portion of global food loss and waste which happens in consumer households is 37%. This is enough food to fill 1.8 million football fields.

Empowering consumers and industry with information on the positive environmental impacts of reducing food waste is imperative to tackle the challenge. Educating people that additional shelf-life days on a product can also mean less waste which has a carbon, water and dollar equivalent. Kerry has launched a first-of-its-kind food waste estimator to do this: a free-to-access tool on the company website that estimates the impact of food waste reduction for food manufacturers and the general consumer. Using just a few simple inputs, the estimator shows a manufacturer the impact additional shelf-life days it will have in terms of production volumes, CO_2, water and number of people fed. For consumers, they can view a version that shows what food waste reduction at home equates to in money saved, people fed, smartphones charged and minutes in the shower. The estimator includes data from over 30 sources and builds on the review of over 50 scientific articles.

The Kerry Food Waste Estimator[42] simultaneously highlights the magnitude of the food waste crisis and the opportunity to make significant changes. It enlightens consumers and industry with the harrowing reality of our food waste problem, while at the same time empowering them to make changes for the better. Tools like the food waste estimator are designed to spark conversations on food waste which may seem rather abstract until the producer can see the value of shelf-life extension for themselves. Some early cases studies on how the calculator translates into actionable insights for the industry include R&D scientists successfully using it to pitch for greater investment in shelf-life extension with their executive and procurement teams, as they had calculated the impact on waste reduction from their production using the estimator. Retailers have also been able to highlight the economic loss from using discount margins on a significant volume of food due to short shelf life.

5.8   From traceability to transparency

Traceability is defined as 'the ability to trace the history and follow the use of a product through identification recorded in relation to material flows and supply chain operators'. The identification and traceability of a product allow us to ascertain its characteristics including constituent parts, production batch and processes used. It also retraces its technical-commercial history such as change in ownership and intended destination and verification of incident causes. Traceability is a legal requirement and a foundational aspect of food safety which ensures controls on processes, and foodstuffs can be correlated to each production phase so that products can be recalled if risks for consumers arise.

Achieving full traceability for a product can be challenging, but the advance of digital technologies is making it easier for information about a food to flow along the value chain, from the ingredient production stage to consumption stage. When a company produces a food product made with ingredients purchased directly from farmers, we can consider this a supply chain product. In contrast, a market product is made with ingredients sourced indirectly, as commodities from the market. Traceability helps us to understand the importance of the distinction.

Just because a product is fully traceable does not imply that it belongs to a direct supply chain. This concept can be explained through the example of pasta. Producers buy semolina (or durum wheat, in case they also manage the milling process) through one of two different approaches: from the market at the best price in accordance to defined requirements or directly from farmers with whom they have established contracts and agreed farming programmes. In the latter case, the resulting pasta can be defined as a supply chain product. Supply chain products use ingredients sourced directly from international supply chains (e.g. an Italian pasta producer might have Canadian farmers it buys from). Even if only Italian ingredients are used, it is a market product if the ingredients are purchased indirectly on the commodities market.

Without the appropriate context, it cannot be said whether a supply chain or a market product is better or worse in terms of its traceability or social and environmental impact. However, supply chain products have several advantageous aspects. A supply chain product requires the identification of all companies involved in the process, from primary production and processing to transport and retail. Companies are normally held to precise contractual obligations and subject to rigorous specifications that often go well beyond the demands of current legislation. This has two key benefits. The first concerns safety, since companies are aware of the strengths and weaknesses of producers in their supply chain and are able to determine critical points on which to focus quality controls. The second is related to overall sustainability. Establishing medium- to long-term agreements along the supply chain facilitates investments in improvements and allows for better control of the raw material at critical hot spots along the supply chain.

Palm oil provides an example, the production of which has seen significant media scrutiny for its ecological impact. Palm oil is a major commodity that food manufacturers typically purchase from trading companies who aggregate supply from many farmers – big and small – across geographies. As a result, it is challenging for manufacturers to have accurate transparency of where their palm oil is coming from, how it is produced and the environmental and social impacts. Organisations such as the Roundtable on Sustainable Palm Oil were established to address the issues. However, challenges in assuring compliance with their certification standards demonstrates that certification schemes can only be complementary and cannot replace manufacturers' own due diligence on their ingredient supply chains, as articulated by a report adopted by the EU Parliament.[43]

Box 5.9   Raw materials traceability: the case of palm oil for Ferrero[44]

What is Ferrero's approach to sustainability and transparency?

Responsible sourcing is at the heart of Ferrero's business and is a non-negotiable requirement in the way Ferrero builds supply chains across all categories. The approach to responsible sourcing is built on strong due diligence and supplier-management practices, traceability and transparency throughout the supply chain supported by certification and standards, partnerships and collaboration.

Traceability is an essential building block for a fair and sustainable supply chain. To meet commitments for quality and responsibility, Ferrero seeks to fully understand where raw materials originate from and how they were produced. Ferrero sources raw materials from a multitude of smallholder farmers and needs to identify and understand the issues they face in order to be able to support them. Ferrero expects suppliers to directly support these commitments by being open about their activities and those of their own supply chains. Farmer mapping is a tool for improving the traceability of raw materials like cocoa, palm oil and hazelnuts. Knowing the location and size of each farm makes it possible to trace raw materials to plantation level, so that any necessary interventions can be identified. Having a greater information, data and monitoring also helps Ferrero to support sustainable livelihoods and address risks and challenges such as deforestation, child labour and forced labour. Certification schemes, where available, are an additional lever that can be used. They provide third-party assurance that suppliers are meeting specific traceability requirements and sustainability standards set by independent bodies.

Palm oil plays a key role in Ferrero's products, enhancing the taste and texture of the other ingredients. It has an excellent yield per hectare compared with other vegetable oils and when cultivated responsibly is an important contributor to the livelihoods of farmers.

Where palm oil is not sourced sustainably, it is associated with negative impacts on biodiversity and can contribute to deforestation, changes of land use and use of chemicals in tropical forests and other species-rich habitats. There are also social issues involved, and it is often difficult to trace palm oil back to its source to address these. In addition, the land rights of indigenous communities are often not recognised, and land clearance by palm oil companies can displace rural farmers. Labour rights is another issue, as workers often live in poor conditions without access to basic facilities. Instead, when sourced sustainably and responsibly, palm oil production can bring economic benefits for producers and consumers and aid the preservation of ecosystems.

Ferrero's palm oil sourcing and sustainability approach is based on a few key principles, including:

- *Sourcing 100% RSPO (Roundtable on Sustainable Palm Oil)-certified segregated palm oil for Ferrero products from a limited number of reliable suppliers, so to trace palm oil back to plantation level.*
  Building on this high level of traceability to plantation level, monitoring full palm oil supply chain for deforestation using Starling satellite technology (covering around 1 million hectares of land).
- *A Palm Oil Charter and a Supplier Code with standards and requirements* that have been developed in collaboration with third parties.
- *Disclosing palm oil supply chain, both for historical Ferrero products and for acquired brands.*

In June 2021, Ferrero updated the Palm Oil Charter, originally published in 2013. The new Charter outlines the ambition to achieve a palm oil industry that is good for both people and nature by going beyond high certification standards. The Charter sets out the aim to be a driving force behind a palm oil industry where production creates value for all: where smallholders and farming communities thrive; where workers in mills, refineries and plantations have rights that are unequivocally respected; and where environmental values are protected and enhanced through sustainable agricultural practices. The Charter is based on three pillars that apply to all Ferrero's palm oil suppliers, the three themes being common to other Ferrero raw materials and commodities:

1. *Human rights and social practices. Ferrero is committed to improve working conditions across its value chain (workers with fair recruitment, working and living conditions).*
2. *Environmental protection/sustainability. Ferrero is actively monitoring and verifying that its value chain is deforestation-free (satellite verification to ensure zero deforestation in the value chain).*
3. *Supplier transparency. Ferrero is achieving a fully transparent value chain (full traceability to plantations, publication of mills and estates list, time-bound Action Plan and Progress reports).*
   Ferrero sources palm oil only from suppliers that have signed and follow its Supplier Code. Ferrero's palm oil supplies[45] come from 100% RSPO-certified and segregated (SG) oil. RSPO-Certified Sustainable Palm Oil is palm oil from different certified sources that is kept separate from ordinary palm oil throughout the supply chain. It differs

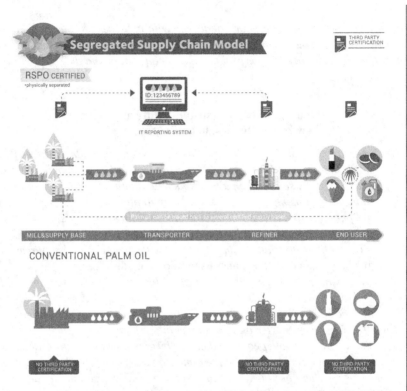

Figure 5.25 Segregated vs conventional palm oil. Adapted from *Annual Palm Oil Progress Report*, Ferrero, 2021, chrome-extension://efaidnbmnnnibp-cajpcglclefindmkaj/https://www.ferrerosustainability.com/int/sites/fer-rerosustainability_int/files/2022-05/palmoilast.pdf.

from Mass Balance palm oil which contains palm oil from certified sources that is mixed with ordinary palm oil throughout the supply chain (Figure 5.25).

Ferrero is increasingly aware of the importance of tracing palm oil to the source as fundamental to understand more precisely the challenges to be addressed and to generate sector-wide benefits. Ferrero works towards further enhancing the visibility of its value chain by strengthening partnerships with its suppliers and by leveraging the most advanced technology available.

Why are some raw materials purchased from a supply chain approach while others are purchased from the market? One reason is essentially linked to costs. In general, supply chain products have higher production costs than market products due to the need to design specifications, share them with suppliers and implement more extensive monitoring measures. Producers also cannot compare suppliers and choose the best available price day to day, as they can with market suppliers.

Another notable aspect concerns the size of the buyer company; a small grocer in northern Italy is unlikely to be able to sell supply chain oranges, whereas a large retailer can afford to do so. In this sense, cooperative purchasing groups that are starting to gain ground can provide a valid alternative.

The product types that tend to be supply chain-based are context-dependent. In principle, when a material is considered strategic – for reasons such as market scarcity, effect on product quality, effect on cost, etc. – it is highly likely that producers will incorporate it into their supply chain and implement controls that go beyond legal requirements.

Key takeaways

- A sustainability transition should be based on reliable data and information that must cover the whole length of the food value chain.
- It is important to recognise that any single step in a food value chain has a strong interdependence with others, given its nature as a biological system and the frequent use of by-products across the industry. It is therefore not possible to consider each food product independently; rather, it should be seen in its context within the rest of the food industry.
- The food industry is a useful instigator for innovation and the use of technology across multiple industries. IT applications in the agriculture sector could help increase sustainability whilst lowering costs for farmers and reducing negative environmental impacts.
- The production of raw food ingredients and animal husbandry are the hot spots for sustainability – that is where the majority of social and environmental impact are often located. A deep understanding and tight control of these phases in the value chain is crucial and a useful foundation for long-term sustainability projects.
- Time is one of the most important variables for improving sustainability processes. While changing an industrial process is a short-term project and the results are immediate, an improvement in agriculture needs years given the time it takes to shift soil production, as well as to influence behaviour change at farmer level.

Key questions for reflection

- What are the areas within your value chain that are real hotspots of environmental and social impact and require detailed analyses and decision-making?
- What are the trade-offs that you need to make, and how are these important to different stakeholders within your organisation and value chain?
- What are the ways you can influence the way your product is used or consumed and disposed of in order to minimise negative impacts and promote the right behaviours along the value chain?

Notes

1 P. Achakulwisut, P.C. Almeida, E. Around, *It's Time to Move Beyond "Carbon Tunnel Vision"*, Stockholm Environment Institute, March 2022, https://www.sei.org/perspectives/move-beyond-carbon-tunnel-vision/.

2 G. Wozniacka, *The Greenhouse Gas No One's Talking About: Nitrous Oxide on Farms, Explained*, Civil Eats, September 2019, https://civileats.com/2019/09/19/the-greenhouse-gas-no-ones-talking-about-nitrous-oxide-on-farms-explained/.

3 *Danone*, Ellen MacArthur Foundation, https://ellenmacarthurfoundation.org/danone.

4 D. Carrington, Glyphosate Weedkiller Damages Wild Bee Colonies, Study Reveals, *The Guardian*, July 2022, https://www.theguardian.com/environment/2022/jun/02/glyphosate-weedkiller-damages-wild-bumblebee-colonies.

5 A. Spanne, Glyphosate, Explained, *Environmental Health News*, March 2022, https://www.ehn.org/glyphosate-explained-2656803555.html.

6 M. Liebman, E. Dyck, Crop Rotation and Intercropping Strategies for Weed Management, in *Ecological Applications: A Publication of the Ecological Society of America*, Vol 3, Issue 1, pp. 92–122, February 1993.

7 In collaboration with *Open Fields*, https://www.openfields.it/en/.

8 *Canale Emiliano Romagnolo*, https://consorziocer.it/it/.

9 Section curated by S. Bosi, G. Dinelli, *Department of Agri-Food Science and Technology (DISTAL)*, University of Bologna.

10 R. Angelini, *Il pomodoro*, Coltura e Cultura, https://www.yumpu.com/it/document/read/9586283/il-pomodoro-coltura-cultura.

11 *Row 7*, https://www.row7seeds.com/pages/our-story.

12 Article 2, Directive 2001/18/EC of 12 March 2001.

13 *Food: Genetically Modified*, World Health Organization, May 2014, https://bit.ly/3zLwaFW.

14 Accomplishment Report, 2019, International Service for the Acquisition of Agri-biotech Applications (ISAAA), https://bit.ly/3f8sO6y.

15 *Biodiversity Loss and the Threat to Food Production*, Croner-i, July 2019, https://app.croneri.co.uk/feature-articles/biodiversity-loss-and-threat-food-production.

16 *Rice and Duck Farming as a Means for Contributing to Climate Change Adaptation and Mitigation*, TECA – FAO, January 2013, https://teca.apps.fao.org/teca/en/technologies/7724.

17 In cooperation with L. Pallaroni, director of ASSALZOO (Italian feed producer association).

18 The European Feed Manufacturers' Federation, for example, has published Soy Sourcing Guidelines that include different criteria aimed at minimising the risk of using non-sustainably produced soy (*Soy Sourcing Guidelines*, FEFAC, 2021, https://bit.ly/3r0n4kA).

19 I. Grégoire, *Insects to Feed the Planet*, IDCR-CRDI, October 2022, https://www.idrc.ca/en/stories/insects-feed-planet.

20 *Making Nature-Positive Food the Norm*, Ellen MacArthur Foundation, https://ellenmacarthurfoundation.org/resources/food-redesign/overview.

21 *Management Intensive Grazing*, Sustainable Agriculture at UGA, https://sustainagga.caes.uga.edu/systems/management-intensive-grazing.html.

22 *Silvopasture*, Agroforestry Research Trust, https://www.agroforestry.co.uk/about-agroforestry/silvopasture.

23 *Guidelines for National Greenhouse Gas Inventories*, IPCC, 2006, https://www.ipcc.ch/report/2006-ipcc-guidelines-for-national-greenhouse-gas-inventories/.

24 J.A. Williamson, *The Benefits of Managed Grazing Systems*, PennState Extension, February 2023, https://extension.psu.edu/the-benefits-of-managed-grazing-systems.

25 FAO, The State of World Fisheries and Aquaculture, Rome, 2020.

26 *Mari e Oceani*, WWF, https://bit.ly/3rafl3J.

27 *IFFO*, https://www.iffo.com.

28 *3D Ocean Farming*, Nourish, https://www.nourishlife.org/2016/12/3d-ocean-farming

29 Food Packaging Sustainability. *A Guide for Packaging Manufacturers, Food Processors, Retailers, Political Institutions & NGOs*, Stop Waste – Save Food, 2020, chrome-extension://efaidnbmnnnibpcajpcglclefindmkaj/https://denkstatt.eu/wp-content/uploads/2020/08/guideline_stopwastesavefood_en_220520.pdf.

30 *The State of Food Security and Nutrition in the World*, FAO, 2021, https://www.fao.org/documents/card/en/c/cb4474en.

31 *5 Facts about Food Waste and Hunger*, World Food Programme, June 2020, https://www.wfp.org/stories/5-facts-about-food-waste-and-hunger.

32 *The European Commission's Knowledge Centre for Bioeconomy*, European Union, 2020, https://food.ec.europa.eu/system/files/2021–04/fw_lib_stud-rep-pol_ec-know-cen_bioeconomy_2021.pdf.

33 *Food Wastage Footprint: Impact on Natural Resources*, FAO, 2013, https://reliefweb.int/report/world/food-wastage-footprint-impacts-natural-resources?gclid=CjwKCAjwq-WgBhBMEiwAzKSH6GF-sNlpBK0xEj1YGni7_49cbcJyfvpv6I-yKF8fZ8HQX4nrN-wZhxoC85QQAvD_BwE.

34 *Introduction to the Food Waste Reduction Roadmap and How to Get Involved*, Wrap, https://wrap.org.uk/resources/guide/introduction-food-waste-reduction-roadmap-and-how-get-involved.

35 *Food Waste Reduction Roadmap Progress Report*, Wrap, IGD, 2021, chrome-extension://efaidnbmnnnibpcajpcglclefindmkaj/https://wrap.org.uk/sites/default/files/2021–09/WRAP-Food-Waste-Reduction-Roadmap-Progress-Report-2021.pdf.

36 *EUR-lex*, https://eur-lex.europa.eu/eli/dir/2018/851/oj?locale=en.

37 *Promoting Sustainable Lifestyles*, UN Environment Programme, https://www.unep.org/regions/north-america/regional-initiatives/promoting-sustainable-lifestyles.

38 *Food Wastage Footprint. Full Cost Accounting*, FAO, 2014, https://www.fao.org/3/i3991e/i3991e.pdf

39 *5 Facts about Food Waste and Hunger*, WFP, June 2020, https://www.wfp.org/stories/5-facts-about-food-waste-and-hunger.

40 *UN Report: Global Hunger Numbers Rose to as Many as 828 Million in 2021*, WHO, July 2022, https://www.who.int/news/item/06–07–2022-un-report--global-hunger-numbers-rose-to-as-many-as-828-million-in-2021.

41 M. Karwowska, S. Łaba; K. Szczepański, Food Loss and Waste in Meat Sector—Why the Consumption Stage Generates the Most Losses? in *Sustainability*, Vol 13, Issue 11, 2021.

42 *What Happens When You Cut Your Food Waste?*, Kerry, https://explore.kerry.com/food-waste-estimator.

43 *European Parliament*, https://www.europarl.europa.eu/doceo/document/TA-9-2020-0285_EN.html.

44 *Sustainability Report*, Ferrero, 2022, https://www.ferrerosustainability.com/int/sites/ferrerosustainability_int/files/homepage-annual-report/2023-06/ferrero-sr22_230621.pdf.

45 Not including recent acquisitions as per transition period.

6 Stakeholder engagement and sustainable marketing

Stakeholder engagement and responsible marketing are critical elements of the journey towards sustainability, ensuring the involvement of all stakeholders – both internal and external – at each stage of the value chain.

Understanding what your stakeholders want is one of the key elements key element to building your strategy and communicating outcomes. There are hundreds of different topics that are relevant across the value chain, and an impactful strategy must take into account the topics that are most important to key stakeholders. We must understand what is important to stakeholders and appreciate the dynamics of communication, avoiding the risk of being accused of greenwashing and the technical tools used to 'sell' a company's sustainability.

Box 6.1 How communication helps sustainability pay off?

Implementation without effective communication limits potential progress, especially in the food sector which is so closely connected to the market. The 4P diagram (for a deep dive on this topic and framework see Chapter 8) shows how to define a strategic roadmap that, moving through the four quadrants, allows a company to promote the sustainability investments and actions it has made to its target market. A useful example is what happened with palm oil (Figure 6.1). It started out in the top-left quadrant as an environmental issue denounced by activists and moved into the bottom-left quadrant as it became a more well-known problem among consumers when possible health risks were hypothesised. At that point, the topic became a fully fledged marketing topic for businesses, typical of the bottom-right quadrant, both as a 'positive' (we use only sustainable palm oil) and as a 'negative' (we are palm oil-free) message.

DOI: 10.4324/9781003449744-6

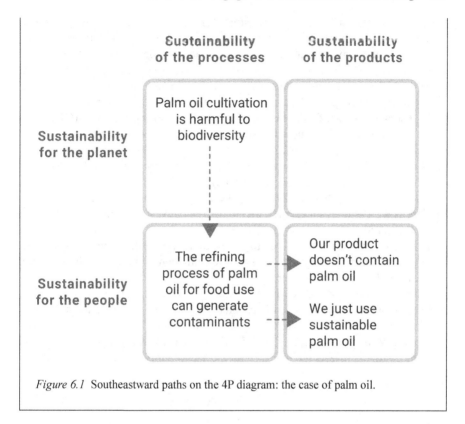

Figure 6.1 Southeastward paths on the 4P diagram: the case of palm oil.

6.1 Identifying stakeholder priorities

A materiality analysis is a useful business management analytical tool to identify the most important, or *material,* topics to your stakeholders in order to prioritise a set of issues to an organisation's effort. As with any business activity, it is important to be strategic, investing targeted resources to achieve the maximum impact. This is especially the case with sustainability where there is a multitude of topics (ranging from paying fair wages to tackling climate change) that a company can affect, and these differ markedly depending on the stakeholders of that organisation: from investors to their consumers. For food-based companies, there are many issues that could be addressed as discussed in Chapters 4 and 5, from land use, pollution and soil health to nutrition and climate change. A materiality analysis is important in this case to help identify those topics that are most salient for the specific company in question, its customers, its market segment and its position in the value chain. A correct identification of the most material topics will allow the impact of its sustainability initiatives to be maximised.

Historically, materiality was meant in the sense of *financial* materiality, a process informing the economic value creation and risks from external factors on the company, mainly for the sake of investors. With the rise of ESG (environmental, social and governance) considerations and the increased expectation that companies should take responsibility for their adverse impacts on the world, the materiality concept evolved into what is now referred to as *impact* materiality, or *outward* materiality. The impact materiality informs on the impacts of the company on the environment, the people and the economy. This process is the cornerstone of worldwide sustainability standards, such as the Global Reporting Initiative (GRI). The combination of financial materiality and impact materiality is referred to as *double* materiality and is expected to become the norm in the future, at the behest of the EU Corporate Sustainability Reporting Directive, which makes double materiality a requirement for big companies (Figure 6.2).

The impact materiality is informed by the company's internal and external stakeholders as well as relevant experts, including, typically, staff members, customers, trade associations, local communities, NGOs, governments, etc. Engaging with them is therefore an important step to understand their concerns and expectations. Furthermore, engagement contributes to informing and building trust between the company and its direct ecosystem.

As a first step, understanding the company's context is crucial: its activities, business relationships, the general sustainability context, and its main stakeholders. In a second step, which builds on the first, the actual and potential impacts of the company should be identified and listed, in order to achieve an overview of the way the company affects the world. This can include topics such as generation of

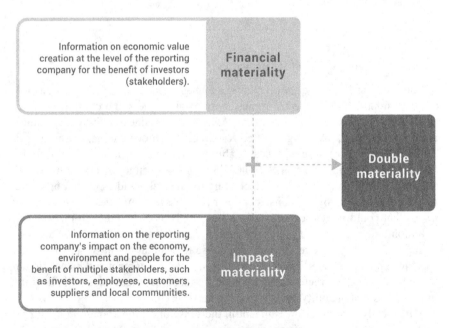

Figure 6.2 Double materiality concept. The GRI perspective. *The Materiality Madness: Why Definitions Matter*, GRI, 2022, www.globalreporting.org/media/r2oojx53/gri-perspective-the-materiality-madness.pdf.

greenhouse gases, health and safety issues, human rights violations in the supply chain, etc.

Assessment and prioritisation are essential to ensure that efforts are made where significant impacts occur. This can happen through consultations with various stakeholders and experts. Hearing stakeholders express themselves on their respective priorities empowers the company to arbitrate between various viewpoints and anticipate potential new trends. A significance analysis based on severity and likelihood also proves useful to assess and compare different impacts.

The result of this process is the identification of the most important impacts, which represent the actual material topics of the company. Plotting them into a materiality matrix is a way to represent them in a visual form and can help in visualising divergent viewpoints between stakeholder groups and/or significance. The material topics of the company are those the company should act on with highest priority (Figure 6.3). Therefore, the materiality process informs the development of a robust corporate sustainability strategy.

Once a materiality assessment is done, this will guide the strategic approach your organisation can take to sustainability. It will likely include a blend of topics that are very important and impactful, with others that are selected primarily to engage with stakeholders and satisfy their priorities. For example, if you are

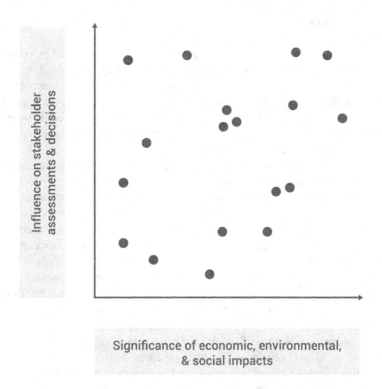

Figure 6.3 Example of a materiality matrix. *GRI 101: Foundation*, GRI, 2016, chrome-extension://efaidnbmnnnibpcajpcglclefindmkaj/https://www.globalreporting.org/standards/media/1036/gri-101-foundation-2016.pdf.

a fresh-food grocery producer, you may work on climate change due to the high environmental impact of farming activities and to satisfy government requirements on net-zero agriculture; but it is not something that customers will be very focused on. However, it will also be important to have plastic-free netting due to customers' priorities, to engage them and communicate that you are a sustainable brand, even though the relative impact of plastic vs non-plastic-free grocery netting will be negligible.

The World Business Council For Sustainable Development (WBCSD) recently launched a report on materiality assessments to provide guidance to companies on different existing methodologies to conduct such an assessment, as well as to evaluate how closely they are representative of truly material topics.[1]

6.2   Evolving consumer perspectives

Consumers are one of the most important stakeholder groups because success is not possible without their support. Consumers have always had strong views on sustainability, especially when it comes to food. But while people claim to be aware of the issues, they tend to act only when they see a sustainable product as having a benefit to themselves. Typically, individual benefits are in relation to the health or organoleptic qualities of a product. When a product's sustainability credentials relate only to environmental or wider social impacts, there is often no correspondence between what consumers say and their purchasing decisions.

Given this premise, the value of sustainability can be interpreted by consumers in different ways. Consumer behaviour can also change quickly based on an emotive response to emergent trends, such as those seen in the media or learned through word of mouth. The best way to avoid being caught out by changing consumer demand is to gather intelligence on the *weak signals* that denote people's core values and, as well as defining consumer profiles, allow businesses to intercept market trends before they noticeably alter the market.

In 1975, Igor Ansoff[2] developed the concept of 'weak signals' to identify seemingly irrelevant information that can be crucial in guiding strategic decisions in uncertain situations. Weak signals are solitary events, or weakly connected events, that could have significant or critical future implications.

In 2020, Coop Italia – a large Italian food retail conglomerate – used a weak signal-based approach to launch its Sustainable Consumption Observatory, developed by Roma Tre University and Sita Ricerca.[3] It defines five values which can generate a response among the population, the attractive power of which may grow or wane depending on the moment in time and culture of the region. For example, in late 2020 the value of 'autarkic defence' was rising, driven by the populist movement that influenced Italian and global politics and by the effects of pandemia. The value of 'prosperous degrowth', which for many years was presented as the main solution to avoid environmental disasters, gave way to technological and innovative solutions such as 'friendly science' and 'pragmatic rationalism'. These were driven by a strong focus on carbon neutrality and the circular economy. Finally, the growing popularity of 'diversity and sharing' was driven by global movements founded to bring the focus onto the health of the planet, for example, the youth-led strike movement, Fridays for Future, launched by Greta Thunberg.

Box 6.2   The concept of sustainability according to the different mindset of consumers[4]

Autarkic defence

'The first step toward sustainability starts with choosing local products, supporting one's region and avoiding the cultural and environmental contaminations generated by globalisation'. During the Covid-19 pandemic, the attachment to local products and communities was further emphasised and brought positive emotional feedback. This highlighted the need to safeguard the local community, localism and own food culture. Distrust of large corporations increased, as did the attraction to small-scale, artisanal production.

Friendly science

'Technological progress and scientific research have always allowed us to overcome humanity's greatest challenges. New technologies, new foods, and new products will allow us to be sustainable without sacrificing our lifestyle'. Many people, despite being aware of the environmental and social problems of our time, are not willing to compromise on their prosperity and see science and technology as a way to reconcile their lifestyle with a focus on sustainability. This idea is espoused primarily by those who tend to be more optimistic about the future and humanity's progress.

Pragmatic rationalism

'Sustainability can be achieved only by enacting behaviours and practices that bring about completely circular production and consumption processes, eliminating waste, recycling and reusing all resources'. This understanding guides people who believe that circular processes and the reduction of waste can be the key to achieving real sustainability. Solutions that can be easily implemented, even by individuals, are promoted by businesses through initiatives or incentives. Examples include food recycling start-ups and new models of sharing or renting economies.

Prosperous degrowth

'Our economic development is incompatible with environmental sustainability. If we want to avoid environmental catastrophes, we must abandon

growth at all costs and implement more responsible consumption choices, cutting out everything superfluous'. This is a minor but nevertheless significant trend that primarily guides those who have developed a greater awareness of the severity of the environmental crisis. These alarmed consumers undertake more extreme consumption behaviours and radical lifestyles, willing to make sacrifices because they believe that it is impossible to reconcile sustainability with our development model, which is based on growth at all costs.

Diversity and sharing

'Sustainability is a collective challenge that can be overcome only if we are willing to adopt an attitude of total openness and sharing between countries and cultures, promoting and defending all types of biodiversity'. This important idea is shared by people who agree that to win the environmental challenge and achieve good long-term effects, we need everyone to contribute and follow common guidelines. The Covid-19 pandemic further bolstered this position, making it clear to everyone that the planet is a single system in which humans are only one of the various components.

Understanding the values people spontaneously attribute to the word 'sustainable' allows companies to decide which features to leverage when making their product range more competitive. If a company that has invested in sustainability wants to gain a competitive advantage, it must ensure that the sustainable qualifier applied to its product meets the higher-order needs set out in Maslow's hierarchy.[5] These needs can be summed up as self-esteem and social status and are subjective in nature, meaning they vary from person to person and evolve over time based on social, cultural and economic factors.[6] For example, adverse circumstances may cause people to become more materialistic and place a greater emphasis on safety, while greater well-being can encourage prioritisation of self-expression (Figure 6.4).

In practice, every consumer adopts their own sustainable consumption behaviours based on the mix of values to which they adhere. Several core values can coexist and overlap, although some are easier to reconcile and provide a characterisation of an individual's behaviour, while others clash and serve to distinguish between the consumption behaviours of different people.

By identifying the core values that guide consumption behaviour towards environmental sustainability, we can define different consumer profiles that share the same combination of values. Each of the five profiles expresses its own interpretation of sustainable food consumption. These can vary depending on geographical and historical context.

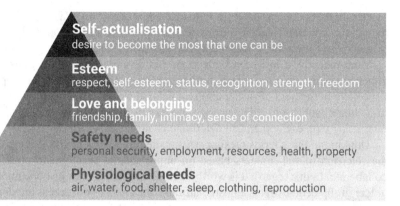

Figure 6.4 Maslow's hierarchy of needs. Widespread representation.

6.2.1 Consumer perspectives around the world

Although sustainability is a global phenomenon, the reasons behind consumer interest vary greatly around the world, depending on cultural legacy and socio-economic context. In a country such as the UK, the sustainability of food may be of interest due to concerns over animal welfare or climate change. At the same time, sustainability can be perceived as a luxury which may alienate some parts of society. In Italy, food is a cultural imperative and sustainability goes hand in hand with quality and nutrition. And in China, mistrust in the quality and safety of certain food products has seen key food products being imported from Hong Kong, such as baby food, leading to the enforcement of quotas.[7] It's crucial to understand how values specific to a market may impact the broader topic of sustainability, as shown by the following examples.

6.3 Developing a communication strategy

Developing an effective communication strategy means accounting for many sustainability factors, which can be technical and not widely understood. Compared to other types of corporate communication, sustainability topics involve sensitive and complex social and environmental challenges that lack simple solutions. The way they are communicated can risk alienating the target audience, rather than generating positive engagement.

As with other forms of communication, it is essential to define who, what, how and how much to communicate when developing a sustainability communications strategy. Below are some useful things to consider.

6.3.1 Who to communicate to?

In the past, communication was understood as the relationship between broadcaster and receiver or speaker and listener. The concept might be illustrated through an archery-based metaphor; in fact, it is no coincidence that 'target' is still a widely used term in this context. Then we moved on to a more symmetrical approach: from 'one to one' to 'one *with* one' in a two-way communication and engagement process.

More recently, it has been understood that in order for the relationship to be effective, it had to go one step further, adopting a multi-stakeholder approach. Especially in the field of sustainability, to obtain a result in terms of the behaviour of a 'target' subject it is increasingly necessary to involve other actors who, by interacting with each other, can determine change.

Thinking in these terms presupposes the definition of a matrix (Figure 6.5) and the selection of stakeholders based on importance to success and propensity to collaborate. In this regard, it is worth highlighting that if even just one main stakeholder group demonstrates a hostile attitude, the chances of success are drastically reduced, even if unconditional support is received from all other parties. Those stakeholders considered to be both important and hostile should be prioritised. To engage and overcome their resistance, a triangulation approach might be useful – a path from A to B, via C. In essence, A communicates to stakeholder B via an intermediary stakeholder C, which makes A more credible and thus more effective. This is the case, for example, with projects that involve an endorsement by environmentalist organisations.

When triangulation is necessary, or in any case where the relationship between stakeholders is complex, an apt analogy is a game of snooker. The goal is to get

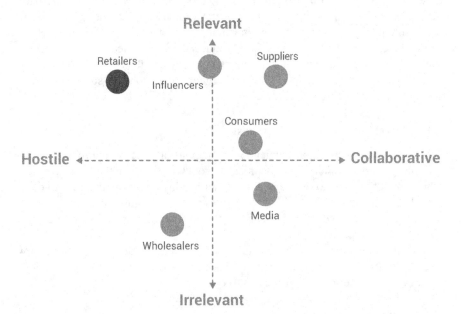

Figure 6.5 A hypothetical stakeholder classification based on importance and propensity to collaboration. Important and hostile stakeholders are the highest priority. Authors' elaboration. Originally published in the first edition of this book, *Il Cibo Perfetto*, published in Italian in 2022.

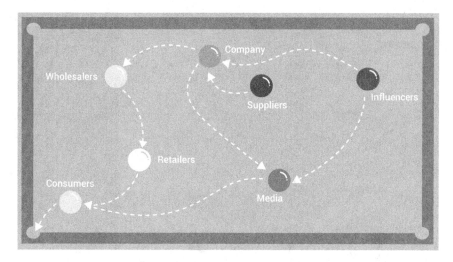

Figure 6.6 Stakeholder and communication strategy. The goal – getting the ball in the pocket – is often achieved through indirect actions, playing off the cushions and using the other balls on the table. Authors' elaboration. Originally published in the first edition of this book, *Il Cibo Perfetto*, published in Italian in 2022.

the ball in the pocket, and it is achieved indirectly through a series of intermediate steps, actions, tactical shots and bounces (Figure 6.6). For example, support from distributors might be gained by first engaging with consumers who, in turn, put pressure on retailers, or by going through the media first and getting influencers involved.

Further complexity in messaging and marketing strategies is driven by the different reaction times of stakeholders. Consumers tend to change their preferences quickly, with some demand trends fading away after just a few months and new trends emerging quickly due to a social media influencer making waves, for instance.

For businesses delivering food products and ingredients, responding to the changing demands of the market in a timely manner can be difficult, because getting a product to market depends on R&D innovation and supply chain changes, which take time to complete. For example, finding an alternative packaging material to replace plastic, or alternative vegetable oils to replace palm oil, is not a simple substitution task. And once an effective and feasible solution is developed, it takes time to be put into production.

It is a bit like having to connect and synchronise gears and cogs in a machine; there are multiple dependencies, and all components need to be properly in place before the machine can work. In this metaphor, communication might represent a drive belt, due to its synchronising role that can be implemented through various means, for instance, educating stakeholders on what is truly sustainable, going beyond ideology and fake news and explaining why some corrective actions are not yet available or announcing when they are likely to be (Figure 6.7).

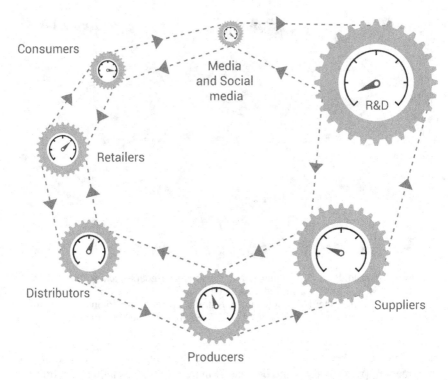

Figure 6.7 The different speeds at which stakeholders move and communication as a drive
belt. Some elements – the larger cogs – move slowly, while others – the smaller
cogs – move more quickly. Authors' elaboration. Originally published in the first
edition of this book, *Il Cibo Perfetto*, published in Italian in 2022.

6.3.2   *What to communicate?*

The question of what to communicate involves taking two key aspects into
consideration: what the context is and what specific interests the consumers have.
Concerning the context, there are many different issues regarding sustainability,
and these can change over time as trends come and go and the science develops.

The Rogers diffusion curve is a very well-known model in the world of traditional marketing which is used to illustrate how innovation is adopted by individuals in a social system. Drawing inspiration from this approach, we can map the
relationship between collective interest in a sustainability issue and the degree of
development throughout the life cycle of interest, which goes from indifference,
through concern and alarm phases to loss of interest (Figure 6.8).

Taking plastic as an example, a decade ago the issue was largely unknown
among the public. It became a matter of alarm before the start of the pandemic
in 2020. At the time of publication, three years after the first lockdown, the issue
still generates interest, but it is undoubtedly less prominent on the agendas of

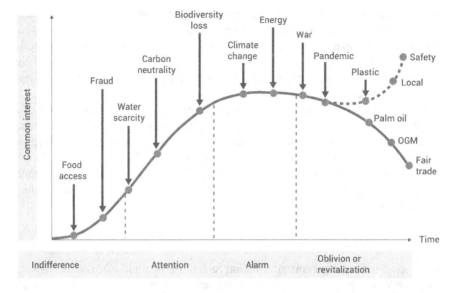

Figure 6.8 The life cycle of environmental concern. Authors' elaboration. Originally published in the first edition of this book, *Il Cibo Perfetto*, published in Italian in
2022.

companies, consumers and institutions as the situation has developed and other
issues have come to the fore. This curve is not based on statistical data, but on
managers' perceptions and the most-cited communication issues. It is always in a
state of flux and must be constantly updated.

Why is this kind of approach needed? Because proactively identifying emerging
problems early on, before they gain mass attention, enables a company to begin to
prepare and develop solutions to bring to market when demand shifts. Given the
R&D and supply chain time requirements discussed, it can be hugely advantageous
to be on the front foot and to anticipate consumer demand shifts ahead of time and
ahead of competitors.

Defining the specific message to be communicated through marketing activities
is crucial. For the successful communication of any message, three key elements
must be conveyed in sequence:

1 the *problem* perceived by the audience
2 the *solution* offered by the company through its product or production process
3 the *reasons why* – namely, the objective factors that support the solution (patents,
   certifications, product impact, features, etc.)

It may seem like an obvious path but, in most cases, communication follows the
inverse journey. A message will start with the technical/scientific characteristics of
the product or company (i.e. the *reason why*, with sentences like 'for 100 years,

our company has produced...'), then move on to the *solution*, which is the new feature being promoted, and finally – though not always – the *problem*. Articulating messages in this manner massively reduces the empathy effect and the likelihood of achieving the desired outcome through the communication. Our audience is not interested in our products, patents or history but they do want to know how we can make their life better.

To make this type of communication appealing, it can be presented as part of a compelling narrative, using storytelling. In addition to fully conveying its content, a well-designed story is more likely to be well-received by the media and to go viral, taking advantage of word of mouth and current use of social media platforms. However, when communicating about sustainability, it is imperative to understand that storytelling without science is greenwashing, and science without storytelling is academia.

6.3.3   How much to communicate?

The issues, data and general information related to the topic of sustainability are countless – ranging from social and environmental topics to economic and political. It is crucial to consider how much information needs to be communicated to reach the intended outcome.

Because of the wide variety of sustainability-related issues, companies often produce excessively long documents (as is often the challenge with sustainability reports) in which they list outcomes and goals they believe to be relevant and interesting to any possible audience. They can undoubtedly be useful and necessary in helping companies take stock of their current situation and progress towards goals – effectively obligating corporate departments (marketing, procurement, production, human resources, finance, etc.) to take an interest in sustainability and record and report on commitments and progress. But, while they are often presented in an aesthetically pleasing way, they can be difficult to read and too long to be used effectively, making these documents far from effective communication tools for a general audience, such as consumers.

When it comes to achieving impact through communication, companies benefit from being highly selective and discerning as to what it is genuinely useful to communicate in the most effective and engaging way. To understand how much to communicate, it is worth keeping in mind two phenomena that, in combination, suggest the right amount of information to convey to the audience.

The first effect, described by the Dunning-Kruger curve,[8] reminds us that – despite what many people think – understanding the actual facts requires a certain level of knowledge and expertise about the issue at hand. Limited knowledge gives people false confidence and provides virality and authoritativeness to fake news, which is often based on partial information and guided by ideology rather than objective data. Paradoxically, the feeling of understanding decreases as knowledge increases, at least in the earlier phases of knowledge acquisition (Figure 6.9).

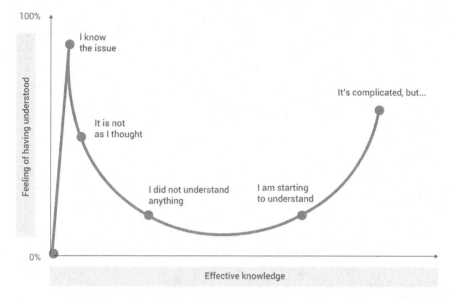

Figure 6.9 The Dunning-Kruger effect: how the feeling of understanding and actual knowl-edge are not in direct relation to each other. Widespread representation. Origi-nally published in the first edition of this book, *Il Cibo Perfetto*, published in Italian in 2022.

The most obvious solution to combat this effect might appear to be for a company to increase the amount of information it conveys to the public. However, going too far in this direction can generate another undesirable effect, which we might call 'gobbledygook'.

To explain this, we can draw a two-axis graph. The vertical axis represents com-municative effectiveness, meaning a company's ability to explain complex con-cepts and information (such as carbon offsetting or ecological footprint). Lower down on this axis is the absence of communication or a 'communication vacuum', while higher up we find 'completeness', which is the perfect conveyance of all content to the audience. In the middle, there is an area we can call 'clarity', which is the result of effective albeit incomplete communication, not inclusive of all the content that the broadcaster would wish to convey (Figure 6.10).

The other axis, meanwhile, measures the number of concepts, or meaning-ful words, that are conveyed simultaneously, or within the same communica-tive instance, from the broadcaster to the audience. To the left, we find few or no concepts and, as we move right, the number of words and/or concepts expressed increases towards a theoretically infinite value.

The two axes can be used to build an asymmetrical bell curve, where the right tail is significantly longer than the left one (in statistics, this is called non-normal distribution). The right side of the curve is where the gobbledygook phenomenon

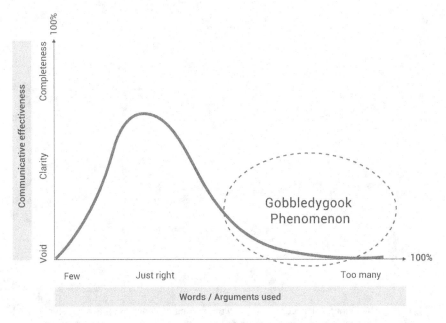

Figure 6.10 The gobbledygook curve. The curve correlates the volume of arguments with communicative effectiveness. Authors' elaboration. Originally published in the first edition of this book, *Il Cibo Perfetto*, published in Italian in 2022.

occurs. In essence, excessive use of words or concepts – which are often tactical – drastically reduces communicative effectiveness.

This is what happens in situations where communicators use many arguments without a clear connection between them. This can be done inadvertently, when a speaker is too earnest or enthusiastic about the issue but, in most cases, it is a defensive communication strategy used when a single argument is not robust enough to convince the audience. Even with the best of intentions, if the optimal level of concept and information is surpassed – and this limit is not especially high – the addition of further content does not improve the quality of communication but reduces it.

Keeping to the left side of the graph, using very few arguments, comes with its own risks. This is the case when companies describe themselves as generically sustainable, without any justification, and end up undermining their credibility and raising concerns of greenwashing.

Evidently, defining the optimal degree of concept communication is difficult. It all depends on the context in which the communication happens and the audience's interest in the topic. As an initial approximation, an 80/20 Pareto allocation might be a good rule of thumb for effective communication, aiming for 80% accuracy while using 20% of the possible content to convey the message to the audience.

Box 6.3   Labelling: a small but crucial detail

Labels are one of the most widely used and valuable tools for communicating a product's characteristics. Label design is very important for conveying relevant content, which might impact perceived value, within a limited space and according to labelling regulations around the world. Labels must be honest, truthful and correct without confusing consumers. The value of labels is to inform customers and influence their decisions, adding significant value per unit of a product (Figure 6.11).

One company with the greatest expertise in this field is Eurostampa, a family business founded in Bene Vagienna, Italy, in 1966. The Cillario family worked to establish itself as a leader in the world of luxury labelling, supplying clients in the wine, liqueur, cosmetics and food sectors. Today, Eurostampa operates from six global locations and has clients in over 40 countries.

Since its founding, the development of Eurostampa was driven by its ability to offer first-rate products and services thanks to outstanding attention to detail, which allowed it to meet the needs of the most demanding clients. In recent years, the company has developed a focus on sustainability-related issues, which is manifested in its interest in technological innovation and renewable energy alongside a constant search for new materials with a reduced environmental impact.

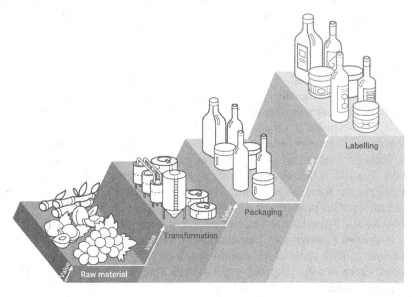

Figure 6.11 The value generated by the label. Authors' elaboration.

> *Eurostampa has nurtured a long-standing collaboration with the University of Gastronomical Science (UNISG) in Pollenzo, with a focus on the circular economy. This collaboration has resulted in the launch of the Circular Economy for Food (CEFF) Hub, a platform that maps and collects the most emblematic applications of the principles of the CEFF. Its aim is to help businesses and institutions adopt strategies for the transition to a circular production model. At the heart of the project are the three Cs advocated by UNISG: capital (natural, cultural and economic), circularity and coevolution. Another outcome is a project designed to promote innovation in the label packaging sector in collaboration with the University is Envelope. This is a creativity lab that engages students in applying their multidisciplinary approach to the realm of label design. Eurostampa, thanks to its expertise and its Innovation LABels (a department fully dedicated to the development of new ideas and the search for technical and creative solutions), aims to enhance its value as much as possible with a view to sustainability.*

6.3.4   Selecting your channels

There are endless channels through which companies can convey their messages, from websites to TV advertising, packaging to call centres and word of mouth to press releases. Aside from the individual means, there are four basic modes of communication, each with its own rules that make it possible to reach different audiences and objectives (Figure 6.12).

A *One-to-many.*
   This is traditional advertising, which involves a broadcaster (the company) speaking unidirectionally and asymmetrically to its audience. It is an affordable and efficient way of reaching many people with a low cost/contact, but the overall investment is generally high. This mode is suited to simple messages that do not require dialogue. It can be the right approach when a company wants to declare its values, mission or purpose, but it is less suited to explaining products. The risk is that claims will not be credible if there is no opportunity for triangulation, where an economically disinterested party (e.g. someone who has already used the product and endorses it) can validate the message.
B *One-to-one.* Symmetric and bidirectional, this mode is suited to launch a discussion such as a custom sale. Communication does not have to be initiated by the company; other stakeholders can do this, for example, through customer care portals such as online support or call centres. Thus, it may be better to call this type of communication 'one *with* one'.
C *Many-to-many.* This type of communication occurs spontaneously between people without the company having much control, despite it having been a catalyst.

Approaches to communication and related objectives			
One to many	One to one	Many to many	Many to one
Target Broad publics (low contact cost but high investment)	LSD, scientific community, influencers, policy makers, journalists	General public, media	General public, groups and associations, media
Objective Communicate company values, mission, etc.	Sales, influencers and policy maker engagement	Word of mouth	Curb accusations of greenwashing or boycotts
Typical instruments Advertising	Sales network, lobbying	Social media, press office	Testimonials, public relations, contact centers, websites

Figure 6.12 Communication approaches and related goals. Authors' elaboration. Originally published in the first edition of this book, *Il Cibo Perfetto*, published in Italian in 2022.

Thanks to social media, word-of-mouth dissemination of information can be extraordinarily viral. Companies invest to ensure that content is positive, while also knowing that bad news tends to be more engaging than good news. When a brand ends up under fire, it is unlikely that it will be able to defend itself alone. Thus, it is best to triangulate the conversation by bringing in third parties – such as experts and influencers – or through organisational endorsements.

D *Many-to-one.* When word of mouth goes beyond a certain popularity threshold, this can lead an entire group of people to demand that a company act – or not act – in a certain direction. One of the most striking examples was the case of palm oil, which ended up being abandoned by many companies due to pressure from the collective.

An outcome of communication approaches that requires stakeholder interaction is the transition away from the dualism of B2B (business to business) or B2C (business to consumer) communication systems towards a more intricate B2B2C system, in which communication between parties that are distant from one another in the value chain – for example, raw material producers and consumers – happens via intermediate steps. This is the case with Skretting Italia, a leader in the production of fish feed, whose long-standing communication process is not primarily aimed at communicating with clients (fish farmers), but at helping clients build dialogue with consumers through their retail partners, in particular large-scale distributors.

6.3.5   *Short-term or long-term benefit?*

One approach that can be helpful is to apply a matrix that traces the marketing journey of a product or service, in setting up the communication strategy and the relationship between businesses and the market more generally over time. In this case, the vertical axis represents the beneficiary (a single individual or the planet) and the horizontal axis shows the timeframe over which the benefit is distributed.

The timeframe can be in the short term (the immediate moment of consumption) or extended over time (the long term). Historically, the sole purpose of marketing was to generate short-term value for the company by ensuring individual consumer satisfaction at the moment of consumption. This implies that any product or service offered on the market is considered a good outcome as long as it is appreciated (and therefore purchased) by the consumer (Figure 6.13). While businesses still use this short-term approach, many incorporate the further goal of ensuring customer satisfaction and benefit over time, including through repeated purchases.

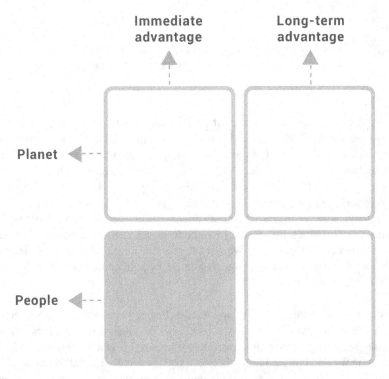

Figure 6.13 Businesses and the market: traditional marketing. The original goal of marketing was to generate value for the company by ensuring individual customer satisfaction at the moment of consumption. Authors' elaboration. Originally published in the first edition of this book, *Il Cibo Perfetto*, published in Italian in 2022.

For longer-term approaches, the bottom-right quadrant includes actions that fall under the label responsible marketing (Figure 6.14). The company takes responsibility for the well-being of the consumer, according to the so-called customer advocacy approach. In some case, this is done at the risk of limiting sales – for example, where excess consumption could have an undesirable effect. This applies to food which, when consumed in an unbalanced way, can lead to obesity, malnutrition and serious illnesses. Viewed through a long-term lens, any form of marketing that drives ever-increasing consumption of a product or service can have negative consequences if not appropriately balanced. To expand their approach into the bottom-right quadrant, businesses must:

- promote products with positive effect on the consumers
- inform and educate people to consume products responsibly
- implement fully fledged de-marketing policies where necessary (understood as practices aimed at reducing or limiting consumption)

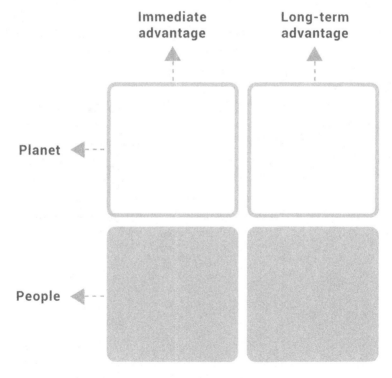

Figure 6.14 Businesses and the market: responsible marketing. The first stage of evolution: a focus on the long-term effects of consumption is added to short-term customer satisfaction. Authors' elaboration. Originally published in the first edition of this book, *Il Cibo Perfetto*, published in Italian in 2022.

In the top-right quadrant highlighted in Figure 6.15, the target of marketing shifts from the consumer to the planet, comprising the environment and society as a whole. This includes the remit of so-called green marketing, which focuses on the effects of production and consumption at the collective level. Where this is prioritised over individual customer satisfaction (the bottom-right quadrant), the economic sustainability of a business becomes more challenging, for example, where consumers are asked to accept a price premium or reduced performance for a product that has a lower environmental or social impact. The consumer receives no benefit of this decision, except indirectly as a member of the collective. With few consumers willing to choose goods that are better for the planet but more expensive and less functional, they end up occupying a small niche in the market.

In practice, it is unlikely that a product can ever have a purely positive impact on people or the planet, and fully reconciling individual demands with those of the planet is virtually impossible. One of the most critical challenges encountered involves the trade-off between human health, multiplied across a multitude of individuals, and the natural environment. Fish is a good example; its consumption once

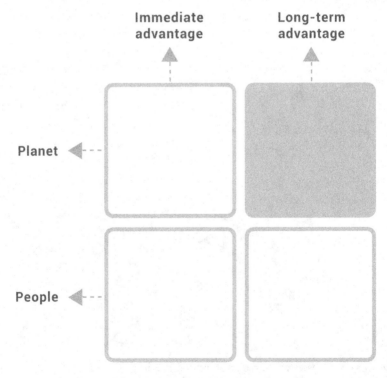

Figure 6.15 Businesses and the market: green marketing. A niche approach that prioritises reducing the environmental effects of production and consumption at the expense of customer satisfaction, in terms of perceived product quality. Authors' elaboration. Originally published in the first edition of this book, *Il Cibo Perfetto*, published in Italian in 2022.

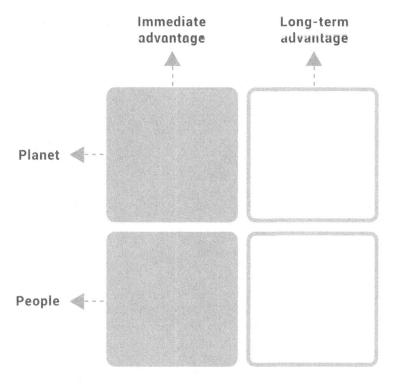

Figure 6.16 Businesses and the market: CRM. A temporary commitment to the environment or the collective is added to short-term customer satisfaction. Authors'
elaboration. Originally published in the first edition of this book, *Il Cibo Perfetto*, published in Italian in 2022.

or twice a week is recommended for a healthy diet, but if everyone on the planet
did this, the entirety of global fish stocks would not meet demand. This topic will
be explored further in the coming pages.

The top left-hand side of the matrix (Figure 6.16) also cannot be considered truly
sustainable because it complements short-term customer satisfaction with a commitment that generates a short-term collective gain. Examples include initiatives that
support non-profit organisations or campaigns through promotion/sales of a commercial product. These strategies are known as cause-related marketing (CRM) and
are often seen as falling under the umbrella of greenwashing, especially when the
campaign target has no bearing on a company's actual business activities.

The true challenge of sustainable marketing is to avoid the small niche of green
marketing and the temptations of greenwashing to embrace, in a single offering, the
entire realm of sustainability. In this case, long-term gain becomes the strategic focus,
benefiting the planet, wider society and the consumer. Short-term customer satisfaction is a prerequisite, and tactical environmental actions (top-left quadrant) are merely
an outcome of developing a solid, long-term strategy (Figure 6.17). All of this should
be taken into account when designing an implementation approach to achieve long-
term sustainability and communicate distinctive information to the market.

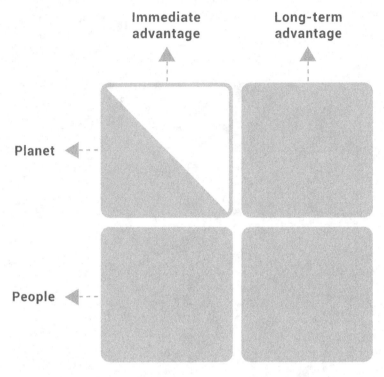

Figure 6.17 Businesses and the market: sustainable marketing. The focus is on long-term gain for the collective, the environment and the consumer. Authors' elaboration. Originally published in the first edition of this book, *Il Cibo Perfetto*, published in Italian in 2022.

Box 6.4   Creating value in the B2B sphere: the case of Skretting Italia

Skretting Italia is part of Nutreco Group, owned by SHV, and a world leader in the production and trade of fish feed. It produces over 2.5 million tonnes of feed every year, operating in 18 countries with its most sustainable facility located in Italy. The company's trading contracts are exclusively B2B and its clients are primarily farmers of marine and freshwater species in countries such as Italy, Greece, Croatia, Tunisia, Bosnia and Herzegovina, Albania, Armenia and Bulgaria. There is a high risk of commoditisation, a process whereby clients see the product (feed) purely from a nutritional properties perspective and other aspects are undervalued. To remedy this, in 2017, Skretting Italia launched an engagement programme for Italian clients, translating its commitment to sustainability into a competitive placement involving the entire supply chain. The project was called 'Acqua in Bocca' and began with a series of workshops designed to engage Italian clients to better understand their needs.

The first meeting was held in 2017 to discuss value creation strategies in the aquaculture sector by leveraging the issue of sustainability. The farmers highlighted the need for greater coordination of communication activities between stakeholders in the supply chain (feed producers, farmers, processing plants, distributors) to give more value to the products of Italian aquaculture.

As a consequence, communication was the focus of a roundtable discussion held in 2018 at AquaFarm, one of the sector's largest international trade fairs. The event was set up to facilitate dialogue and discussion between large-scale distribution companies and the farmers. The roundtable highlighted the need to improve consumer perception and shed light on the efforts of the entire value chain, which is committed to constant product quality improvement.

In late 2018, Skretting went back to work on the topic of communication, particularly to convey messages to the market to address prejudices and misconceptions regarding aquaculture across the variety of stakeholder expectations. The company held a public event, inviting fish farmers and a panel of media professionals (bloggers, journalists, writers) and representatives from the worlds of large-scale retail and haute cuisine. The main outcome was the drafting of a communication handbook (Acqua in Bocca! Guida pratica per non diffondere... illusioni ittiche), designed to help farmers better communicate the value of aquaculture products and debunk fake news and misconceptions. The production of the communication handbook strengthened the relationship between Skretting and its clients, who were directly involved drafting its content.

In 2019, the Acqua in Bocca handbook was reviewed and updated, and Skretting offered its clients the option to create personalised copies with their company logo and overview.

The project (https://bit.ly/3AlND8j) involved several innovative elements, particularly given Skretting Italia's positioning as a company operating in the B2B sector.

Points of contact

As often happens in a B2B setting, even at Skretting Italia the relationship with clients is mostly centralised and entrusted to the sales network. The Acqua in Bocca project made it possible to broaden the audience that clients can communicate with and multiply the points of contact with the company.

B2B2C approach

While there is no lack of initiatives in the agri-food sector to engage stakeholders upstream in the supply chain, it is more difficult to find the right reasons to involve clients, who are often in competition with each other, in dialogue. In this case, there was a nonpartisan need shared by all clients that the company could fulfil. The matter was resolved by adopting a B2B2C approach, supporting clients in communicating and influencing their end market.

Focus on the target market

Acqua in Bocca is an example of a strategy that bases its success on ideas that are designed and tailored to the target market. In multinational companies, marketing strategies are often approached from the top down, with global corporate inputs only partially adapted and revised for local contexts. With this initiative, the dynamic was overturned, because the input started with Skretting Italia. The Italian Operational Company thus became a reference point for other members of the group.

Pre-competitive action

Skretting Italia acted as a hub in the collection of information and analysis of difficulties concerning aquaculture, creating a shared, pre-competitive base for its clients. It made the Acqua in Bocca communication handbook freely available online, allowing anyone wishing to convey accurate and reliable information about aquaculture to access a useful and user-friendly tool.

6.4   Avoiding greenwashing

Greenwashing is a term used to highlight the communication activities of organisations aimed at garnering a 'green' reputation without truly deserving it. Concern over greenwashing is on the rise as awareness has grown that some companies use green communication as a way to divert attention from the true impact of products and operations, which may be far from sustainable. One sign that can distinguish this type of practice is the absence, within corporate communication, of a clear description of the impact of sustainability activities undertaken and concrete actions implemented.

Aside from a few clear-cut cases, establishing whether a company is culpable of greenwashing is no simple matter. Regulations, market demands and public opinion can change over time, so activities that might have seemed legitimate once – or even commendable – may come under fire. This is at times the case with philanthropic activities – typically in the form of donations to NGOs and charitable contributions to individuals, communities or institutions – which were a main indicator used to define a company as 'responsible' in the 20th century. Nowadays this can appear at times as greenwashing, seeing as financial contributions to worthy causes which buy a company the opportunity to continue with harmful core business activities.[9] Although during the Covid-19 crisis, corporate donations – particularly in a healthcare context – became popular once again and seemed to elicit approval from public opinion, these are still considered parallel activities that do not represent a truly sustainable firm.

Greenwashing is not necessarily a symptom of opportunistic behaviour, it can also be inadvertent due to lack of expertise at both company and market level, from sudden scares conveyed by the media that inflame public opinion, controversial scientific evidence regarding environmental management and even poorly written legislation.

In essence, the line between effective actions concretely linked to sustainability and greenwashing is vague and changeable, shifting as the awareness and demands of markets evolve. In addition to everything that is already being done (such as third-party certification, labelling, sustainability budgeting, etc.), the concept of sustainable category management[4] can help bring more clarity and cast more definitive judgements on questions of greenwashing.

From a scientific perspective, in assessing the life cycle of products, so-called *hotspots* can be identified within each product category. These are often the environmental and social impacts that are objectively the most considerable. Aside from general principles, each product represents a world unto itself, featuring specific elements that determine profitability and environmental and social impact. There are value chain variables that make all the products in a specific sector more or less sustainable, regardless of any specific differentiation that may exist between branded products.

For some product categories, the hotspots are located at the beginning of the value chain in the raw materials or components used. In food, this is the production of raw ingredients. In other cases, industrial processing is the most problematic phase, such as is the case with chemical products which require a lot of energy to manufacture and generate considerable emissions. Issues can also relate to worker well-being, as with illegal hiring practices, or animal welfare in the animal husbandry sector. For other products, logistics or consumption involve hotspots, for example, generating food waste. Often, end-of-life management gives way to problems such as packaging waste or domestic food waste.

Typical sustainability indicators (carbon footprint, water footprint, ecological footprint, etc.) and the types of impact (climate change, pollution, biodiversity loss, animal welfare, etc.) are easy enough to list and, in some sense, they concern almost all products. However, only careful analysis based on scientific literature and data can guide industrial and distribution strategies by indicating the hotspots for a specific category. Without this information, institutions, businesses and consumers may make decisions regarding sustainability in a self-referential manner, measuring and acting on factors that might be misleading and not representative of the most critical point for that specific product or sector. For instance, if a company producing dairy products communicates only about reducing plastic packaging when the main impact is linked to the pollution of groundwater, it could be an example of greenwashing. The same applies to highlighting the environmental qualities of an organic product whose farming involved illegal hiring practices.

Ultimately, for companies to avoid accusations of greenwashing, they need a general commitment to sustainability (which, by now, is in their economic interests if they want to remain competitive in an increasingly well-informed marketplace) and credible proof that they have implemented, and are planning all possible actions, to address the environmental and social hotspots in their product categories.

6.4.1   *Reducing the risk of greenwashing*

Communicating sustainability is not just costly (in terms of time and resources) but also risky: the danger of being accused of greenwashing is always just behind the corner. Therefore, it is important to carefully establish which channels to use and what messages to convey. One of the ways to minimise the risk of greenwashing is to communicate using tools recognised by international standards. A possible approach that might be adopted (typical of the field of industrial security) is risk analysis.

It is a well-known fact that the risk associated with an event is calculated by multiplying the probability that it will occur by the damage it will generate, or the

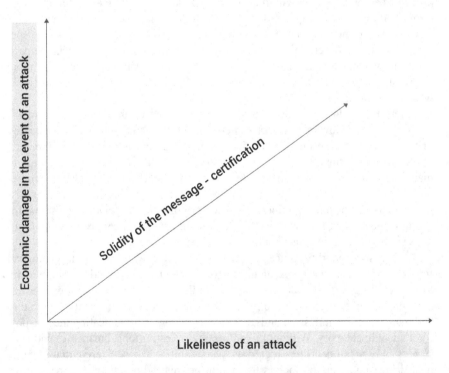

Figure 6.18 How to reduce the risk of greenwashing. When communication is potentially at risk of greenwashing accusations or the damage from these allegations would be considerable, it is worth ensuring that the message is very solid and, ideally, certified by a third party. Authors' elaboration. Originally published in the first edition of this book, *Il Cibo Perfetto*, published in Italian in 2022.

magnitude thereof. Applying this process to sustainability communication might lead us to say that the risk of greenwashing can be calculated by multiplying the probability of being accused by the economic damage that such allegations might generate (Figure 6.18).

If a company communicates that it is producing recycled paper packaging to 'save the trees', this statement is very low-risk and there is no need to have dedicated scientific evidence or certifications that corroborate the message. But if what is being communicated has a high risk of coming under fire – such as an advertisement stating 'our product A is more eco-friendly than our competitor's product B' – the message must be substantiated as much as possible, even using third-party certifications, to avoid generating damage that might be unsustainable for the business.

6.5   Communication tools and accreditations

There are many communication tools and initiatives that can be used to substantiate the sustainability efforts of organisations. These can be applied to the brand, operational facilities, the product along its value chain and individual ingredients and their purpose differs: whether it is to provide trust to customers and improve brand equity (e.g. B Corp) or whether it is to provide compliance to important minimum standards (e.g. ISO certifications) (Figure 6.19). For each area, there are many tools which are often based on international standards that allow them to be certified by credible bodies.

The use of one or more of these tools depends on the content of the communication and on the recipient. The scope of the communication must consider the interest of stakeholders. It is unlikely, for example, that food consumers are interested in the environmental management system of a production site (ISO 14001), but their attention is focused on the product and its ingredients.

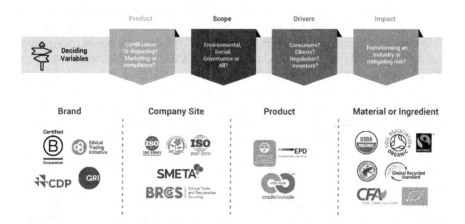

Figure 6.19 The use of communication tools depends on the scope of the communication. Authors' elaboration.

Regarding environmental product claims, for example, ISO 14020 is the standard published by the International Standard Organisation that groups environmental labels into three categories:

- Type I require meeting minimum requirements in terms of environmental impact (emissions below a certain threshold, for example) that are more stringent than legal requirements. These can be understood as indicators of excellence.
- Type II are self-declared environmental claims made by the producer regarding the product's characteristics.
- Type III are represented by verified declarations relating to a product's environmental impacts. These might be defined as transparency labels.

While Type I and III labels require third-party verification, for Type II the veracity of claims is down to the compliance of producers with specific requirements to make the declarations verifiable, not misleading or vague, and not liable to be misinterpreted. For example, Type II labelling includes claims about the compostability, biodegradability, recyclability or recycled material content of products, with the relevant branding. In all cases, the credibility of declarations depends on who sets the rules and who verifies the claims. For this reason, international certification schemes are preferable, defined by independent or institutional organisations that have well-defined and selective accreditation criteria for verifiers.

The most widespread and well-developed categories are excellence and transparency labels. For example, Environmental Product Declarations (EPDs) are becoming increasingly widespread. They provide objective, verifiable and credible information about a product's environmental performance over the entire life cycle. They are designed to be informational and to describe product performance concerning all environmental matters and potential impacts. These declarations require verification and validation by accredited third parties to ensure the credibility and veracity of the information declared. The keyword is transparency. The purpose of EPDs is not to indicate excellence in terms of a product's environmental sustainability but to provide transparent information to consumers. While the tool was originally created as a business-to-business communication tool, many companies – especially in the agri-food sector – use EPDs in their consumer-focused communications. In some cases, a logo is placed on the product label to draw the consumer's attention and invite them to read the published EPD to increase their knowledge of that specific product.

The International EPD® System (www.environdec.com) is one of the most active programmes globally. Launched in Sweden in 1999, it received EU funding in 2003 through the European Commission's LIFE project, allowing it to gain international standing. It has developed the International EPD® System to a level of technical expertise that makes it a reference point for all new initiatives emerging in the field. At the end of 2021, the system had enabled the publication of approximately 2,500 EPDs, over 150 of which were linked to the food sector.

Box 6.5   The B Corporation certification

B Corp is a unique certification that is awarded to businesses that meet high standards of verified performance, accountability and transparency on factors ranging from employee benefits and charitable giving to supply chain practices and input materials. It is holistic in its approach, taking into account not solely a single social or environmental factor but challenging business impacts across all stakeholders.

Where does it come from and what does it stand for?

A US-registered non-for-profit organisation called B Lab manages the certification. Born out of the belief that 'Shareholder Primacy' leads to 'toxic short-termism'[10] and is outdated, there needed to be something that could be awarded to companies that take seriously the notion whereby all stakeholders — not just shareholders – are valued and prioritised. This leads to the Theory of Change guiding the mission of B Lab to 'transform the economic system into a more inclusive, equitable, and regenerative global economy'[11] and ultimately where stakeholder governance ensures we have better businesses that are accountable to both people and planet.

B Corp growth

There has been a rapid rise of interest in the certification over the last five years. With over 6,000 businesses now globally certified 'as a force for good', B Corp has become a truly credible and valuable certification for businesses to aspire to achieve. Although still in its infancy, the certification and associated 'movement' (as B Lab likes to refer to it as) is becoming increasingly desired by consumers, clients, investors and workers alike. To put the growth into perspective, over 1,000 of certifications have come in the past nine months.

What type of business can become a B Corp?

The B Corp certification is only for 'for-profit' companies, but it is not limited by industry. That said, there are certain industries that are deemed controversial and are therefore ineligible for B Corp certification or require additional requirements to be met. For example, agribusiness producers in Brazil need to meet specific requirements regarding deforestation and land conflicts to be eligible; and bottled water companies need to meet requirements around sustainable water usage, fair water access and waste management. The full list can be found on the B Corp website. There are some additional considerations regarding eligibility for complex structures and for those operating within conflict zones. Furthermore, as the certification relates to impact, a company must have been operational for at least 12 months to be eligible.

So what do you have to do to become B Corp certified?

The broad requirements of the certification relate to verified performance, accountability and transparency; but more specifically, this boils down to three steps:

1   reach the verified 80-point threshold on the B Impact Assessment (BIA)
2   meet the legal requirement as determined by Country of Incorporation and Corporate Structure
3   be transparent – by publishing scores, disclosures and, if required, BIA assessment

To maintain B Corp certification, a company has to recertify every three years as well as pay the certification fee (which is based on revenue) annually.

B Impact Assessment

The BIA is the free-to-use digital tool currently being used by over 200,000[12] businesses worldwide to measure their positive impact performance across all stakeholders – from supply chain governance, carbon footprint, to inclusion policies and employee engagement. The BIA is tailored to companies based on sector, size and location and requires each business to answer approximately 200 questions, broken down into two categories: Operational Questions – covering day-to-day policies and practices; and Impact Business Model questions: these are awarded to businesses which are deliberately set up to create high levels of social or environmental impact for the specific stakeholder group. Within the F&B industry, common considerations would be worker ownership, conservation action, organic produce and/or serving customers in need.

The pillars that make up the BIA are:

Governance: code of ethics; financial information disclosure; whistleblower policy; mission and engagement

Workers: career development; health, wellness and safety; tracking satisfaction and engagement

Environment: environmental management system; recycling materials; water, waste and energy usage

Community: civic engagement and giving; diversity, equity and inclusion; supply chain management

Customers: customer feedback or complaint mechanisms; regularly monitoring of customer outcomes and well-being

Once the self-assessment has been completed this is submitted for verification by B Lab's independent Standards Team where answers are considered and supporting documentation is required to confirm. In short, you are audited!

Legal requirement

The legal requirement ensures that B Corporations remain legally accountable to all of their stakeholders – workers, communities, customers, suppliers, and the environment – not just to shareholders. Certified B Corporations are legally required to consider the impact of their decisions on all of their stakeholders – a model known as stakeholder governance. The B Corp legal framework allows companies to protect their mission and ensures that the company will continue to practise stakeholder governance even after capital raises and leadership changes.

Transparency

All certified B Corporations share their BIA overall scores and category scores on their public profiles on B Lab's website. Public companies' wholly owned subsidiaries have extra transparency requirements to make their entire BIA public. As a side note, an additional benefit of the transparency requirement is that it allows businesses who have completed the BIA to be able to benchmark against B Corporations within their industry or the same geographical location.

Why do companies become a B Corp?

Benefits:

- It preserves their mission.
- It gives business credibility and has become an effective marketing tool.
- It makes a company more attractive to employees and new hires.
- It helps a company connect with like-minded businesses and investors and to benchmark against other businesses in the industry or region. The B Corp movement is more than just a certification to be proud of another label for products. There are forums designed to build partnerships and events annually to address environmental and social issues as a collective.
- A marketing tool – It is undoubtedly on a trajectory to become a household reference point for businesses that are a force for good.

Drawbacks and limitations:

- A company needs to consider the non-financial impact of its actions.
- A company is open to ongoing scrutiny.

- B Corp certification does not replace industry-specific certification – B Lab tends to build partnerships and the standards team will consistently refer to other certifications; but as a general business certification it will not replace them. Advice would always be to consider doing both, especially as B Corp is still becoming fully established and recognised. However, the certification does credit these third-party certifications. Furthermore, reporting frameworks such as GRI are not (yet) aligned with B Corp and therefore duplication of work is to be expected.
- The time it takes – Due to the increased interest in recent years, there can currently be a significant wait for verification; in certain regions companies have been known to wait over a year. There are plans in place to bring this down; but currently the process to B Corp certification can be something of a marathon rather than a sprint.

Key takeaways

- Priority stakeholders and stakeholder's priorities. Understanding who your stakeholders are and what their priorities are is very important. There are some topics that your organisation may need to work on purely because of the degree of social and environmental impact, and others that will need addressing due to the importance key stakeholder groups place on those topics.
- Communication for sustainability is never one to one: a multi-stakeholder approach is always needed. And the starting point is those stakeholders who are relevant but unfriendly to us, and therefore need to be reached indirectly.
- We need to be aware that the sustainability values to which consumers refer are different (and not always compatible with each other).
- Various environmental concerns change and follow one another over time, forcing industries to innovate. But along the value chain, the reaction times of the actors are different; consumers are the fastest to adopt and forget concerns owing to the conditioning of the media and public opinion, while companies need a lot of time to adapt products and processes. This generates frictions that must be managed through communication.
- In the evolution from 'traditional' marketing to 'sustainable' marketing, two variables change: (a) the time perspective, from 'now' to 'always', and (b) the focus from 'consumer' to 'community'.
- Avoiding greenwashing is difficult because over time the rules (increasingly restrictive) and the sensitivity of public opinion (less and less tolerant) change.

- There are a number of certifications that can be used to verify and signal the sustainability credentials of your business or product. These vary, from brand-level certifications to ingredient- – or material-specific certifications. A blended approach is likely needed to speak to different stakeholder groups.

Key questions for reflection

- Who are your organisation's key stakeholders (thinking well beyond customers, employees and investors and considering other groups that are connected to and influence the value chain)? What are their priorities and why?
- What are the most material topics to your identified stakeholder groups? Which environmental and social topics is your business likely to be able to impact the most? What is your 'basket' of topics to work on that satisfies both potential for impact and stakeholder priorities?
- How much information and data on your sustainability do you think your stakeholders are interested in receiving and able to manage?
- What certifications are important for your business that complement the key messages you want to deliver to your stakeholders, from customers to investors and suppliers?

Notes

1 WBCSD, *The Reality of Materiality: Insights from Real-World Applications of ESG Materiality Assessments*, 2021, https://www.wbcsd.org/Programs/Redefining-Value/Redesigning-capital-market-engagement/Resources/The-reality-of-materiality-insights-from-real-world-applications-of-ESG-materiality-assessments

2 H.I. Ansoff, Managing Strategic Surprise by Response to Weak Signals, in *California Management Review*, Vol 18, Issue 2, pp. 21–33, December 1975.

3 Over 700 markers from desk research and 40 interviews were selected to identify the key values that guide the sustainable purchasing behaviour of Italian consumers in the food sector. Through five design thinking workshops, the markers were summarised into 30 keywords that were grouped into 5 customer values. Subsequently, thanks to research institute Sita Ricerca, the results were validated by a consumer survey (*Osservatorio Consumi Sostenibili COOP*, Roma Tre, Sita Ricerca).

4 *Ibid.*

5 Psychologist Abraham Maslow proposed a system to hierarchically organise human needs in the shape of a pyramid, with basic needs, such as hunger and thirst, at the bottom, and more complex, higher-order needs – which, for the sake of simplicity, we might call psychological – towards the apex. The latter category includes the need for esteem, status and self-actualisation. In a nutshell, the key intuition is clear: we all start to fulfil our needs by starting with the basic ones and depending on the resources at our disposal, move on to higher-order needs. See A.H. Maslow, A Theory of Metamotivation: The Biological Rooting of the Value-Life, in *Journal of Humanistic Psychology*, Vol 7, Issue 2, pp. 93–127, October 1967.

6 R. Inglehart, W.E. Baker, Modernization, Cultural Change, and the Persistence of Traditional Values, in *American Sociological Review*, Vol 65, Issue 1, pp. 19–51, February 2000.

7 S. Xinqi, Hong Kong's Limit on Baby Milk Formula to Stay as Fears Grow Demand from Mainland China Could Cause Repeat of Shortage, *SCMP*, February 2019, https://www.scmp.com/news/hong-kong/hong-kong-economy/article/2187581/hong-kongs-two-tin-ban-baby-milk-formula-stay-amid.

8 D. Dunning, The Dunning-Kruger Effect: On Being Ignorant of One's Own Ignorance, in *Advances in Experimental Social Psychology*, Vol 44, pp. 247–296, 2011.

9 This is demonstrated by the bestselling book *No Logo*, in which Naomi Klein warns companies against working on projects that are typically in the purview of the third sector.

10 R. Feloni, *More Than 2.600 Companies, Like Danone and Patagonia, Are on Board with an Entrepreneur Who Says the Way We Do Business Runs Counter to Human Nature and There's Only One Way Forward*, Insider, December 2018, https://www.businessinsider.com/b-corporation-b-lab-movement-and1-cofounder-2018-11?r=US&IR=T.

11 *Imagine a World Where All Stakeholders – Not Just Stakeholders – Are Valued and Prioritized*, Bcorporation, https://www.bcorporation.net/en-us/movement/theory-of-change.

12 *The UK B Corporation Movement*, https://bcorporation.uk/.

7 Sustainability solutions

Accelerating your journey

We have now identified many of the environmental impacts generated throughout the agri-food value chain and understood the complex interconnectedness between different parts of the food system. We have also outlined approaches for setting up a strategy to improve food sustainability, how to communicate on the topic and the importance of establishing robust targets and metrics to credibly report progress.

Once a strategy, targets and measurement systems are in place, the most challenging part is putting them into practice and beginning to deliver results. Where do you start? What approaches can do you take? Which of the many potential solutions do you choose to invest in? And which ones are likely to be the most effective and impactful given your context?

Driving meaningful progress towards sustainability demands taking risks, since the solutions and technologies are often at the forefront of innovation and have yet to be tried and tested for several years. Businesses play a pivotal role in shaping and accelerating progress. Every time they choose to invest in a solution, they can help to ensure it delivers the scale, affordability and capabilities needed to have a true impact across the value chain.

In this section, we investigate three principal solutions that have gained traction within the food industry: decarbonisation strategies, regenerative agriculture and circular economy approaches.

We selected these aspects because they offer the potential to generate significant positive impact. They are mutually reinforcing and can be carried out in combination because they are not isolated and distinct, but deeply interrelated. Further, solutions within each approach can be pursued sequentially and simultaneously. For example, a decarbonisation strategy can be established to help a business articulate its climate goals and how it will achieve them. This strategy can include ambitions for implementing regenerative agriculture and circular economy solutions within the supply chain, generating benefits that support decarbonisation and broader outcomes such as cost savings, enhanced biodiversity, water conservation and more nutrient-dense foods.

Sustainability is a journey, and there is no such thing as perfection. This is true in many contexts, but all the more so in the food sector for two key reasons. The first is that food consumption is closely connected to human health, which must be considered as the foundational value; above all, sustainable diets must be healthy.

DOI: 10.4324/9781003449744-7

The second is that food production is the result of an extremely intricate network that links many different systems. These must be considered organically, attempting to find, for example, a balance between agriculture and animal husbandry. There are decisions to be made between alternative forms of sustainability. Which one is more wasteful – bagged salad or loose salad? Can palm oil be truly sustainable? Are locally sourced products always better for the planet? Many businesses and consumers are asking questions like these, and the answers are often based on hearsay and incomplete information, guided by ideology instead of reliable data.

Box 7.1   Stages of a sustainability transformation

If we examine traditional corporate strategies focused on profits and costs, we see various combinations of five levels of implementation of the concept of sustainability.

The first is the broad and superficial realm of corporate philanthropy, a feature of companies that invest in strategic actions in favour of social or environmental causes. Generally, it takes the form of patronage or sponsorship of NGOs or associations, publicised by advertising campaigns to increase public awareness. When the operation is linked to a marketing campaign (as in the case where a company donates a percentage of the proceeds from the sale of a product), this can be defined as Cause-Related Marketing (CRM).

Then there is the more advanced formula of Corporate Social Responsibility, which requires a company to support external causes and also make a commitment that directly affects its activities. Social and environmental responsibility exists alongside the core business, which remains the company's primary responsibility. There is no true integration of the three spheres.

With an awareness that social and environmental issues can have severe economic impacts, companies can opt for a more detailed and structured risk management strategy approach to prevent crises.

Next, we have the business sustainability approach, which presupposes a newfound awareness: that the only way to guarantee profits over time is to reduce – and, where possible, eliminate – all negative impacts. In other words, there can be no economic sustainability without social and environmental sustainability.

Finally, the fifth stage is regenerative business.[1] This approach is necessary to reverse the environmental degradation that has taken place, recognising that businesses need to contribute to regenerating soils, ecosystems and communities if we are to achieve long-term well-being and thriving industries. The assumption is that we need companies to go well beyond maintaining the status quo, to having a positive impact (the term sustainable can now be seen as too passive). This is the most ambitious commitment a business can make.

7.1   Decarbonisation

One of the main challenges on the sustainability journey is reducing GHG (greenhouse gas) emissions. This can be pursued by developing a decarbonisation strategy and defining and implementing actions that fall into four specific categories:

- Process efficiency – reducing, wherever possible, energy and resource consumption while maintaining the same rate of production. In many cases, efficiency can be improved by altering the organisation of production, for example, by improving the structure of processing cycles.
- Technology – improving process engineering by investing in more advanced technology components and systems. A classic example is the installation of systems for the independent production of electricity from renewable sources, such as solar panels.
- Procurement – when an organisation has no direct control over the resource production process, it can improve the sustainability of its products by setting up procurement strategies that take into account CO_2 emissions or sustainability more generally. This is the most common case in the agri-food sector, because many companies involved in the production of consumer products do not manage the cultivation of raw ingredients and can act only by choosing suppliers that meet specific sustainability criteria.
- Innovation – addressing everything that is not yet known. It is worth remembering that innovation is not just technological, it also can be organisational. Using electric heavy goods vehicles (HGVs) as sustainable transport is not especially innovative. Much more innovative, for example, is the design of logistical models that do not require the use of road freight at all.

Which of these categories is the most important? None, as a matter of fact. Based on the type of production in question, many actions can be implemented, all having different effects. Regenerative agriculture and circular economy (detailed in the next sections) are examples of decarbonisation solutions across these categories.

A possible approach to a diagrammatic analysis of the topic can be found in Figure 7.1, where two variables are displayed: one that relates to economic effects and the other concerning effectiveness in terms of true environmental benefits. Each of the four quadrants represents one possible situation.

- Win-win. These actions enable both economic savings and a significant reduction in emissions. Actions that maximise production efficiency typically fall within this quadrant.
- Nice to have. Emission reduction is minor but still leads to savings, as with turning off office lights when they are not needed. These actions are important because, despite not having major environmental effects, their educational potential is considerable.
- Unavoidable. These actions come at a cost and provide a limited reduction of emissions – in some cases, these can even increase. In agri-food production,

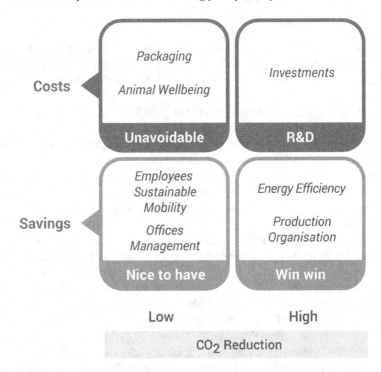

Figure 7.1 Possible organisation of environmental impact reduction actions. Even quantitatively minor actions can have a considerable effect in terms of communication. Authors' elaboration. Originally published in the first edition of this book, *Il Cibo Perfetto*, published in Italian in 2022.

animal welfare is a classic case, with interventions that are often necessary even though they lead to increases in per-unit GHG emissions.
- Research & development (R&D). This includes all actions that lead, or will lead, to significant reductions after economic investment, which can be considerable – for example, the construction of renewable energy plants.

7.1.1   *Scope of emissions*

According to the leading GHG Protocol,[2] a company's or product's GHGs are classified into three scopes (Figure 7.2):

- Scope 1: direct emissions from company-owned and controlled resources. In other words, emissions that are released into the atmosphere as a direct result of firm-level activities. They could arise from stationary combustion (e.g. fuels, heating sources), mobile combustion (e.g. vehicles owned or controlled by a firm), fugitive sources (e.g. refrigeration, air conditioning units) and process emissions.

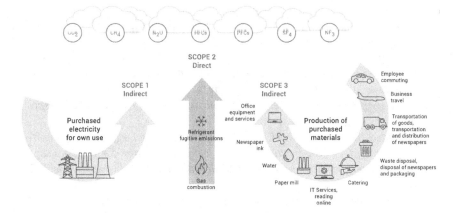

Figure 7.2 Boundaries in the GHG assessment. Widespread representation.

- Scope 2: indirect emissions from the generation of purchased energy.
- Scope 3: emissions from all other indirect sources that occur in the value chain.

In the food industry, Scope 1 and 2 are mostly related to the efficiency of the industrial processes where the aim is to reduce the energy consumption per unit of product. The most important and critical emissions are Scope 3 for two main reasons: amount of the emissions typically represents more than 50% of the GHG emissions of a product and involves complex supply chains with many farmers located around the world. Because of this, any reliable reduction targets must include Scope 3 evaluation.

Box 7.2   A strategic framework: the case of Zespri

Renowned for its delicious taste and nutritional boost, Zespri kiwifruit is trusted and sought out by millions around the world.

We take our role as 'kaitiaki' (guardians) for our future generations seriously. While playing that role, we tread lightly on the land and support communities both in New Zealand and globally but know we can do more. Our consumers expect that of us as we do ourselves.

Our ambition is to make sure we continue to grow in a way that respects and enhances our people, the environment and the communities around us, helping them thrive and grow stronger.

That is why we have established 'Better tomorrow' as one of our four core strategic priorities, underpinned by our company values and purpose.

Better tomorrow is about developing new sources of value, improving our business for the long-term and leading sustainability in our industry.

We have developed a Kiwifruit Industry Sustainability framework that defines our top sustainability priorities.

The framework has been developed through conversations with key stakeholder groups in New Zealand and internationally based growers, packhouses and cool stores representatives, industry representative groups, Māori kiwifruit growers, Zespri's global distribution partners and Zespri employees (Figure 7.3).

Guided by the framework, we have set ambitious targets and commitments which focus on creating a more sustainable future for our industry. Linked to our priorities, our eleven sustainability targets cover Scope 1, 2 and 3 emissions (Table 7.1).

Behind the delivery of our corporate targets, there are natural cycles to consider. Nature is variable by definition, and variability plays a key role when long-term strategies are applied on ground, because every season has different challenges in an interconnected global supply chain. Sometimes, variability can be standardised – like in logistics and packaging – sometimes not so much, as in the orchards where weather events can require new adaptation strategies to maintain the high reputation of the top-quality brand.

Climate change impacts are now tangible, with strong weather events like summer-long heat waves season after season. These affect volumes and also quality, taste, appearance and storability of the fruits.

Zespri takes the role of 'kaitiaki' (guardians) for future generations by defining sustainable priorities and also adaptation strategies to increase resiliency to ongoing global changes.

Figure 7.3 Zespri's sustainability framework. Adapted from Zespri's website, https://www.zespri.com/it-IT/zespri-sustainability.

Table 7.1 Zespri's priorities and goals

Our kiwifruit	Health	• We will offer over 6 billion healthy eating occasions to people around the world by 2025
Our environment	Packaging	• Our packaging will be 100% recyclable, reusable or compostable by 2025
		• If we use plastic packaging, it will be made from at least 30% recycled plastic by 2025
		• We will reduce our packaging footprint, per kg of fruit, by 25% by 2030 (footprint means carbon impact (Global Warming Potential) as defined by a life cycle assessment)
	Climate change	• We will work with our partners to be carbon positive by 2035, including the key milestones of:
		• Zespri corporate will be carbon neutral by 2025
		• Our industry will be carbon positive to our retailers by 2030
		• We will report on our climate risks and opportunities by August 2021 and will build an industry wide adaptation plan by 2022
	Water	• By 2025, Zespri growers will be
		• Protecting water quality by demonstrating alignment of nutrient inputs and losses to good practice limits
		• Using monitoring technology to actively manage and demonstrate efficient use of our precious water resources
Our communities	Growers	• People want to work in the kiwifruit industry and every employee will be valued, safe and supported in their jobs
	Workforce	• We will attract talent and continue to build a thriving workforce amongst our value chain by 2030 (thriving means continually improving social practices in relation to working conditions, pay, health & safety, development and diversity and inclusion)
	Markets	• We will partner within communities on healthy lifestyle programmes in our major markets by 2022

Adapted from Zespri's website, https://www.zespri.com/it-IT/zespri-sustainability.

7.1.2 *Emission-reduction targets*

Once all possible emission-reduction actions have been taken, the final step a company that wishes to be climate-friendly can take is carbon offsetting. The great excitement surrounding this topic comes with risks, because use of incorrect terminology can lead to misunderstandings, accusations of greenwashing or, worse, violations of legislation. The most widely used terms in relation to CO_2 are net-zero, carbon neutral and carbon positive.

To best understand the term net-zero, it is worth starting with the Paris Agreement target which aims to keep global temperature increase to below 1.5°C compared to preindustrial levels. To achieve this, CO_2 concentrations in the atmosphere must not increase and every organisation must implement abatement actions to contain emissions within certain limits. These abatement targets are sometimes very ambitious and are set according to rules determined by the Science-Based Targets initiative (SBTi), which also includes an assessment procedure. To be defined as net-zero, an organisation must follow an abatement plan aligned with the Paris Agreement and integrate CO_2 removal actions by intervening in its supply chain, for example.

An intermediate step, which has become the target for many organisations, is to achieve carbon neutrality. In this case, unavoidable GHG emissions are offset by purchasing certified carbon credits created through carbon abatement projects outside an organisation's value chain.

The most ambitious and still evolving target is to become carbon positive, whereby emissions removed are greater than those needed to achieve net-zero. Unlike the carbon neutrality and net-zero targets, climate positive status does not yet have internationally shared methods or standards, but some situations in the world of agriculture are starting to come close (Figure 7.4).

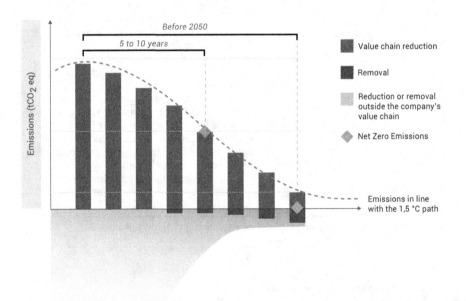

Figure 7.4 The ideal carbon management strategy. *SBTi Corporate Net-Zero Standard,* SBTi, 2023, https://bit.ly/3qdk5Gg.

7.1.3   *Carbon credits and offsetting*

Formalised under the Kyoto Protocol in 1997, carbon credits are a tool that allows industrialised nations to partially offset their emissions by funding climate change mitigation projects in lower-income countries. The 2015 Paris Agreement and decisions made at COP26 in Glasgow in 2021 marked the beginning of a new chapter for climate action in which all countries have their own emission-reduction targets and can cooperate through the exchange of certified carbon credits.

In addition to providing climate and environmental benefits, projects can have positive social and economic effects on countries and local populations. In quantitative terms, one carbon credit equates to 1 tonne of CO_2 equivalent reduced, avoided or removed by these projects.

Not all environmentally beneficial activities can generate carbon credits. Indeed, this is the key element in distinguishing between reduction actions and actions capable of generating credits. Key factors include recognisability, transparency and additionality.

Additionality is the most critical feature, so much so that various international initiatives are working to constantly improve the definitions and methods that distinguish carbon credit mechanisms. Based on the current definitions, the main features are[3]:

- additional – the abatement of emissions must be greater than with business as usual, meaning that it would not occur if the project was not implemented
- real – the abatement must be the result of concrete, proven and ex-post certified physical action
- quantified – the abatement must be measured using quantitative methods formulated and recognised by international standards
- permanent – the abatement must not be reversible, and the project must be designed to account for possible adverse developments
- verified – the carbon credit derived from the abatement of one tonne of CO_2 equivalent must be uniquely issued and tracked through a third-party electronic registry. The guarantee is provided when internationally recognised methods developed by scientific committees are used. Continuous updates and regular certification of the methods ensure the quality of the credits. International standards such as the Gold Standard and Verra are among the best-known and most trustworthy

The use of carbon credits in the offsetting actions is often a critical point since it could be considered as greenwashing if not properly used.

One of the most important points is to understand that the carbon credits originate from projects that are designed and developed to ensure CO_2 reduction or removal compared to a baseline – or business as usual – value. The main types of projects are the following.

Renewable energy projects, namely, the development of solar, wind, geothermal or hydroelectric power plants that increase the proportion of electricity generated from renewable sources and contribute to the gradual replacement of fossil fuel power.

Emissions reduction projects, such as those providing access to water and efficient cookstoves. These are community-based projects that enable the abatement of emissions by providing local communities with clean water, when normally they would have to boil water to make it drinkable, or more efficient cookstoves that allow communities to use less wood and coal for their daily needs. These projects lead to improvements in the management of ecosystems key to human health, environmental sustainability and economic prosperity.

Reducing Emissions from Deforestation and Forest Degradation (REDD+) projects. Forest cover is a crucial factor in the fight against climate change. As well as capturing and storing carbon, forests have a massive impact on local ecosystems and can be a powerful tool for the protection of biodiversity and indigenous peoples.

The world of carbon credits is constantly evolving at the international level due to countries' and companies' increasing desire to pursue Paris Agreement targets and the need to maintain high levels of quality in the market, while guaranteeing social and environmental benefits. In the net-zero transition, high-quality offsetting and carbon credits play an important, complementary role. They are a bridge between what is feasible today and what must be built for the future, allowing us to channel private sector investments towards the mitigation of climate change and activities that promote sustainable development in line with UN Sustainable Development Goals.

As the importance of decarbonisation has evolved at national levels and, especially, within individual companies, carbon offsetting is increasingly seen as not enough, being highlighted as greenwashing by campaign groups such as Greenpeace as it is seen as a way to carry on polluting activities by simply paying or outsourcing or 'offshoring' decarbonisation. Meaningful change to product design, operations and supply-chain structuring are required to make tangible GHG emissions across a company's value chain. The implementation of mitigation projects within supply chains is especially important, which allow companies to actively engage their suppliers and improve their Scope 3 figures. A great example of this within the agriculture and food industry is the development of carbon insetting projects. These have evolved organically within organisations, though the International Platform for Insetting (IPI) has made significant contributions to support the carbon accounting methodology in this space as well as the approach to innovation.

Box 7.3   *Carbon insetting as a powerful tool for decarbonisation in Food & Beverage*

Tilmann Silber is Global Lead Thriving Nature at the global chocolate manufacturer Barry Callebaut. He also serves as Strategic Program Lead at the IPI.

As terminology, insetting first occurred in 2009 in an article by the consultancy Econometrica.[4] It was developed as a reaction to offsetting – the use of carbon credits to compensate GHG emissions and thus achieve 'climate neutrality'. Such carbon credits are typically sold by international project developers from pre-existing projects. Developed opportunistically around the world, these carbon projects have typically little or no relation to the business or supply chain of the company aiming to offset its emissions. This led to an impression of alienation, particularly for companies in land-based sectors such as food, cosmetics, textile and retail, which had an existing long history of engaging in supply-chain sustainability through local projects and engagements.

Insetting then provided the opportunity for 'bringing the compensation topic home'. It refers to taking climate action where it matters most: in a company's own supply chain, typically at the level of farming or early-stage processing of agricultural raw materials. The benefits include much clearer and stronger communication benefits, as well as synergies around the so-called co-benefits of carbon projects. Next to mitigating climate change, such projects typically provide significant other sustainability benefits such as improved livelihoods and resilience of farming communities, increased productivity, biodiversity and water benefits, to name a few. Whereas in off-setting, these co-benefits are solely of communicational value, in insetting they offer the opportunity to catch several birds with one proverbial stone by contributing to other supply-chain-related sustainability targets, next to GHG reduction.

Operationally, insetting typically takes significantly more resources than offsetting, as projects need to be developed from scratch, with little co-funding and thus requiring higher costs of carbon and longer financial commitments on behalf of the company involved. For almost a decade since its inception, insetting therefore remained a niche climate strategy, used primarily by high-value consumer-facing brands that aimed to offer their consumers a form of 'premium compensation'. A well-known example is Nespresso. Together with its partners, the premium coffee brand of Nestlé between 2014 and 2020 planted almost 3.5 million trees in its coffee farming communities in Latin America and Africa.[5] Most of these trees are planted in the coffee fields themselves, as agroforestry. Such systems can help to improve soil health and increase yields, as well as help farmers to adapt to climate change. Towards consumers, Nespresso is aiming to achieve full climate neutrality, based on a mix of in- and offsetting.[6] Other companies that pioneered insetting include the luxury brand Chanel, cosmetic giant L'Oréal and Unilever's ice cream brand Ben & Jerry's.[7] Many of these companies are members of the IPI.[8] Next to agroforestry, commonly applied insetting techniques include efficient cookstoves, regenerative agriculture and rotational grazing in livestock farming.

In 2015, WWF, UN Global Compact, CDP and other organisations launched the Science-Based Targets initiative (SBTi), an analogue to the Paris Climate Accord, designed for companies. It requires committed companies to include their value chain emissions (Scope 3) in their targets, *which was not common until then. Interestingly, the SBTi does not accept offsetting as a means to achieve set targets. Since most emissions (and reduction opportunities), particularly for companies in the land sector, are related to farming, the SBTi gave a massive boost to insetting strategies. As a consequence, today the carbon benefits of insetting are chiefly no longer claimed as to compensate for a company's carbon emissions and therefore to achieve climate neutrality (and thus as a direct alternative to offsetting), but as a decarbonisation mechanism within their value chain and thus reduction of Scope 3 emissions. This change entails a range of technical accounting questions, not all of which are fully answered today. Also, some companies still opt to use insetting to claim climate neutrality due to a higher familiarity of consumers with the concept vs SBTi. Regardless of the detailed carbon accounting approach, all insetting strategies share common features: Direct investments into positive impact in the communities and ecosystems that global agricultural value chains critically depend on. As a strategic mechanism with growing momentum, insetting still has a lot of untapped potential.*

Further Reading: S. Brandt, T. Silber, *A Practical Guide to Insetting*, International Platform for Insetting (IPI), 2022, https://www.insettingplatform.com/insetting-guide/

7.2   Agriculture: from problem to solution

Because of its large emissions footprint, solutions in the agricultural sector play a critical role in supporting progress towards decarbonisation. In this section, we focus on production solutions, including regenerative agriculture. Before looking at the solutions, it is useful to understand how best to approach transforming agricultural production into a solution to the environmental challenges we face.

Strategy and tactics are terms used to define actions aimed at achieving a goal. Strategy refers to actions implemented with a medium- to long-term outlook, while tactics are short-term decisions that take practical and contingent factors into consideration. The challenge of improving agriculture's environmental impact requires the effective combination of strategies and tactics.

Committing to sustainable production is a strategic farm-level decision which must be taken in line with a medium- to long-term vision (at least four to five years) including economic considerations. Taking steps towards this strategy requires new ways of working and highly collaborative dynamics between different actors in the supply chain. In this sense, working the supply chain – with direct communication between growers and the agri-food industry – can enable all stakeholders to make mutually beneficial decisions.

At the farm level, the plots can be redesigned to generate better outcomes for the environment while cutting costs for farmers. Many approaches can be employed. For example, the ancient practice of crop rotation involves growing different crops on the same plot of land over a sequence of growing seasons and is one of the most useful practices to improve agri-food sustainability. The sequence of chosen crop species has a considerable impact on the environment, because what happens in a field one year has a major influence on what will happen the next year. In the case of wheat, for example, there is an increased risk of certain plant diseases (and thus the need for more frequent treatments) if the previous crop was corn. But if the previous crop was a legume, there will be minimal or no need for fertilisers because of legumes' nitrogen-fixing properties.

In addition to crop rotation, selecting varieties consistently within a medium-term plan can help farmers more efficiently manage their land. An example is thoughtfully selecting crops that are planted in rotations to build resilience of production and support soil health. Staying with wheat as an example, certain varieties are more resistant to specific diseases and others are less so, making it advantageous to plant disease-resistant varieties. Farmers can also opt for perennial species and varieties, such as Kernza,[9] which is a grain high in protein and antioxidants that, unlike annual crops like wheat, does not need to be replanted each year. This saves GHG emission and farmer costs, as tilling isn't required, while protecting soil from erosion.

Once the strategy is developed, there are the tactical decisions to be made nearly every day. Is it worth spraying fertiliser if it is about to rain? Is it appropriate to use a certain treatment against a disease? And so on. These tactical decisions need to be made quickly while considering contingent factors like the weather, the risk of infection, etc. And because they can have considerable environmental and economic impacts, they require tools and information that more traditional farmers often do not have at their disposal. For this reason, Decision Support Systems (DSSs) are increasingly used.

Box 7.4   Capital markets and the future of food

The food and beverage (F&B) industry is at the centre of many sustainability issues and globally shared objectives, including climate change, biodiversity loss and food security.[10] With a global market value of >$6 trillion,[11] and as the source of one-third of global anthropogenic GHG emissions,[12] the industry is well-placed to provide high-quality investment opportunities that build multi-stage resilience across the food supply chain[13] and simultaneously address global sustainability goals. As an industry that is deeply impacted by vulnerabilities to climate, water and other shocks and stresses on the natural system, the F&B industry itself is also in need of critical and expansive transformation to remain productive. All of this opens doors for the industry to capitalise on growing investor demand for climate-smart investments and the groundswell of sustainable finance more generally.

Global capital markets are increasingly interested in how sustainability or environmental, social and governance (ESG) issues can mitigate risks and create holistic value for portfolios and entities that they finance, invest in or underwrite.[14,15] *However, they have not yet reached the level needed to effectively address the pressing sustainability issues faced by F&B companies. This represents an opportunity for new investment vehicles to fund transformational solutions.*

One critical area of opportunity to capitalise on these trends and invest in system transformation at the very roots of the value chain is regenerative agriculture. In addition to potentially increasing yields by up to 300%,[16] *regenerative practices deliver monetisable co-benefits like ecosystem services that can range from water conservation to consumer health improvements. Real assets, such as agricultural land, are the main asset class through which regenerative food and agriculture is currently financed; current annual capital flows are estimated at $20 billion. But this figure accounts for a mere 4% of total climate finance capital flows and is far from sufficient to transform the food system: it is estimated that investments totalling $350 billion are needed by 2030 to transform the food system in line with global climate and sustainable development goals.*[17]

In addition to investments in how food is produced, companies will also need access to capital to transform how food is processed, packaged, delivered and even consumed to combat issues like resource intensity, waste reduction and food justice. There is said to be a $4.5 trillion opportunity to evolve consumer industries by harnessing the power of circular and regenerative principles in product and process development,[18] *and the F&B industry is well-positioned to attract such investments. Moreover, by its very nature, the F&B industry is exposed to a global and complex supply chain. By working with capital markets, F&B companies can create opportunities to scale up private capital to innovate, meet sustainability objectives and finance adaptation strategies.*

Additionally, the F&B industry has an important role to play in the financing and realisation of a Just Transition, one that seeks to incorporate social and cultural considerations as integral to the journey to a low-carbon economy. While climate change affects food production worldwide, there are significant disparities in impacts across geographies. Emerging economies are the most vulnerable to climate impacts[19,20] *and most challenged to attract such sustainability-driven investments,*[21] *so incorporating Just Transition principles into financing considerations is imperative. On average, 59% of the populations of low-income countries is employed in agriculture, compared to 38% in lower-middle-income countries.*[22] *Additionally, emerging markets also lack the funding necessary to meet the scale of change required to transform the F&B sector,*[23] *and they face even greater challenges in attracting financing for solutions at scale. Considering irrigation as a fitting example for an increasingly drought-stricken world, it has been estimated that more than $10 billion of annual investments is needed in developing countries to expand and upgrade irrigation to meet the projected surge in global food demand by 2030.*

The F&B industry is fertile ground for investment that enables meaningful progress on some of the world's greatest challenges. But doing so will require (1) investors to understand the particularities of the industry – especially in regard to investments in agricultural transformation, and (2) a variety of financial products tailored to the challenges and opportunities therein. In particular, they should (1) include longer investment timelines and (2) a more holistic approach to value creation, and (3) consider both land management and restoration. The case studies provided offer a glimpse into the types of innovative financial transactions that are needed at scale to transform the food system in line with global sustainability imperatives.

Examples

- ***Blended Finance – Mirova's Land Degradation Neutrality (LDN) Fund***: The LDN Fund was launched in 2017 to provide long-term loans or equity to profit-generating companies in emerging markets to finance projects that improve sustainability and efficiency through sustainable land use and restoration. In March 2021, the fund reached its final closing, with over $200 million. The fund invests in companies involved in agroforestry, regenerative and sustainable agriculture, and sustainable forestry on degraded land. This impact investment fund is committed to investing in eight countries in areas ranging from sustainable coffee and cocoa production, restoring deforested areas in Latin America, to sustainable forestry and nut production projects in Africa and Asia, focusing on smallholder inclusion.[24,25]

- ***Partial Guarantee Mechanism – Promoting the Use of Agricultural Technologies and Practices among Small Farmers in Guatemala***: The project aims to strengthen the capacity of Guatemalan farmers to adapt to and mitigate the effects of climate change. The IDB Lab and the Green Climate Fund will contribute $2 million as a conditionally recoverable investment grant for an automated partial guarantee mechanism administered by the National Federation of Credit Unions of Guatemala. The automated partial guarantee mechanism will leverage artificial intelligence, Big Data and/or data analytics to promote a financial risk mitigation instrument to encourage credit unions to increase their agricultural credit portfolio. Complementarily, IDB Lab and the Green Climate Fund will commit $675,000 to provide technical assistance to farmers, focusing on farmers' adoption of climate-smart technologies and agricultural practices.[26]

- ***Natural Capital as an Asset Class – Climate Asset Management Natural Capital Fund (Global)***: In 2020, HSBC Global Asset Management and Pollination joined forces to create the world's largest dedicated natural capital asset management company, Climate Asset Management. Its investment solutions are based on nature-based investments, including sustainable forestry, regenerative agriculture and nature-based carbon projects. At its inception, Climate Asset Management announced its intention to raise up to $1 billion for its natural capital fund and $2 billion for the carbon credit fund. In December, CAM raised $650 million for its 15-year natural capital fund, which targets a 10% return on *investment on regenerative agriculture and forestry projects in developed markets*.[27,28,29]

- **Private Equity, Growth Equity, Real Assets – AXA, Unilever and Tikehau Capital Regenerative Agriculture Fund**: *In May 2022, Axa, Unilever and Tikehau Capital signed a memorandum of understanding to launch a €1 billion impact fund focused on regenerative agriculture. According to* New Private Markets *magazine, this will likely be the first private market vehicle to carry such a brand. The vehicle will be endowed with €300 million by the partners (€100 million each), with the aim of raising €1 billion and the fund targets conventional private equity returns of between 15% and 20% IRR.*[30]

Box 7.5   Developing strategic policy: the case of Barilla

Barilla began to focus its attention on the environmental impact of its products, raw ingredients and supply chains in 2000 with its first life cycle assessment (LCA) analyses of pasta. The results, which were surprising at the time, showed that the main source of GHG emissions per kilogram of product throughout the life cycle of pasta was home cooking, followed by cultivation of durum wheat. This awareness led to the launch, in 2010, of the Barilla Sustainable Farming project. It allowed the company to gain a competitive advantage thanks to four foundational pillars.

***Varieties research**. For a long time, Italian crop production was unable to consistently guarantee the quantity and quality of durum wheat. This made wheat imports inevitable. Today, research into the selection and improvement of exclusive wheat varieties has made it possible to adapt production to environmental requirements, meaning that only Italian wheat is used in products sold on the local market.*

***Technological innovation**. The possibility to support farmers with expert technologies, such as Decision Support Systems (DSSs), has enabled resource optimisation – for example, of fuel and fertilisers – without affecting the quantity and quality of wheat production. In addition to DSSs, Barilla provides farmers with artificial intelligence systems for recognising and monitoring the most important wheat adversities, thus helping them in determining the most appropriate interventions. This has clear benefits for the environment and for the balance sheet.*

***Cultivation methods**. Traditional practices, passed down through generations of farmers, are no longer fit for purpose. Part of the BSF project, the 'Handbook for the sustainable consumption of durum wheat' is a collection* *of rules and recommendations for reducing environmental impacts and optimising total income, providing a practical tool to guide farmers' operational and strategic decisions.*

Horizontal agreements and supply-chain contracts. *Even though the European Union's Common Agricultural Policy incentivises crop rotation, farmers often persist with monocultures because they are not always able to sell products other than durum wheat. Barilla set up horizontal agreements between different supply chains to allow durum wheat producers to access other contracts (such as sugar beet, tomato and peas, with Barilla itself – involving other raw ingredients it needs for its processes – and other businesses).*

The implementation of the BSF approach to durum wheat has brought considerable environmental benefits. Taking into account only GHG emissions, it is estimated that an average 11.5% improvement over traditional methods has been achieved.

The durum wheat project was ground-breaking within Barilla's sustainability policies. The excellent results led the company to increase its focus on suppliers of raw ingredients. These are key partners with whom relationships are formed based on dialogue and transparency, in accordance with the Barilla Sustainable Agriculture Code. This document contains guiding principles for managing stakeholder relationships and procurement.

In addition to durum wheat, Barilla's attention is focused on all strategic raw ingredients including soft wheat, rye, eggs, cocoa, tomatoes, meat, vegetable oils and basil.

Work on the durum wheat supply chain continued through the Handbook project and the use of a tool designed to analyse objective parameters (such as weather, agronomic and crop data), and to support farmers in making tactical field management decisions.

The sustainability of the soft wheat used in bakery products is managed thanks to the adoption of two production guideline documents focused on protecting plant and animal biodiversity: the Carta del Mulino and the Charte Harrys. Their use has been gradually extended to a growing number of Italian and European farming businesses.

Rye, which is the basic ingredient in crispbreads, has several environmental advantages. As a crop, it has low water and fertiliser requirements. Additionally, the BSF programme launched an experimental regenerative agriculture project aimed at restoring the soil's natural ability to absorb CO_2.

Basil is the main ingredient in Barilla's pesto sauces: this is grown according to Carta del Basilico, a strict agronomic specifications aimed at optimising water use, preserving biodiversity and with varieties resistant to the most important crop diseases.

Finally, tomatoes and vegetable oils are procured primarily to produce sauces and pesto in certain countries. The crops undergo international certification protocols such as Global Gap and ISCC Plus.

7.2.1   *The role of technology*

Improving the sustainability of food requires integrating skills and expertise from different sectors. The traditional image of farming as a lagging sector operating in a rustic setting is no longer accurate. Similarly, the highly critical view of farming as an industry that has no restraint in its use of chemicals to supply raw ingredients to a cynical system is also inaccurate. The farming industry comprises highly skilled professionals who increasingly understand their role as stewvards of the natural environment and deserve to be rightly valued for the services they provide, both food provision and ecosystem services.

Collaboration between agronomists, computer scientists and communication specialists is promoting the development of technological platforms to help farmers make ever-more rational and robust decisions. Is using agrochemicals to control a specific plant disease the right decision? Yes, if there is a real, measurable risk. Otherwise, it is a waste. How much fertiliser should be applied to plants? It depends on their requirements which can vary across different areas in a field. This information, and much more, can be gained using systems that help farmers make well-informed decisions.

Box 7.6   On-farm technology: the case of xFarm

Farm is a platform designed to support farmers in managing their business easily and efficiently. Using smartphones, computers and tablets, farmers can directly oversee the management and organisation of crop-related activities (field mapping, recording of processing actions…), logistics (warehouse inventory, real-time tracking of vehicles and harvest progress…), compliance (report production, data digitisation…) and machinery management (maintenance planning, data collection via installed tracking devices).

In addition to its core functions, xFarm offers specific packages to meet different business needs, such as the use of advanced sensors to monitor soil moisture and plan disease prevention strategies, or the provision of budgeting and financial planning support. The benefits include reductions in agricultural inputs, costs and GHG emissions.

The app now includes a sustainability package that, using data provided by farmers about the amount and type of work done in the field and the use of agrochemicals and fertilisers, provides insight into environmental impacts such as CO_2 emissions, soil acidification, eutrophication and water use. The feature is certified according to ISO 14040. The app is also able to determine the soil carbon sequestration potential according to the agricultural interventions of the farmer. Storing carbon in the soil reduces the CO_2 present in the atmosphere. Many soil benefits also arise including

---

water-holding capacity, microbial activity, nutrient release and resilience to external factors. The app allows farmers to simulate best practices in terms of carbon storage that eventually benefit crops, soil health and the environment. Thanks to this tool, farmers are able to access a digital report of their environmental performance and gain a detailed understanding of activities and products that have a greater environmental impact, while tracking progress over the years.

Box 7.7   Cooperation along the chain: the case of AgroCO$_2$ncept

*In 2011, a discussion took place among farmers who were part of a land consolidation project in Switzerland about making farmland available to create an ecological network according to the specifications of the Nature Conservation Office of the Canton of Zurich. Interest in building up soil organic matter for carbon sequestration triggered the creation of the **AgroCO$_2$ncept Association**, which is committed to reducing CO$_2$ emissions in agriculture.*

What started with 3 farmers is now a network of 24 farmers with different operations including livestock, vineyards, staple crops and specialties like asparagus. They each select measures that are suitable for their unique situation from a stock of 42 mitigation and efficiency measures.

The farmer set goals for 20% less on-farm CO$_2$ emissions, 20% lower expenses through cost reductions and efficiency increases and 20% more added value through better-priced climate-friendly products and brand reputation gain for the participants and the region by 2020 (known as the target formula 20/20/20).

These objectives make it clear that climate protection in agriculture cannot be about reduction of emissions alone. It must combine the farm and technical-level measures with a regional view that includes marketing and cross-farming and cross-sector cooperation. This allows the system boundary and the scope of action to expand. Increased cost efficiency and added value from climate-friendly products play a major role, especially in the associated investments. Added to this, energy is not only a climate factor but also a cost factor that ultimately affects value creation.

The project is based on a bottom-up approach with farmers at the centre. Key elements beyond technical interventions include the creation and exchange of knowledge among farmers, and between researchers and farmers, and development of a collaborative network of cross-farming and cross-sector actors. The project played a pioneering role at the national level, as there is limited experience with practical climate protection at the farm level in Switzerland.

Media interest was also high, with some 50 newspaper articles and television reports on the project. In 2019, the project received the title of Ambassador for Rural Innovation, awarded by the European Liaison Project in Brussels which encourages farmers to develop innovative solutions together with representatives from science, consulting, associations, federations and companies. Selected from over 200 entries from all over Europe, Liaison called AgroCO$_2$ncept an 'inspiring and ground-breaking initiative'.

In 2016, the AgroCO$_2$ncept became part of a Resource Project of the Swiss Federal Office for Agriculture. It selected 12 mitigation measures to be applied and developed for a future standard Swiss-wide application. This project came to an intermediate end in 2022, followed by a final GHG accounting and inventory to assess the impacts of the measures applied in 2022. Outcomes included:

A reduction of 314 tCO$_2$eq/year, or 5%, within the project region between 2015 and 2021 (the year of third accounting).

GHG emissions per farm varied from −46% to +45% compared to 2015. Thirteen farms were able to reduce their emissions, five by over 10% and two by over 20%.

At the farm level, GHG efficiency (GHG emissions per unit of product) improved on many farms. In crop production, 8 out of 17 farms improved their GHG efficiency compared to 2015, 7 of them by more than 20%. In dairy production, nine out of ten farms improved their GHG efficiency between 1% and 16%, and for beef fattening/suckler cow herds, five out of six farms improved between 5% and 11%.

The diversity of these results reflects the individuality of each farm and their combination of selected measures. The selection of those measures is influenced by the actions of farmers, which depends on the reduction potential, economic efficiency, weather conditions, the experience of other farm managers, positive side effects, strategic considerations and more.

Now that the results are available, the project can move into the next phase of establishing mitigation measures as an inherent component of a climate-friendly agriculture.

In summary, there is no single or universal solution when it comes to reducing GHG emissions at the farm level. However, there are key levers to reduce GHG emissions in agriculture. Over the last five years, some of the levers that were shown to have the greatest reduction potential among the list of selected measures were in the three areas of livestock, crops and soils and energy. Unsurprisingly, these include measures impacting herd and manure management such as low-carbon feed with climate-friendly feed composition of concentrates and roughage. Other high-impact measures are soil cover with intercropping, management of crop residues, pyrolysis for biochar production, optimisation of fertiliser use, humus build-up/carbon sequestration and all measures related to energy efficiency and the production of renewable energy, such as biogas plants and solar power. However, because these measures require time, investment, innovation and expert advice, their application is not a foregone conclusion.

Agriculture can clearly make substantial contributions to global GHG reduction, but this contribution is inadequately reflected if we look only at individual measures. We must see the farm as a whole, open system and as part of a network of farms. In line with target formula 20/20/20, this includes the non-technical side by considering social networks leading to better knowledge dissemination and continuous learning, adaptation and optimisation of mitigation measures.

Many farms were proud to have improved their GHG efficiency and made progress in net reductions and carbon sequestration. The latter played an important role in the overall combination of potentially suitable measures and many farmers decided to continue applying the mitigation measures without receiving subsidies.

Part of this success was the Agri Climate Change Tool (ACCT). This allowed the farmers to gain a holistic view of their farm. They called this the climate/mitigation lens, through which the interfaces between climate change, mitigation and operational processes became visible. Reduction potentials could be identified and utilised, and it provided common ground for exchange of information and knowledge. As a GHG accounting tool, the ACCT was ideal for positioning a farm on its way to reducing emissions, but it is not suitable for calculating the emissions of specific measures.

The farmers involved became aware that climate protection in agriculture requires the commitment of individuals and also teamwork among farms and with the economy, society and politics. In this sense, AgroCO$_2$ncept is not a completed project but a programme to be continued. While it has a strong focus on the farm level, it links on-farm measures with strategic corporate sustainability strategies of agri-food industries as well as communities, regions and entire countries. Thus, the approach has the potential to be applied on a larger and more international scale. It can be combined with tools like xFarm to become a true measure-oriented on-farm support for GHG reduction and sustainability strategies in general.

It also becomes even clearer that the success factors of a climate-friendly agriculture extend far beyond the farm (see Figure 7.4). Society and consumers need to be partners of climate-friendly agriculture because they can achieve substantial changes by changing their consumption patterns (e.g. by paying more attention, buying climate-friendly products; Figure 7.5).

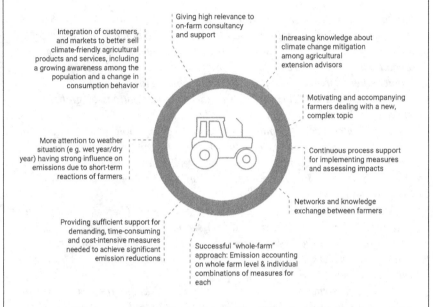

Figure 7.5 The success factors for a climate-friendly agriculture going beyond the farm level. Authors' elaboration.

7.2.2   *Capturing CO₂ in soil*

Carbon sequestration is a natural process whereby plants, via photosynthesis, use CO_2 as nourishment. There is a growing interest in this phenomenon as a critical part of the solution to the climate crisis. Farming has a key role to play as research-ers believe that sustainable agronomic practices have a positive impact[8] because the soil can perform a key function within the climate change mitigation process, thanks to its potential for storing enormous amounts of carbon.

When it comes to the sustainability of primary production, a key topic of discus-sion is regenerative (or organic-regenerative) agriculture. This explains how crop farming can be organised in ways that are mutually beneficial with the surrounding environment, according to a long-term vision.

Regenerative agriculture involves employing practices such as crop rotation, cover crops and less invasive techniques. A good example is minimum tillage, which involves minimising soil processing as much as possible (never ploughing deeper than 20 centimetres, for example) to avoid uncovering too much soil and unnecessarily releasing stored carbon. Another option is to use cover crops which serve no commercial purpose but are used solely to protect and increase fertility of the soil and biodiversity. Green manure is a great example; it consists of one or more crops planted for the sole purpose of improving soil organic matter content by storing carbon and other nutritional substances that will improve yields in the subsequent crop cycle.

In addition to the reduction of environmental impacts, another aspect of regenerative agriculture that is generating interest is the potential to adopt these approaches for the production of carbon credits due to its carbon storage potential. These can provide an economic advantage when sold as part of carbon offsetting or insetting (when a company offsets carbon within its own value chain). Many organisations are looking into this matter and, as we saw in the section on carbon credits, is additionally a key requirement. Only emission reductions from an innovative project, set up specifically for this purpose, can be used to generate certified and tradable carbon credits.

7.2.3   *Biochar as a possible solution*

Biochar is a form of carbon that has undergone a stabilisation process at high temperatures in the absence (or at very low concentrations) of oxygen. It looks like charcoal even if it is obtained from biomass. Biochar is not a modern invention; rather, it is a product of an ancient process that used to take place frequently in the Amazon Forest. Amazonians would dig holes in the soil, fill them with organic waste and biomass in general, light it up to let the temperature rise and cover it with soil to create an anoxic environment. This resulted in the rich dark soils that we call 'terra preta', meaning 'black soil' in Portuguese. After all this time, these soils remain fertile, demonstrating that biochar is more stable than any other soil amendment.

The common carbonisation process for preparing biochar is pyrolysis. Pyrolysis proceeds under oxygen-free conditions at the temperature ranging from 300°C to 600°C. The char obtained by gasification and hydrothermal carbonisation generally does not meet the definition of biochar. During the pyrolysis process, solid, liquid and gas products are formed. The solid and liquid are usually called biochar and bio-oil and the gases are called syngas, which usually contains carbon dioxide, hydrogen and nitric oxide. Temperature is the main condition that determines the product efficiency of pyrolysis; the pyrolysis reaction becomes exothermic after a certain threshold is passed, reducing the required energy input to maintain the reaction.

Figure 7.6 shows how important temperature control is to obtain biochar.

While the effects are still under study, the use of biochar in agriculture has two main long-term benefits: increased soil fertility and carbon sequestration. Biochar production is sensitive to technological variables such as pyrolysis temperature and biomass used. Yet the same biomass does not show the same properties each year, as they depend on the climate conditions the biomass was grown in. It is agreed in the literature that this affects the carbon sequestration potential, but long-term studies are needed for this to be validated.

Soil fertility: Biochar has the ability to improve the physical properties of soil, including its structure, surface area, porosity, bulk density and water-holding capacity. This increases plant water availability, nutrient retention capacity and root penetration. Additionally, the surface areas of amended soils can favour microbial communities. Being alkaline, biochar acts as a liming agent in acidic

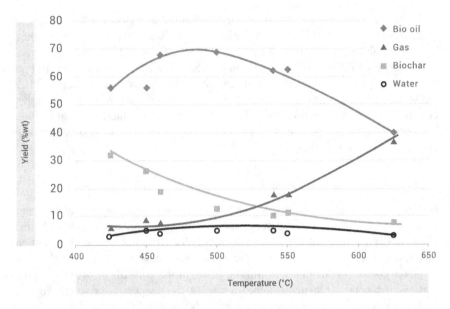

Figure 7.6 Temperature is an important variable for process control. Increasing the temperature reduces biochar production in favour of the liquid and gaseous fractions.
Maximising biochar is therefore at the expense of usable energy in gaseous and
liquid forms and has an opportunity cost. F. Verheijen, S. Jeffery, A.C. Bastos,
M. van del Velde, I. Diafas, *Biochar Application to Soils. A Critical Scientific
Review of Effects on Soil Properties, Processes and Functions*, European Commission, 2010, https://publications.jrc.ec.europa.eu › JRC55799.

soils. Depending on the soil texture, biochar can positively affect sandy soils by
improving water-holding capacity and clay and loamy soils through improved
aeration.

Carbon sequestration: Biochar is stable in nature and could have long-term
carbon sequestration value. Studies of charcoal tend to suggest stability in the order
of 1,000 years in the natural environment – a win-win strategy for climate change
mitigation and food production on a global scale.

Biochar usually has a high resistance to biodegradation due to its highly con-
densed aromatic structure. However, no consistent result has so far been provided
because both increased and decreased emissions of carbon dioxide were observed.
The carbon in the biochar can be divided into liable carbon and recalcitrant carbon. Liable carbon can be utilised easily by soil microorganisms when biochar is
added to the soil, resulting in increased carbon mineralisation at the beginning.
This explains why biochar addition stimulates carbon mineralisation. In fact, the
contents of recalcitrant carbon in biochar are far higher than that of labile carbon.
The recalcitrant carbon can last for a long time in soil, and the carbon input caused
by the addition of biochar is higher than the carbon output caused by the mineralisation of liable carbon.

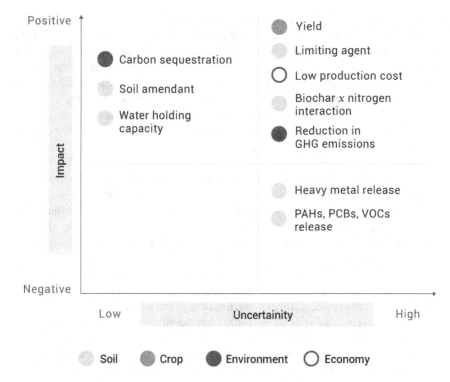

Figure 7.7 This figure summarises the impact of biochar, both positive and negative, and its uncertainty, given its agreement among studies present in literature. It is worth noting that the negative-low uncertainty box is empty, resulting in positive or neutral impact associated with the use of biochar in soils. Authors' elaboration.

Diverting biomass that would have normally been composted, landfilled or incinerated to biochar production would produce a carbon-stable contribution to soils and avoid emissions that would have occurred during conventional biomass treatment (Figure 7.7).

7.2.4 *Regenerative agriculture*

Inspired by the principles of organic farming, regenerative agriculture goes further by operating according to natural biogenic cycles, producing with few or no external inputs, without over-exploiting, polluting and impoverishing lands. Regenerative and organic-regenerative[31] agriculture promote beneficial ecosystem outcomes such as healthy soil, improved air and water quality, enhanced biodiversity and carbon sequestration. This conserves agricultural lands and their ecosystem, avoiding excessive degradation and loss of fertility. Beyond environmental benefits, regenerative agriculture offers benefits for farmers' long-term livelihoods due to reduced costs and increased food output, as well as more nutritious foods.[32]

Regenerative agriculture is in deep contrast to the industrial forms of agriculture used widely today. It is an approach that aims to work with nature rather than against it, moving away from the linear, extractive and polluting farming model to one that is life-affirming. Regenerative agriculture draws from preindustrial techniques and approaches used for centuries by ancient civilisations who lacked the agricultural machinery, chemical pesticides and synthetic fertilisers of today. It is applied using techniques that are based on the same principles of ancient agriculture, while embracing modern technologies which can accelerate progress towards sustainable food production.[33]

The principles of regenerative agriculture propose to carry out cultivation operations in a more respectful way of the surrounding environment, according to a long-term vision to restore the soil's natural capacities to absorb CO_2 emissions, support local biodiversity and be capable of producing food far into the future. The most important interventions are diversifying and rotating crops, using of cover crops, minimising soil disturbance and integrating livestock with crop systems. This requires farmers adopt an entirely different mindset and to see their role as stewards of the land. It means listening to what the plants and soil need and supporting life – beginning with alive soils – rather than dousing virtually dead soil with fertilisers to provide sufficient nutrients for plants to survive.

Cultural diversification is an essential component of regenerative agriculture. It is fundamental to restoring fertility, obtaining good yields and limiting the need to use pesticides, while boosting resilience to climate shocks, pests and disease.[34] With crop rotation, soil structure is improved, and biological activity is stimulated while avoiding erosion, increasing water security and preventing loss of biodiversity. Cover crops – such as green manure – protect the soil by ensuring soil is never left bare and vulnerable to erosion from winds and water. They help to retain water, nutrients and organic matter to improve and protect the soil structure while waiting for the next production cycle. Here, the presence of grazing livestock is fundamental to contributing to the biological vitality of soils, organic reconstruction and the natural mineralisation of soil.

Minimum soil disturbance is another core pillar of regenerative agriculture.[35] Reducing the tillage and the mechanical impact on soils to a minimum helps retain the organic substance and recover fertility. Minimum tillage is a practice that limits the tillage of the soil, for example, ploughing no deeper than 20 cm avoids uncovering too much of the earth and losing the protection of the carbon stored on the ground. In practice, it is necessary to prevent the intense movement of the soils that invert their layers, as happens with deep ploughs. The aim is not to have excessive oxygenation of the earth, but to practise less intense processing. This protects the habitat and organisms that inhabit the soil, such as earthworms which, together with the roots of the plants, contribute to its structure. In regenerative agriculture, we can reach the total elimination of tillage, a practice that drastically reduces the fuel consumption, emissions and environmental impact.

In addition to making an environmental contribution, regenerative agriculture arouses economic interest thanks to its potential to increase farmer income through increased food output[36] and produce carbon credits. Its practices increase the absorption of carbon dioxide and the sequestered carbon, representing a financial advantage for the farmer who can sell his or her credits for compensation. Regenerative agriculture is also being adopted because it offers a pathway to increased resilience in the face of increased extreme weather events and plant and animal diseases. One of the indirect benefits is improved water management and protection from floods and droughts; increasing the organic carbon content of soil by 5% enables it to hold about 30 m^3 more of water per hectare. Regenerative agriculture can also generate significant health benefits through increased nutritional density of the foods produced[37] and decreased health costs for farmers (e.g. due to decreased exposure to pollutants and pesticides).[38]

The outcomes of this regenerative agriculture generally begin to materialise after three to five years after they are adopted, and planning needs to be for the long term. It is essential to put into practice new agronomic knowledge, which is constantly evolving, such as plant protection based on integrated biological control. The direct and indirect benefits of wide-scale adoption of regenerative agriculture are many. Still, it is essential not to remain anchored in the past and to collaborate with modern technologies to use resources efficiently, while respecting natural balances and biodiversity.

7.3   The path to a circular economy

Whether or not we accept it, we are called upon to change our economic model because of increasingly scarce finite resources and ever-rising consumption levels driven by a global population that could soon surpass 9 billion people. Today's economic model is highly 'linear' – a take, make, waste system where finite resources are extracted to make products for a growing population and massive volumes of waste are generated.

The concept of a circular economy is based on the recognition that this linear model cannot work long term. Rather than aiming to do less harm, we can create good by fundamentally redesigning the products, services and systems we use every day. A circular economy recognises the objective limits of our planet's carrying capacity, accounting for the number of human beings that inhabit it and their lifestyles, production levels, energy and resource use, consumption and waste production. With this economic model, stability does not depend on a constant increase in consumption of virgin materials, but on the sustainable preservation of good environmental and social conditions by decoupling growth from resource extraction.

The circular economy comprises a framework based on three core principles: eliminate waste and pollution, circulate products and materials at their highest value and regenerate natural systems.[39] While many solutions within the food sector already align with these principles – such as regenerative agriculture – we focus here on solutions that target elimination of waste and circulation of nutrients and materials within the agri-food industry. These not only reduce waste, but support decarbonisation and generate co-benefits such as restored natural resource stocks. They also contribute to the delivery of the UN Sustainable Development Goal target 12.3, which aims to reduce food waste by 50%. For example, developing more sustainable agricultural practices will play a vital role; a report from WWF[40] found that 1.2 billion tonnes of food produced globally is lost before it even leaves the farm.

The change that businesses and consumers are being asked to bring about requires a complete rethinking of business models and consumption patterns. The majority of today's production is not sustainable due to the resources it consumes and the enormous amount of waste generated and not recovered. It is a highly linear, take-make-waste economy. The new model takes inspiration from nature and physics to create self-sufficient, zero-waste systems that involve no energy loss. In a circular economy, waste is eliminated, materials and products are circulated at their highest use for as long as possible and natural systems are valued in the use of inputs (raw materials and semi-finished products) and outputs (waste and emissions) at every phase of the production, consumption and post-consumption. This is how we will realise an economy that operates within planetary boundaries (Figure 7.8).

Under the circular economy approach, the concept of waste can be completely eliminated. When excess edible food is prevented in the first place, any extra is redistributed for human consumption and the remaining inedible by-products are

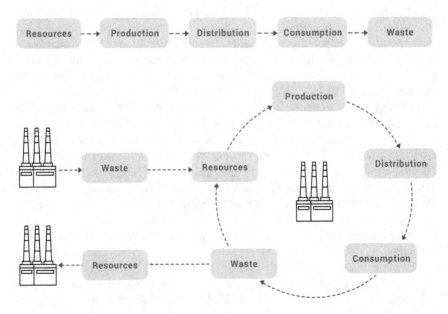

Figure 7.8 The transition from linear to circular economy. Authors' elaboration. Originally published in the first edition of this book, *Il Cibo Perfetto*, published in Italian in 2022.

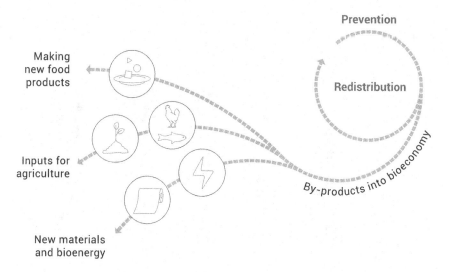

Figure 7.9 How to redistribute by-products into the bioeconomy. Adapted from *Cities and the Circular Economy for Food*, Ellen MacArthur Foundation, 2019, https://ellenmacarthurfoundation.org/cities-and-circular-economy-for-food.

circulated at their highest value (see Figure 7.9). Food products can be designed to minimise unused materials and by-products can be captured and used as feedstock for new cycles. At the same time, post-consumption systems ensure all further waste and residues become new resources (input) for the production processes of other businesses and sectors.

The benefit of adopting a circular economy approach is clear, both in terms of waste reduction and disposal costs and because it recovers raw materials which will become increasingly scarce in the future. It is important to explore all possible solutions for circulating materials, both within the food sector and in other areas of the bioeconomy.

The correct implementation of a circular approach requires innovation, an entrepreneurial approach and creative collaborations between actors within sectors and across seemingly distant sectors spanning the entire value chain – as is demonstrated in the case of animal feed.

7.3.1   Circularity in the feed production

One of the most important examples of the circular economy in the food sector involves feed production. Most animal feed recipes include by-products of other agri-food production sectors, made possible through cooperation across different food production realms. An interesting case is the use of formerly inedible foodstuff as valuable feed ingredients. This supports the sustainability of feed production and reduces food waste (Figure 7.10).

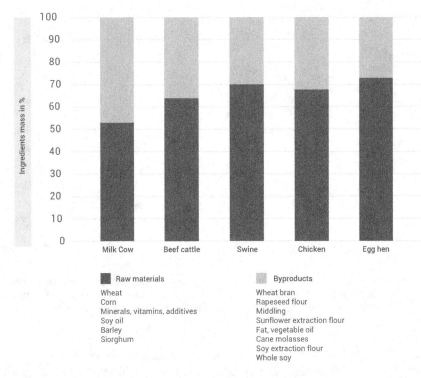

Figure 7.10 Animal feed and the circular economy. *Report Ambientale*, Assalzoo, 2020, chrome-extension://efaidnbmnnnibpcajpcglclefindmkaj/https://www.assalzoo. it/wp-content/uploads/2021/06/ASSALZOO_Report_Ambientale_2020.pdf. Originally published in the first edition of this book, *Il Cibo Perfetto*, published in Italian in 2022.

Box 7.8   Former foodstuffs as feed ingredients

by Valentina Massa (President of EFFPA, European Formers Foodstuffs Processors Association)
Feed producers have always practiced a circular economy in the agri-food sector. The use of wheat chaff from flour mills is a classic example. Wheat chaff bran is the external part of wheat and has very limited application because it is mostly inedible to humans, but it is valuable in an animal's diet due to it being a useful source of fibre (also known as roughage). When processing wheat flour, the chaff can be captured and – rather than go to waste or be turned into biofuel via anaerobic digestion – be used as an ingredient for animal feed. Strong logistical organisation and plant engineering are critical components for ensuring high-quality feed is produced.
*   One of the innovations in this sector is the use of former foodstuffs[41] such as those derived from the processing and sale of products such as biscuits,*

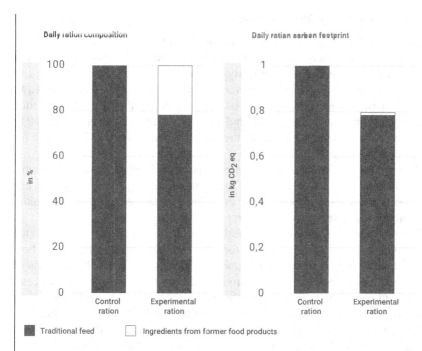

Figure 7.11 Two alternative rations. *Report Ambientale*, Assalzoo, 2020, chrome-extension://efaidnbmnnnibpcajpcglclefindmkaj/https://www.assalzoo.it/wp-content/uploads/2021/06/ASSALZOO_Report_Ambientale_2020.pdf. Originally published in the first edition of this book, Il Cibo Perfetto, published in Italian in 2022.

pasta, snacks bread, biscuits and cookies. These are processed into feed ingredients that can replace some of the main traditional ingredients in feed recipes such as cereal grains, sugars and oilseeds. Since they usually have already been cooked and contain more fats and less fibres than raw cereals, these ingredients improve digestibility and add useful energy to each meal.

This is a win-win process; in addition to the benefit of preventing food waste, the inclusion of feed made of former processed foodstuffs in animal diets reduces CO_2 emissions, water consumption and land use, depending on the type of animal husbandry value chain. Figure 7.11 shows the results of an experiment carried out in the dairy cattle sector.[42]

It is important to remember that former foodstuffs are neither waste nor by-products; they have simply gone from being foodstuffs to animal feed in full compliance with food safety regulations. The inclusion of this type of ingredients in feed production is promoted by the European Commission for two reasons: the prevention of food waste and the decreased need to use traditional agricultural raw ingredients, which generate negative environmental impacts when produced conventionally. This consequentially reduces competition within the food value chain and promotes a more efficient and sustainable food system.[43]

7.3.2   *Circularity in animal husbandry*

There is a well-known saying in Italy's culinary tradition that '*no part of the pig is thrown away*'. This harks back to farming families during wartime when concern for sustainability was driven by poverty and hunger. Those who could afford to raise and slaughter a pig would use every last part of it. Today, we are called to debate the issue of sustainability while taking into consideration other factors, such as the welfare of humans and animals and the environment. However, one certainty has remained – even today, no part of the pig is thrown away. This is also true for other types of livestock.

Meat production chains are deeply interconnected with other economic systems, both at the farm level and at the level of industrial processing. Farming systems can have local or systemic interactions, for example, a farmer can use excreta (manure and slurry) to fertilise the soil where crops or fruit trees are grown.

Dairy farmers provide an example as their products enter several different value chains, within and beyond the food sector (dairy products, meat, leather). The beef slaughter industry generates a considerable range of residues and by-products of animal origin that can be repurposed through recovery systems and further processing, instead of going wasted. One of the greatest technological challenges is the ability to recover proteins and other nutrients suitable for human consumption from the by-products of the beef slaughter processes. For example, the possibility of incorporating animal tissue in the design of medical devices (such as heart valves) is highly interesting. It is also worth remembering the more traditional uses of animal bones in pet food and gelatine for use in foodstuffs, leather and the abomasum – a part of the stomach used in the production of rennet for the dairy industry. When materials cannot be recovered for other uses, they can be repurposed for energy production. This is the case with fats and rumen, which can be transformed into biogas. One of the highest-value solutions for generating biogas is anaerobic digestion which produces a nutrient-rich digestate (remaining part of organic matter) which can be used in organic fertilisers, in addition to biogas.

Box 7.9   The circular economy of meat and poultry production

BONES are used in the production of pet food, feed, fertilisers and gelatines used in food and pharmaceuticals.

COW AND PIG SKIN is used in the production of leather goods; calfskin for luxury items (shoes, handbags, belts, etc.); bullock leather for the automotive sector (car seats); cow leather for sofas and other goods and pig leather for the inner lining of footwear.

FAT is used in the cosmetics and chemistry sectors (soaps), as well as in feed for use in animal husbandry systems.

PIG SKIN AND CARTILAGE are used in the production of food products, thickening agents and pet food.

PIG SKIN AND OTHER TENDONOUS PARTS are used in the production of gelatine, used in the production of food (mostly from pig parts) and pharmaceuticals (mostly from cattle), to create films in which drugs are encapsulated.

BLOOD AND ENTRAILS – pig entrails are used as casings for sausages and cured meats, while cow blood is used to produce fertilisers and food protein and poultry blood for pet food.

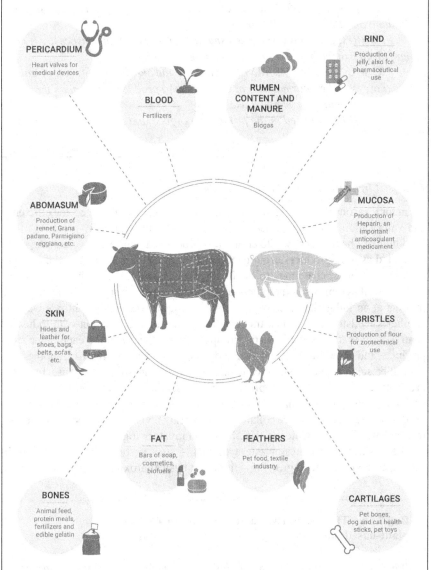

Figure 7.12 Main uses of slaughter by-products. E. Bernardi, E. Capri, G. Pulina, *La sostenibilità delle carni e dei salumi in Italia*, FrancoAngeli, Roma, 2018. Originally published in the first edition of this book, *Il Cibo Perfetto*, published in Italian in 2022.

THE PERICARDIUM taken from pigs and cows is used to create medical devices (heart valves).

FAT DRIPPINGS AND RUMEN CONTENTS are used alongside other waste as sources of renewable green energy (biogas cogeneration).

THE ABOMASUM (the last of the four cavities in a ruminant's stomach) is used to produce rennet (e.g. it is the only coagulant permitted in the production of protected designation of origin (PDO) cheeses such as Grana Padano and Parmigiano Reggiano).

PIG BRISTLES that were once used in the production of brushes are now employed primarily in the production of feed flours.

PIG MUCOSE MEMBRANES (extracted during the production of casings) are used by pharmaceutical companies to produce heparin, an important anticoagulant for medical use.

FEATHERS are used in the production of feed and in the textile industry (Figure 7.12).

7.3.3   Circularity at scale: industrial symbiosis

As natural resources become scarcer and more expensive, the need for efficiency and valorisation of materials becomes increasingly important. By-products of the food industry have given way to entire new product categories. For example, whey generated as a by-product during cheesemaking is often dried and sold as a high-protein powder for customers to use in other foods, such as smoothies.[44]

Industrial symbiosis is the practice of making use of every single material and product at an industrial scale so that nothing goes to waste. One entity's waste is another's feedstock. In China, this has taken on a new dimension with industrial centres built that combine industry groups that together leverage each other's by-products and take the waste of one industry as a material input of another. On a smaller scale, there is significant movement among start-ups to use food by-products as an input. For example, B Corp Toast Ale[45] uses leftover bread to brew beer and Mush Foods[46] makes a burger with 50% mycelium grown on food by-products. These start-ups are collaborating to bring a vision of industrial symbiosis to life. The plant[47] in Chicago, US, brings innovators together under one roof to enable business-to-business waste synergies – such as brewery waste to mushrooms, carbon dioxide to growing – through physical proximity and collaboration.

Box 7.10   The circularity challenge: The case of the plant-based industry

While we have seen a growing shift in consumption of plant-based protein products, the plant-based manufacturing sector is some way behind its traditional meat counterparts when it comes to by-product valorisation.

The sector could face increased scrutiny over the use of its by-products, making it important to develop a strong knowledge of the supply chain, from field to fork, to ensure plant-based products are not falsely marketed or over-sold as better than animal products. As the plant-based protein sector looks at how to optimise the use of its by-products, there are significant learnings that can be taken from animal-derived protein producers and manufacturers.

One of the challenges for plant-based protein manufacturers is to find a use for by-products without compromising on values. For instance, while plant milk alternatives – such as oat and nut beverages – help reduce con-sumption of high-carbon dairy milk, they generate significant volumes of by-products. In 2020, oat milk brand, Oatly, produced 41,000 tonnes of oat pulp.[48] This contains valuable fibre and nutrients which can be upcycled into ingredients for human consumption, rather than downgraded to animal feed.

The protein market structure has shifted towards plant-based proteins as health and environmental considerations lead to more widespread adoption of vegan, vegetarian or flexitarian diets. As this trend continues, manufac-turers will need to develop more efficient supply chains which can deliver sustainability and financial benefits. Animal by-products, sometimes known as the 'fifth quarter', are already used across a range of sectors. This has resulted in strong supply chains, developed over decades, and benefited the bottom line for manufacturers.

Key drivers of change

Plant-based protein manufacturers might find it challenging to utilise by-products which do not compromise their values. Most waste material, such as pulp from plant-based milk production, is currently used as animal feed. However, this could be interpreted as plant-based protein manufacturers indirectly supporting the traditional meat and dairy industry which would be in conflict with vegan consumers' values.

The good news is that there are other options for use of plant-based by-products including textiles, packaging, building materials, biofuel and pet food. But using plant products in non-food applications is second-best and can still be seen as food waste or food loss. The best option is to divert it to feedstock for the creation of new proteins using biomass fermentation or insect bioconversion. This increases the protein output per hectare and the by-product is able to sell at a higher economic value than it currently achieves as animal feed. New innovations are enabling products to come to market that 'upcycle' by-products as high-quality ingredients for human consumption. The Upcycled Food Association[49] has a membership of 150+ innovators who are working to create upcycled food products labelled with a standard certification established by the Association. Consumer recognition and appetite for such products is growing, with the global upcycled foods *market valued at $52.91 billion in 2022.*[50] *This trend provides an economic incentive for companies to turn waste streams into new food.*

Develop a strategy from field to fork

The first practical step for plant-based protein brands and manufacturers is to develop knowledge of the supply chain to understand where waste streams arise and opportunities to create value exist. Once they have visibility of their waste streams, manufacturers can also review their sustainability, assessing which waste products could be eliminated, reduced or reused. While they may have solutions to circulate by-products within their own supply chain, some companies will benefit from external solutions. EverGrain,[51] *for instance, takes the spent barley from beer breweries and transforms it into a high-nutrient powder ingredient that can be sold to food manufacturers to use in their products.*

Localised approach and co-located businesses

Because food is a biological material, the elements of time and space are critical components for preventing waste from arising and capturing by-products to be valorised at their highest value. Putting the right systems and structures in place will be increasingly important for optimising the output products. Although the by-products market for traditional meat products is global, a localised approach focused on symbiotic relationships between manufacturers could deliver significant benefits for the plant-based protein sector. As the strategic players in the market look to achieve greater efficiencies and increase margins, site selection will be an important consideration. While plant-based protein supply chains remain relatively fragmented, there is an opportunity for small, high-growth manufacturers to achieve much greater value for their waste streams if manufacturers and brands can coordinate and co-locate businesses. This could be highly beneficial for planet health and for the growth of the plant-based sector.

Food Strategy Associates – Nigel Devine, Associate Director of Integrated Food Projects

Key takeaways

- The scale of the sustainability challenges may seem intimidating, though there are already existing and promising solutions that can be adopted that tackle many issues at once: circular economy, regenerative agriculture and decarbonisation solutions are some of these.

- Decarbonisation, or achieving net-zero, is quickly becoming a universal goal by mid-century to mitigate and adapt to climate change. It comprises a process of comprehensively calculating an organisation's GHG emissions across its value chains, adopting a mix of technological solutions, product design changes, change in energy sources used, carbon offsetting and carbon insetting projects to achieve carbon neutrality.
- Agriculture can be considered a problem but it can also be a solution. Regenerative agriculture is a powerful proposition: revising agriculture practices to prioritise soil health and biodiversity, such as no-tilling, cover-cropping and crop rotation, has many benefits such as increasing carbon absorption in the soil, increasing soil fertility, increasing crop nutrition, increasing water retention and natural pest management. Regenerative agriculture as a study of scientific enquiry is still relatively recent, so these impacts are still to be measured carefully – though major food conglomerates and governments around the world are quickly setting it as a strategic imperative.
- Circular economy is a framework for companies that use by-products as raw materials, so waste and use of resources are reduced. It does this through principles in the use of ingredients (e.g. renewable, recycled materials), business model innovation (prioritising re-use and re-pair of products) and designing products for durability, to ensure they have long lives and cycle through multiple consumers before needing to be repurposed or recycled into something else. The food production chain is a pioneer of the circular economy and feed production is always one of the best examples of how circular systems are put into practice.

Key questions for reflection

- How can you use circular economy principles to re-design or launch new products or services that help keep materials in use?
- What is the circular economy industry vision for your particular industry segment, and how can you be part of it?
- What is your stage of maturity with regard to understanding your carbon footprint and identifying solutions towards net-zero?
- How can you leverage both carbon insetting and offsetting approaches to decrease your environmental footprint?
- How can you integrate regenerative agriculture into your value chain? What benefits that regenerative agriculture can provide (from carbon sequestration to soil fertility and nutrition) are most important to your different stakeholder groups?

Notes

1 I. Carlisle, P. Pivcevic, *Design for a Regenerative Doughnut*, Doughnut Economics Action Lab, December 2021, https://doughnuteconomics.org/stories/140.
2 *Greenhouse Gas Protocol*, https://ghgprotocol.org/.
3 Voluntary Carbon Markets Integrity Initiative (VCMI), Taskforce on Scaling Voluntary Carbon Markets (TSVCM).
4 R. Tipper, N. Coad, J. Burnett, *Is "Insetting" the New "Offsetting"?*, Ecometrica Press, April 2009, https://ecometrica.com/assets/insetting_offsetting_technical.pdf.
5 *Global Assessment Report*, 2014–2020, Nespresso, https://www.nespresso.com/agit/app/uploads/2020/08/Pur-Projet_Nespresso_Global-Assessment-14–21_0.pdf.
6 *The Positive Cup*, Nespresso, https://www.sustainability.nespresso.com/our-climate-commitment.
7 M. Wilcox, *L'Oreal, Chanel and Nespresso Pioneer "Carbon Insetting"*, Green-Buzz, February 2017, https://www.greenbiz.com/article/loreal-chanel-and-nespresso-pioneer-carbon-insetting.
8 *The International Platform for Insetting (IPI)*, https://www.insettingplatform.com/.
9 D. Lev-Tov, *Your Guide to Kernza: A Super Grain That's Good for You and the Planet*, The Land Institute, January 2022, https://landinstitute.org/media-coverage/your-guide-to-kernza-a-super-grain-thats-good-for-you-and-the-planet.
10 https://www.bsr.org/reports/BSR_Climate_Adaptation_Issue_Brief_Food_Bev_Ag2.pdf
11 https://www.thebusinessresearchcompany.com/report/food-and-beverages-global-market-report#:~:text=The%20global%20food%20and%20beverages,(CAGR)%20of%208.7%25.
12 https://www.climateaction100.org/wp-content/uploads/2021/08/Global-Sector-Strategies-Food-and-Beverage-Ceres-PRI-August-2021.pdf
13 https://www.ncbi.nlm.nih.gov/pmc/articles/PMC8452525/
14 https://capitalscoalition.org/guide_supplement/finance-sector-supplement/
15 https://www.oecd.org/finance/ESG-Investing-Practices-Progress-Challenges.pdf
16 https://www.ifad.org/thefieldreport/
17 https://gfpr.ifpri.info/2022/05/11/climate-finance-funding-sustainable-food-systems-transformation/
18 https://regeneration.vc/strategy
19 https://www.brookings.edu/research/renewing-global-climate-change-action-for-fragile-and-developing-countries/
20 https://www.europarl.europa.eu/RegData/etudes/etudes/join/2007/393511/IPOL-ENVI_ET(2007)393511_EN.pdf
21 https://www.imf.org/en/Blogs/Articles/2022/10/07/how-to-scale-up-private-climate-finance-in-emerging-economies
22 https://basis.ucdavis.edu/developing-countries-and-future-small-scale-agriculture#:~:text=A%20significant%20share%20of%20people,in%20lower%20middle%20income%20countries.
23 https://www.g20-insights.org/wp-content/uploads/2018/07/TF3-3.5-Task-Force-3-FINAL-v4-EDB-revised-after-peer-review.pdf
24 https://www.mirova.com/sites/default/files/2021–06/Mirova%E2%80%99s%20Land%20Degradation%20Neutrality%20Fund%20exceeds%20%24200m%20of%20commitments%20for%20its%20final%20close_0.pdf
25 https://www.greenfinanceinstitute.co.uk/gfihive/case-studies/land-degradation-fund/
26 https://www.iadb.org/en/project/GU-G1012?_gl=1*1nhh5w0*_ga*MzQ2MjEwNDE0LjE2NzM0NzM4ODk.*_ga_D6RZQTPGY5*MTY3MzQ3Mzg5MC4xLjEuMTY3MzQ3NTA3Ni41Mi4wLjA
27 https://www.bloomberg.com/news/articles/2022-12-13/natural-capital-funds-backed-by-hsbc-raise-650-million

28 https://www.reuters.com/business/sustainable-business/climate-asset-management-raises-650-mln-invest-nature-projects-2022-12-13/

29 https://pollinationgroup.com/climate-asset-management/

30 https://www.newprivatemarkets.com/axa-unilever-and-tikehau-capital-partner-for-e1bn-ag-impact-fund/

31 P. Newton, N. Civita, L. Frankel-Goldwater, K. Bartel, C. Johns, What Is Regenerative Agriculture? A Review of Scholar and Practitioner Definitions Based on Processes and Outcomes, in *Frontiers in Sustainable Food Systems*, Vol 4, October 2020.

32 A. Sharma, L. Bryant, E. Lee, C. O'Connor, *Regenerative Agriculture Part. 4: The Benefits*, NRDC, February 2021, https://www.nrdc.org/experts/arohi-sharma/regenerative-agriculture-part-4-benefits.

33 K.E. Giller, R. Hijbeek, J.A. Andersson, J. Sumberg, Regenerative Agriculture: An Agronomic Perspective, in *Outlook on Agriculture*, Vol 50, Issue 1, pp. 13–25, March 2021.

34 G.N. Furey, D. Tilman, Plant Biodiversity and the Regeneration of Soil Fertility, in *PNAS*, Vol 118, Issue 49, December 2021.

35 *Healthy Soils, Profitable Farms*, Soilcapital Farming, https://www.soilcapitalfarming.ag/regenerative-agriculture.

36 *Making Nature-Positive Food the Norm*, Ellen MacArthur Foundation, https://ellenmacarthurfoundation.org/resources/food-redesign/overview.

37 D.R. Montgomery, A. Biklé, R. Archuleta, P. Brown, J. Jordan, Soil Health and Nutrient Density: Preliminary Comparison of Regenerative and Conventional Farming, in *Peer J*, January 2022.

38 *Cities and Circular Economy for Food*, Ellen MacArthur Foundation, https://ellenmacarthurfoundation.org/cities-and-circular-economy-for-food.

39 *What Is a Circular Economy?*, Ellen MacArthur Foundation, https://ellenmacarthurfoundation.org/topics/circular-economy-introduction/overview.

40 *Over 15% of Food Is Lost Before Leaving the Farm*, WWF, July 2021, https://www.wwf.eu/?4049841/fifteen-per-cent-of-food-is-lost-before-leaving-the-farm-WWF-report.

41 The European Commission defines former foodstuffs as 'foodstuffs, other than catering reflux, which were manufactured for human consumption in full compliance with the EU food law but which are no longer intended for human consumption for practical or logistical reasons or due to problems of manufacturing or packaging defects or other defects and which do not present any health risks when used as feed' (Regulation (EU) 68/2013).

42 A. Formigoni, *Piano di ricerca su: Recupero zootecnico ex-alimenti. Relazione finale*, Department of Veterinary Medical Science, University of Bologna, 2020.

43 European Commission, *Guidelines for the Feed Use of Food No Longer Intended for Human Consumption*, April 2018, https://bit.ly/3CkejJo.

44 *What Are Whey Products and How Can They Be Used in Meals?*, The Dairy Alliance, https://thedairyalliance.com/blog/what-are-whey-products-and-how-can-they-be-used-in-meals/.

45 *Toast Ale*, https://www.toastale.com/.

46 *Mush Foods' Mycelium Brings Umami-Flavored Protein to Hybrids Meat*, PR Newswire, February 2023, https://www.prnewswire.com/il/news-releases/mush-foods-mycelium-brings-umami-flavored-protein-to-hybrid-meat-301751642.html.

47 *Plant Chicago*, https://www.plantchicago.org/.

48 *Pulp Fiction? What Oatly, Califia and Alpro Do with Their Oat Milk By-Product*, Food Waste Stories, November 2021, https://foodwastestories.com/2021/11/21/pulp-fiction/.

49 *Growing the Upcycled Food Economy*, Up Cycled, https://www.upcycledfood.org/.

50 *Products from Food Waste Market*, FMI, March 2023, https://www.futuremarketinsights.com/reports/products-from-food-waste-market.

51 *Evergrain*, https://evergrainingredients.com/.

8   Activating the transformation

Transforming the food industry is a complex, long-term journey that requires the concerted effort of all players along the value chain and across industries. Where there is complexity and a need for change, there is also opportunity to reimagine business models, improve products and processes and create disruptive innovation.

We are at a stage where many companies have been able to adopt a strong sustainability vision and tools to understand their impact. They now find themselves with ambitious, long-term targets and a less-than-clear plan of how to achieve them. There are insights that can be gained from organisational transformation approaches that can help to address this and drive real-world change.

As we have discussed, there is no one solution for any food value chain and no single idea of the perfect food. Just as understanding a company's impact within the food system requires unique analysis – relative to its specific context, product, market and consumer profile – identifying an effective solution requires understanding the specific strengths and capabilities of the organisation. Each individual company must look at its own context to understand and define what sustainability means for them. This has a significant advantage as each organisation can develop its own unique response, tailored to its strengths and opportunities as well as the specific customer demands it faces.

This process of looking inwards to identify a company's unique role is an important step. The transformation journey will be easier when it is driven by the specific strengths of the organisation's culture and employee skillset, its brand and the role it plays in the market. Transformation cannot happen without change and this will be motivated by the energy and dynamism of employees and by leveraging their know-how and position in the market to influence the value chain.

The journey may require upskilling workforce capabilities and even changing your organisation's structure and business functions. As detailed on the previous chapters, this must be based on a thorough evaluation of what sustainability means for your organisation, products, services and business processes so that it can drive you to greater competitiveness, resilience and brand loyalty.

The decision to embark on such a sustainability transformation can be daunting – from knowing where to start to implementing change at scale. Delivering both impact and value takes commitment and dedication and there is no single, one-size-fits-all way to integrate it into your business operations. You will face numerous

DOI: 10.4324/9781003449744-8

operational and mindset challenges as you orchestrate the journey and having a strategy is only the start. Here, we take you through three key enablers for compa nies to successfully implement the sustainability transformation.

Legislation, market or science: how to be distinctive in your value proposition

When choosing which values will guide your strategy, there are four key conditions to consider:

1 What the market (retailers, consumers, public opinion, etc.) considers relevant. Even if this is conditioned by fads, ideologies and, sometimes, fake news, it is crucial to be successful on the market.
2 What research identifies as hot spots of the industry, i.e. scientific evidence of the real environmental impact of a product. This may align with the previous point, but not always. For example, plastic is an issue which may be opposed by consumers without being the real problem of the specific industry or product.
3 What the law imposes, or will impose, for the market/industry. This could align with the scientific evidence, but it does not always, as policymakers base deci- sions on their own political values or on the values of the majority of citizens.

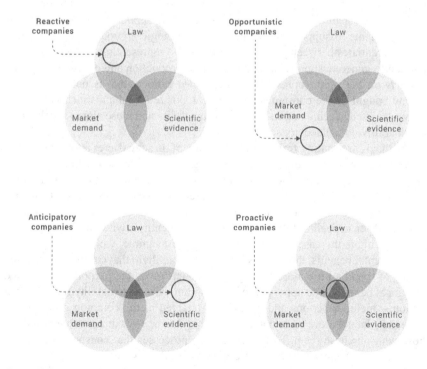

Figure 8.1 Approach to the sustainability from different companies. Authors' elaboration.

4   What the company has an interest in promoting. This depends on what it can do better than its competitors and the requirements of the previous three points.

Figure 8.1 shows how companies can be placed in four different positions with regard to these four considerations, depending on their core sustainability values:

- *Reactive*. They value only compliance with the law, with the risk that sustainability will only ever be a cost and never an opportunity to differentiate themselves from competitors.
- *Opportunists*. They follow market trends and demands, with the risk of falling into the greenwashing trap.
- *Anticipators*. They may arrive on the market before others, but risk taking paths that will never lead to a real competitive advantage.
- *Proactive*. They reconcile all three positions in the best possible way, reducing risks and enhancing opportunities.

Mapping your approach – people, plant, product, process

As an organisation defines its sustainability priorities and the strategic approach it wants to take to achieving a sustainability transformation, it is important to have the right mix of activities that address each stakeholder priorities, the level of impact that needs addressing in the company-specific context and the organisation's unique capabilities. The 4P matrix in this case applies two axes to map different elements to support the definition of a strategic approach. The horizontal axis differentiates between *processes* on the left – representing everything that is required to generate supply, such as farming to production and distribution – with *products* on the right, representing the finished product that is put on the market and bought by the consumer. The vertical axis retains the distinction between actions targeted at achieving individual sustainability and those aimed at delivering sustainability on a planetary scale.

The diagram resulting from the combination of these two axes allows us to map actions that support the strategic path towards sustainability across the 4Ps of people, planet, products and processes. The bottom row includes actions that, in some way, benefit those who implement them (in terms of health, taste or cost savings, for example) and can easily be transformed into value for customers (such as nutrition, health or appealing to a person's sense of identity), with ensuing economic benefits. This is the case of organic farming, for example, which has significant environmental benefits, though it is important to highlight that consumers are often willing to spend a little more for organic products given the purported health and nutritional benefits. The upper part of the diagram – the sustainability for the planet section – includes actions and behaviours targeted at the common good, which make the product more sustainable overall but do not offer direct value or gain to those who purchase them. Examples include processes that consume less water, cause fewer CO_2 emissions or use recycled materials (Figure 8.2).

The easiest actions to market to consumers are those in the bottom right, where sustainability is visible in the product itself and directly benefits the consumer. This

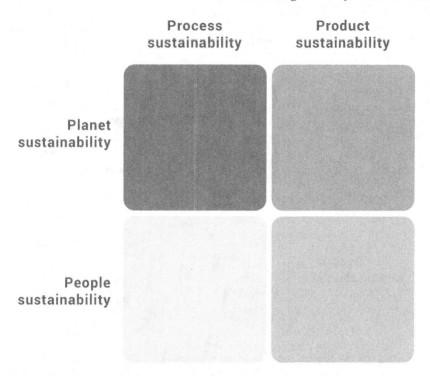

Figure 8.2 The 4P diagram: connecting the different areas of sustainability. Authors' elaboration. Originally published in the first edition of this book, *Il Cibo Perfetto*, published in Italian in 2022.

benefit can often be related to the sphere of health, for example, a certain food is perceived as healthier or more flavoursome (e.g. organic or non-GMO). In other words, the benefit is to what Maslow calls basic needs – namely, physiological and safety – and these inform messages that can be easily communicated.

The top-left quadrant generally requires the largest investment, such as reducing energy consumption or resource use. In the best-case scenario, this can bring down costs for the business in the long term, but it is unlikely that the initial investment will be recovered on the market by applying a price premium or tapping into customer preferences. Consumers are less willing to purchase something due to its production process being more sustainable considering that this does not provide an explicit, direct benefit to them. For activities placed in this area, investing in environmental certifications and labels that increase visibility can help stimulate the higher-order needs that Maslow classifies as social and self-actualisation.

The most ambiguous areas are the top-right and bottom-left sections. The former includes actions that make the final product more sustainable, but which do not provide explicit benefits to individuals. This includes using eco-friendly packaging which is easier to communicate because it is effectively part of the product, but which only affects the choices of the most responsible consumers.

Process
sustainability

Product
sustainability

Planet
sustainability

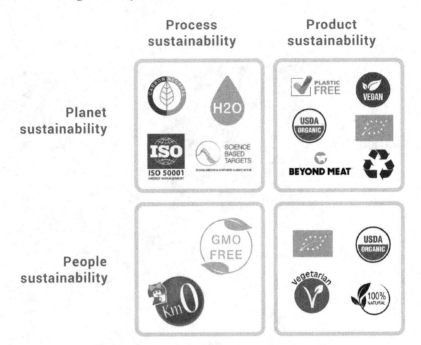

People
sustainability

Figure 8.3 The 4P diagram and some of the main 'sustainable actions' in agri-food production. Authors' elaboration. Originally published in the first edition of this book,
Il Cibo Perfetto, published in Italian in 2022.

Similarly, the bottom-left section concerns processes that primarily impact
production, rather than the characteristics or quality of the product, and are perceived by the customer as beneficial to them. Examples include animal welfare
(including some vegan products) and local sourcing[1] (Figure 8.3).

8.1   Identifying your unique levers

One of the most important accelerators of the transformation is identifying your
specific strengths – or levers for change. What lever will you pull to mobilise
and catalyse change across the organisation or value chain? What does your
company culture thrive on and what drives and engages the people within your
organisation?

This clarity is important to spark the transformation and support it in a way that
honours, builds on and reinforces your organisational culture. If change is driven
by pulling the right levers, employees will naturally feel motivated to be part of the
transformation through shifting mindsets and behaviours. Developing new initiatives or products should be less daunting as these will fit in with the organisation's
overall change or product development process.

Impossible Foods is a science- and innovation-driven organisation. It is at the forefront of food science, combining technical prowess in the laboratory with visionary thinking to create a plant-based burger that 'bleeds'. As a start-up, Impossible Foods is leveraging its key strengths in innovation and science to design products that have never existed before, opening the plant-based protein market and steering the food sustainability conversation away from meat.

In contrast, Whole Foods Market – the US-based food retail store – is driving change in a different way. Leveraging its commitment to sustainability, unprocessed fresh produce and nourishing healthy food, it is driving change through its sourcing practices and high-quality standards – setting the tone for the industry in the US, Canada and the UK. Innovation is not part of its DNA, nor does it need it to build a brand or have a transformative impact on the food industry.

Companies across all sectors are leveraging their unique skillsets and cultural identity to drive unique and ambitious sustainability journeys. Nike and Adidas have positioned themselves at the forefront of athletic wear, powered by innovation in product design as shapers of fashion. Nike has developed a specific website called Nike Grind, fronted by the tagline '30 years of relentless innovation'.[2] It uses this platform to share the leaps it has made on building a palette of sustainable materials for their product ranges. Adidas has pioneered 3D knitted shoe manufacturing techniques, cutting fabric waste by using only the material needed for the final product.

Similarly, The Body Shop has focused its efforts on being activist and revolutionary. It is a loud voice when it comes to fair trade and ethical practices in the beauty products industry. This has led it to concentrate its sustainability efforts on a few, radical projects that are heavily marketed and set an example for the industry. This was at odds with L'Oreal, the Group who once owned the brand, whose research focus and scientifically minded employees led them to adopt a more data-driven approach to sustainability focused on product bio-degradability and defining the naturality index, greatly influencing the ISO 16128 industry standard defining natural cosmetic products.

Finally, Kerry has a vision for a new food future – creating a world of sustainable nutrition. Sustainability is a key part of its heritage and purpose, and it is important to its employees, who can see their own values reflected through the company's activities. Its purpose was built on the company's history and culture, focusing on ongoing and inclusive stakeholder engagement. Sustainable nutrition is not new, but Kerry is working to cement its role in helping customers advance in the nutritional space without compromising on sustainability.

These examples show that a company's levers for change can be varied and extend well beyond its product and position in the market. They can also concern structural elements of what drives change within a firm that can be invisible from the outside. Unilever famously became a pioneer of sustainability change, largely through the leadership of Paul Polman who was instrumental in positioning Unilever to be a driving force of sustainable product innovation. The history of Danone's brand has always involved balancing economic growth and social good, set in motion by the CEO Antoine Riboud in 1972[3] and established by law as a 'société à mission' by inscribing in the company statutes its social, environmental and economic objectives.[4]

It is crucial that a thorough understanding of stakeholder expectations and priorities – from investors to customers, employees, suppliers and others– informs the direction and strategy for change. This can also help to identify the best levers to pull. Setting a clear strategy and assessing the levers should be a deliberate exercise. It is an opportunity for engagement and transparency that is powered by not just the company's desire for change but to marry different stakeholder priorities with the company's unique potential for impact. Importantly, this process is key to empowering the company's leadership and stakeholders and such a process may lead to unexpected insights and opportunities.

8.2   Embedding sustainability in your core business

Having identified your unique levers for change, the challenge becomes how to integrate sustainability into every core process, role, metric and way of working of your company.

Over the last decade, a major shift has taken place in how the sustainability agenda is perceived and managed within an organisation. Companies that have led successful sustainability transformations have integrated the sustainability agenda into the heart of their business structure and overall strategy. Instead of sustainability being driven by a separate team, it is embedded in core business functions – from product development to innovation, strategy and marketing communications. This is reflected in people's job titles – adopting sustainability as an additional remit, such as 'R&D & Sustainability Lead' – in KPIs and remuneration policies and in core business processes. It is no longer sufficient for a sustainability team of experts to sit to the side of a company's core business functions. This leads to inertia in scaling initiatives and results in the leadership of different business functions not fully integrating the company's sustainability agenda into their own targets. The risk is that the sustainability agenda remains deprioritised compared to what are seen as core commercial priorities.

Start-ups lead the way in showing how products and services can have sustainability embedded into their DNA from the outset, irrespective of whether products and services are marketed as sustainable. They set an important example by demonstrating how sustainability can be integrated at every step of the process from procurement and product design to legal, HR and office management. This has put pressure on more established organisations to fully integrate sustainability into their business as increased awareness of the topic and what can be achieved has led customers to challenge more companies, for example, seeing an investment in charitable or sustainability projects that sit apart from a company's core operations as a form of greenwashing.

Integrating sustainability may appear intuitive, but it isn't sufficient to simply overlay new sustainable technologies onto existing processes and people. The transformation requires embedding new ways of working into the operations of a company. There must be a fundamental shift in how people think and act for these efforts to live up to the full potential for positive impact. This needs a practical plan, capacity to implement the sustainability transformation and integration personalised to each user's needs to deliver a change that lives up to its potential.

Organisations continuously learn, evolve and change; this is how they stay relevant and competitive. Leadership may instigate change by announcing a new business model or changing decision-making and other processes in a piecemeal way. These may be the right strategic decisions, but they will not be sufficient for a sustainability transformation. For change to take root, it requires shifting ways of working across all business functions in a coordinated way so that each change is reinforcing. It also requires embracing change as a constant which will take time and need updating and evolving. A top-down approach may be necessary, but you cannot rely on individuals or sustainability champions to change core ways of working across a whole organisation. For real change to happen and to be sustainable over time, it required an 'all-hands-on-deck' approach as applicable to the company.

As Serafeim says,

> A strategic goal, accountability from the top down, and a top-to-bottom culture built around purpose are not always enough to actually get things done. The other piece of the puzzle is operational. The structure of a sustainable company needs to have sustainability infused into everything it does.
>
> George Serafeim, 2022. Purpose + Profit, Harper Collins

In other words, you need to enable long-term change within your organisation, across your value chain and, perhaps, even at a systemic level. These are some practical examples of how to enable long-term change:

- **Sustainable product development**: Integrate sustainability at different stage-gates during the product development process. Include sustainability objectives during requirements gathering, build a sustainability scorecard that is leveraged to evaluate design concepts, include sustainability guidelines on marketing materials at product launch to minimise waste. The criteria should be all-encompassing, ranging from packaging (such as recyclability or biodegradability) to product composition (e.g. nutritional content, origin and sustainability of ingredients) and commercialisation (e.g. affordability considerations).
- **Sustainable sourcing and procurement**: Embed sustainability criteria at each step of the procurement process from supplier identification to material or product requirements, negotiation and contracting. Commercial negotiations can include incremental improvement or innovation targets, contractual requirements for sustainability standards and certifications and strategic partnerships aimed at driving change across the value chain.

- **Legal teams**: Support cross-functional conversations to understand how legal teams can support and facilitate sustainability objectives such as waste prevention (due to liability around sell by or due by dates) or food waste management (allowing for food to be re-sold safely to second-value uses).

A strong governance structure is key to orchestrate, activate and sustain the transformation journey. How a business is managed and structured is fundamental to the outcomes of companies of all size, from small start-ups to complex multinationals. Key governance elements should be factored in to ensure that management at each level is accountable for integrating and driving sustainable change. These can be reinforced through a strong performance and reward system. Sustainability should be included in KPIs, internal commercial reporting and external reporting to allow for visibility and tracking improvements.

8.3   Empowering your employees to drive culture change

Given the complexity of undertaking the successful implementation of a sustainability transformation, people are an essential driving force. We can look to people and culture to drive and sustain change over time.

When considering a company's ambition for positive impact and how to sustain such a transformation, we must consider how best to adapt roles and responsibilities, integrate sustainability into business processes, metrics and targets, and how to innovate on the front of product design and commercial strategies.

The essential, and often overlooked, foundation of such a transformation is culture and behaviour change. This means working with employees to get them excited about this shift and committed to delivering it. This is not a one-off exercise, but long evolution that will see people internalise sustainability, so it is reflected in every decision they make, and every aspect of their role.

Transforming a business or a value chain is not achieved overnight. It is a slow process which requires the ability to solve complex problems, form new partnerships and design new products and services. It requires certain skillsets and momentum and enthusiasm for change, distributed over a long timeframe. Employee training, engagement and empowerment are key to sustain and drive transformation; they are the people who will come up with the ideas, do the work and make change happen.

The critical factor is to adapt your business culture to sustain the transformation by changing underlying mindsets. Individuals and teams need to be empowered, motivated to be a part of the transformation and enabled to think differently. What is requested of them is to do their job differently and to question, at each step of the way, how their work can be shifted or innovated to be more sustainable, from decarbonisation to upholding human rights.

In 'Making Sustainability Work',[5] authors Marc J. Epstein and Adriana Rejc Buhovac explain that success requires both formal and informal systems to support change – but that 'soft' systems are more important than most realise. That is why your people and organisational culture are so intrinsic to success. For example, companies normally driven by performance targets leverage them fairly successfully as levers for change, usually strengthening those formal systems with informal engagement activities. There must be a process whereby you think, as an organisation, about what the transformation means for you and your workforce, who need to understand what it means for their day-to-day activities and broader business partners. You need to create an environment that drives change and embraces continuous improvement – and ensure that your culture integrates these elements too.

This requires a culture shift – a holistic and coordinated activation. Your company's leadership and employees need to view problem-solving and everyday business through a new lens. Incentives will need to evolve accordingly. By recognising your organisation's competencies and resources, you can activate the passion that will be the engine for transformation and sustained change. The idea is not only to spot opportunities to reduce negative impacts, but to see how to generate value out of what was previously labelled 'waste', innovating with new products and different business models to fuel responsible growth.

As George Serafeim states in his book *Purpose + Profit: How Business Can Lift Up The World*, 'You need pressures from both ends – top-down and bottom-up; two forces pushing on the organisation to make things work and make them stick'.

We know that learning and capacity building are best integrated and 'sticky' when they take place over time, are highly relevant, applied to real work and reinforced and supported by managers. What is more, when employees are presented with personalised content that embeds their environment, terminology and procedures in the learning, they tend to be more motivated and engaged.

It is key not to underestimate the challenge and importance of activating and engaging your people. This will require multiple solutions, starting with training and capacity building to catalyse new mindsets and the accompanying skillset. Activation will need continuous interactions throughout the company to keep people energised, engaged, motivated and empowered. Serafeim's research shows the importance of the middle management layer, as that is where strategy and vision meet execution. If a consumer goods company talks about providing healthier products but doesn't put the right financial incentives in place to get the middle managers to develop and market these products, the effort will fail.

All of this applies irrespective of your industry or market and whether your motivation for change stems from regulatory compliance, investor pressure, a desire to tap into ESG (environmental, social and governance) investing or response to consumer pressure. The right way to implement the approach will depend on many variables, the combination of which gives every company a unique challenge – from aiming to transform its sourcing practices to improving its product portfolio and competitiveness.

A mindset must be taught where people critically analyse the decisions they make in their everyday business through a sustainability lens, factoring in environmental and social factors to lead to better outcomes.

Chapter 8 Summary

Key takeaways

- Sustainability transformations are complex and long-term; they do not happen overnight. They require significant orchestration between people within different business functions and partners along the value chain.
- There are frameworks that can help identify strategic priorities, ensuring that an organisation addresses simultaneously what is important to different stakeholder groups as well as what needs to change due to its social and environmental impact. The 4P diagram helps identify priority activities across operational processes and product design, important either for the environment or for people.
- A company is more likely to succeed if their sustainability transformation is driven through their identified 'levers for change': the aspects of their culture, organisation or brand that are unique to them, that makes their people 'tick': whether it is being activist, scientific, process-driven or having charismatic leadership.
- Implementing a sustainability strategy requires a holistic orchestration of effort across all business functions, as it is less likely to succeed if it is piecemeal.
- Sustainability must be integrated at every step of the organisation, in terms of both governance and accountability of results, as well as being factored into every process, tool or individual role.
- In order to activate and sustain the transformation, your people are fundamental as it is their energy, mindsets and capabilities that will drive change, innovation and continuous improvement.

Key questions for reflection

- What is unique about your organisation? What is it known and valued for within the market, across the value chain and amongst its employees?
- What makes your organisation 'tick'? What usually drives change, leveraging its unique culture, ways of working or skills of its employees?
- Have you put together a comprehensive view of the change journey to integrate sustainability across the whole organisation? What would it mean for each function, role, process, tools? How would you motivate your people and sustain the momentum?
- How are you going to not only upskill people's sustainability knowledge, but also work on their mindsets and capabilities to problem-solve and innovate? Have they been given the autonomy to propose and enact change?

Notes

1 In this regard, it is worth noting that, despite locally sourced products generally being perceived as more environmentally sustainable, there is no guarantee that they are. As we will see further on in the text, the 'transport' variable can have a minimal impact compared to other phases of the life cycle.

2 *Nike Grind*, https://www.nikegrind.com/.

3 *Our epic History*, Danone, https://www.danone.com/about-danone/ourhistory.html.

4 *"Raison d'être"*, Danone, https://www.danone.com/fr/about-danone/sustainable-value-creation/danone-societe-a-mission.html.

5 M.J. Epstein, A. Rejc Buhovac, *Making Sustainability Work: Best Practices in Managing and Measuring Corporate Social, Environmental, and Economic Impacts*, Berrett-Koehler, UK, 2014.

Acknowledgements

We would like to acknowledge the valuable insights and contributions of the industry and sustainability experts that we interacted with in our search for the Perfect Food. Their purpose and achievements encouraged us to develop this guide to share the best practices of a rather challenging ambition. Their practical contributions were essential to consolidate the guiding principles towards Perfect Food.

Barilla
Beth Derry
Clara Maffei – INALCA
Cristiana Peano – UniTo
Emma Cahill – Kerry
Emma Chow
Fabio Colli Medaglia – Eurostampa
Giovanni Dinelli – UniBo
Giuseppe Garcea – Zespri
Juan Aguiriano – Kerry
Kiran Mohan, Fauna & Flora International
Lea Pallaroni – Assalzoo
Lorenzo Nannariello
Marco Bassan – Università Roma Tre
Matteo Vanotti – xFarm
Mr Yoo – Pulmuone
Nigel Devine – Food Strategy Associates
Pattie O'Keefe – Kerry
Roberto Ranieri
Sara Bosi – UniBo
Silver Giorgini, Orogel
Simona Fontana
Simone Agostinelli
Tilmann Silber – Barry Callebaut
Umberto Luzzana – Skretting Italia
Valentina Massa – Dalma Mangimi
Ylenia Tommasato – Bolton

We also want to acknowledge the incredible support and collaboration from our colleagues from dss⁺, who wrote key portions of the text, checking solutions feasibility and shaping some of the thinking on sustainability transformation: Ana Mundim, Francesca Berretta, Georgia Young, Jessica Martin, Hannes Zellweger, Laura Burger, Lorenzo Mazzola, Marco Meloni, Martin Fritsch, Tania Montesin, Tobi Karim, Tom Stewart, Thais Mustafa, Victoriana Gonzaga and John Michael Kern.

Index

Note: **Bold** page numbers refer to tables; *italic* page numbers refer to figures and page numbers followed by "n" denote endnotes.

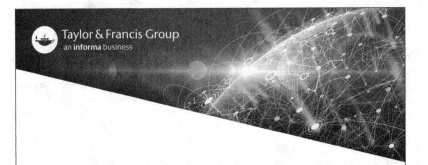

Printed in the United States
by Baker & Taylor Publisher Services